BECOMING A SPIRITUAL LEADER

Becoming a Spiritual Leader
A Life of the Apostle Peter

Patrick Whitworth

Terra Nova Publications

First published by Terra Nova Publications 2005

Published in Great Britain by
Terra Nova Publications
PO Box 2400, Bradford on Avon, Wiltshire BA15 2YN

Cover design by Lion Hudson
Cover illustration:
St Peter's Denial, Rembrandt
© Rijksmuseum, Amsterdam. Reproduced by permission.

ISBN 1901949346

Printed in Great Britain
by Bookmarque Ltd, Croydon.

Contents

Foreword

The Rev Dr Russ Parker

It was Dietrich Bonhoeffer in his book *The Cost of Discipleship* who pointed out that when Jesus calls us to follow him, he is calling us to die! But, you may ask, "Die to what?" Certainly not to being truly human, if Patrick Whitworth's book is anything to go by. What he brings alive are the dynamic encounters between Peter and Jesus. Here we witness the growth and development of this first leader of the fledgling church, which seems to be more a case of painfully won insights from the school of hard knocks than clinical reflections from a rabbi's seminar. This is a book about developing a quality of leadership that Jesus would be pleased with. It is earned through enduring dialogue in which we get increasingly honest and vulnerable with God, with ourselves and with others. Patrick paints a wonderfully alive picture of Peter journeying from professed strength to confessed weakness. It is here that he makes a key statement about godly and effective leadership, when he writes that a sense of personal inadequacy is a far better quality for leadership than a sense of one's abilities.

This book invites us to walk alongside Peter and learn from his struggles to come to terms with his true humanity and calling, as well as feel the full impact and depth of Jesus, the man who is God. On the way we learn the value of not being afraid to ask difficult questions which reveal our inner battles: I wonder who Peter was thinking of when he asked Jesus, "Lord, how many times shall I forgive my brother when he sins against me?" (See Matthew18:21.) Far too many of us think that the issue is about how strong are we to take the responsibilities of a leader, when in fact it is about how weak we need to be in order to be of service for God. As Patrick's book will remind us, only the broken are called into God's ministry to others.

What I also like about this book is that it has the effect of showing us what went on behind those letters which Peter wrote later in life, and which carry the hallmarks of costly wisdom. Peter's dogged trail to maturity and passion for Jesus are culled from a determination to hold on to the love which captured his heart, and it was strong enough to survive his own betrayal of the Lord of heaven. Here is a book which challenges us to be as real and open as a broken Peter, and learn to be as truly human as the Lord who also calls us to share in his marvellous care of others. I warmly commend it to you.

Russ Parker

Preface

Perhaps this is unfair but I have often wondered in writing this book whether Peter would have been accepted for ordination in the Church of England! I can see him being turned down, especially in his earlier years, for any number of reasons. He might have been turned down for leadership in your own church denomination too, and for similar reasons! He was an uneducated fisherman and as the Jewish council observed after Pentecost, "When they saw the courage of Peter and John and realised that they were unschooled, ordinary men, they were astonished and they took note that these men had been with Jesus" (Acts 4:13). So initially Peter might have been overlooked because of his lack of education. Or again he might well have been turned down for his failure to grasp Jesus' mission in going to the cross, or above all for his denial of Jesus in a moment of crisis. He was impetuous, outspoken and sometimes rash and these traits might not have commended him to those who select ministers for our churches now, who may be tempted to look more for managers than leaders, facilitators rather than preachers, and for well-rounded characters rather than blunt-tongued enthusiasts.

Am I being unfair? But there is a danger that, in the search for a well-adjusted, capable, self-aware, technologically literate leader, we may overlook some of the fundamental characteristics that are really needed. Among these are: a clear sense of vocation; a developed faith, which grasps the elements of Christian truth; a solid spirituality, capable of sustaining the ups and downs of ministry; an ability to relate to and lead others; and, finally, the capacity to work as part of a team. These are essential features of spiritual leadership for Christian ministry. This book is an account of how these characteristics grew in one man, as God changed him.

There are hundreds of books available which are manuals on leadership, but I am afraid this is not one of them. Many such books are written from an administrative or business point of view, with sleek points about how to be a good leader; but becoming a spiritual leader — for Peter, as for most others — is about painful formation, and lessons learnt in times of pressure and occasional failure. The French have a phrase which Henri Nouwen uses in his writing, *reculer pour mieux sauter*, meaning to step back, to jump forward again, and that is a fair description of the way Peter developed as a spiritual leader. So in Peter's case, rather than see some straight graph of steadily increasing leadership, we see hard won gains after moments of failure. It is because of this that Peter provides such a pattern of growth in spiritual leadership with which we can identify. My hope is that all those who are engaged in spiritual leadership — whether of five, fifty, five hundred or more — will gain insight and encouragement by re-visiting the biblical account of Peter's life and ministry. Spiritual leadership is both a privilege and a responsibility, and it is made more complex by the age in which we serve. We need all the help and insight we can get!

I would like to thank all those who have helped me to appreciate what is involved in spiritual leadership, including the congregations amongst whom it has been my privilege to serve, and I remember with gratitude those who led them and helped me: David Watson, Raymond Turvey and John Collins.

I would like to thank my publisher, Terra Nova, for all their encouragement; Russ Parker, for his generous foreword; and my family, for their patience and encouragement. Of course, all the deficiencies in this survey of Peter's life are mine. This is the second in a trilogy of *Becoming* books, which is something of a motto for me since, in an age in which we expect so much to be instantaneous, we do well to remember that most of us become over time what we are intended to be —whether "fully human" or a "spiritual leader" or, next, "a citizen of the Kingdom". I hope that Peter would not feel misrepresented by what I have written, and that this study leads to greater maturity in our leadership of the flock of God, for which Christ died.

Patrick Whitworth

St Patrick's Day
17th March 2005

Part One
FORMATION

1

BEGINNING WITH A CALL
Luke 5:1–11, John 1:19–42

The apostle Peter occupies a unique position in the story of the Christian faith. John wrote more of the New Testament. Paul led the mission to the Gentile world, became the most prolific correspondent in the New Testament and was the teacher of the faith. But Peter's life and ministry uniquely spans the ministry of Jesus and the birth of the early church at Pentecost, as well as providing some important instruction to the dispersed Christian communities in Pontus (the coastal strip around the Black Sea), Cappadocia, Galatia and Bithynia.[1] John was more reflective and visionary; Paul more able to explain the gospel to the Gentile mind but Peter was, and remains, the living embodiment of a disciple's struggle to become both the person and spiritual leader he is intended to be.

This is the story of one person's well-documented life, his highs and lows as well as his struggle to become a spiritual leader. As such, it is one in which all who aspire to spiritual leadership can see some of the outline of their story too. The book divides neatly into three parts corresponding to the development of Peter's leadership: the time spent with Jesus; the time around the birth of the church at Pentecost; and lastly, the mature teaching of Peter laid out in his two epistles. Each chapter will focus on a particular aspect of spiritual leadership taken from the life and teaching of Peter.

Leadership is at a premium in our present age as in every age. But what is good leadership? What makes for effective leadership? It seems as though societies rise and fall on the quality of their leadership. It is required in every walk of life: in parenting, teaching, business, administration, politics, sport, science, the military, exploration and the church. Without good leadership, communities decline, gifts are squandered or abused, and the potential of many people is wasted. Of course, the particular type of leadership we are looking at in this book is spiritual leadership or leadership of the church in its life and mission. What we are studying here is how a man chosen in the raw by Jesus became one of the great leaders of the church. It is a story worth retelling in its entirety because it will give hope and substance to our own development as leaders. How much they are needed now —and will be needed in the future!

It all began with a meeting, and to make it more vivid we will imagine the opening of Simon Peter's story in a narrative form, with some poetic licence, before drawing out its significance. Perhaps the day which Luke described in chapter 5:1–11 may have started like this....

Children were playing in the dusty streets. Women were busy fetching wood and water to produce an early morning drink. Men were doing what they did best, sitting and talking in the doorways as if the entire world depended on their conversation! The actual place might have been a village near Capernaum on the shore of the Sea of Galilee. There was a cove nearby, where fishing boats were moored. Some of the fishermen were still mending their nets after a hard but fruitless night's fishing; others were still lying on the beach enjoying the morning sunshine and resting their aching backs and arms.

A crowd began unexpectedly to gather near the water's edge. Peter, who was himself lying on the beach, sat up and rubbed his tired eyes to see more clearly what was going on. Then he caught sight of Jesus amongst one of the groups which had just arrived from Capernaum. He was easy to recognise, not because he was taller than any of the others, nor because he was more good looking, but there was an attractiveness and authority about him which distinguished him from the rest. Peter recalled the first time that they had met. It had been a few months earlier.

At the time there was a frisson of excitement that ran throughout Israel. For years now there had been no word from the Lord but there was a growing sense of anticipation and expectation throughout the community that things were about to change. Rumours coming from the temple in Jerusalem based on stories emanating from two ancient priests and a still more ancient prophetess were flying around. Pundits were saying that the Messiah would come soon, to liberate them from the long years of occupation by the Romans. Many were scouring the Scriptures, expecting that the words given to the prophet Daniel in exile would be fulfilled and that the occupying Roman power would be overthrown. "In the time of those kings", Daniel had prophesied, "the God of heaven will set up a kingdom that will never be destroyed, nor will it be left to another people. It will crush all those kingdoms and bring them to an end, but it will itself endure for ever."[2] Many longed for the end of "exile", which had begun when Jerusalem was sacked by the Babylonians but now continued in another form in their own occupied homeland.

It was in such an atmosphere that Peter had heard of the one crying in the wilderness, "Prepare the way for the LORD."[3] Every Jew knew this was a message of hope. This call to preparation was a part of Isaiah's great prophecy. Isaiah had written, "Comfort, comfort my people, says your God. Speak tenderly to Jerusalem, and proclaim to her that her hard service has been completed, that her sin has been paid for, that she has received from the LORD's hand double for all her sins."[4] So, like many others among his contemporaries, Peter, with his brother Andrew, went down to the Jordan, excitement stirring in his heart. Who was this man whose voice cried, "Prepare the way for the Lord"? He was not to be disappointed. In fact his life took on a sudden and almost violent new direction.

The sequence of events, which led to Simon's first meeting with Jesus, was both strange but typical. It was strange in that there appeared to be a sense of destiny in the ordinary everyday occurrences which led him to be in the right place at the right time; typical, because Peter had come to recognise over time a recurring pattern when it came to his relations with Jesus. It was as if, having been in a backwater for years, he was now being caught up into a current over which he had little control and which was also gathering ever-greater force. It was both exciting and daunting. As a fisherman he thought he knew about currents and winds, but this was different. He also thought that he knew about fishing, but he was to learn much more from an unexpected quarter.

To return to his first meeting, Peter had decided to go down with his brother Andrew to the river Jordan at Bethany where John the Baptist, as he had become popularly known, was baptising. John had burst on the scene a few weeks before. Apparently, he had lived in the desert for years, had existed on a diet of locusts and honey, wore the most rudimentary clothing and had the most uncompromising message, telling soldiers not to extort money but to be content with their wages, and teaching tax collectors not to collect more money than was allowed.[5] But John's main message was to the whole Israelite nation: to repent and be baptised, as preparation for the coming of the one who was mightier than him, and whose sandals he was unworthy to untie. It was hard to exaggerate the impact that John was making; there were delegations sent from Jerusalem to find out who he was and how *bona fide* were his credentials.[6] Peter had heard that this teaching was like nothing anyone had heard before, so he went down to the Jordan with a sense of excitement. Being an enthusiastic man he did not want to miss out!

So it was that Simon and Andrew, with very many others, were baptised at Bethany on the east side of the Jordan. It was an extraordinary moment. John preached about repentance and about changing lives so that they would be ready for the coming kingdom and the coming king. It was both exhilarating and revolutionary. It also made Simon think that the Romans' days of occupation were numbered. A day or so later, Andrew had left Simon and gone with a friend to spend the day with John the Baptist. It was while they were with him that John had suddenly stopped preaching and, in a dramatic manner, had pointed at another man in the crowd whom Andrew had not previously noticed. John had pointed at him and said, "Look, the Lamb of God, who takes away the sin of the world!"[7]

16

The following day, Jesus was, once again, identified by John as the "Lamb of God."[8] This time, Andrew decided to follow Jesus to find out more. Soon afterwards they had their first conversation with Jesus, and had gone to the place where he was staying. They had spent the afternoon together. Andrew knew that he could not keep the experience to himself; in fact he was so excited by this meeting that the very next day he went and fetched Simon and brought him along to meet Jesus too. He even blurted out his estimation of Jesus to Simon: "We have found the Messiah."[9] Simon was mystified, but decided to humour his brother and go with him. Simon would never forget that first meeting. Jesus simply fastened his eyes on him as if he had all along been expecting to meet him and said, "You are Simon son of John. You will be called Cephas."

Since then he had seen him around a few times, and now as he raised himself on the beach that day and rubbed his eyes, he knew somewhere deep down that this day was going to be life-changing.

The thought had barely passed through his sleepy head when Simon would have heard a by now familiar voice calling him Simon Peter. There was still only one person who called him that, although it would only be a matter of months before he was known more as Peter than Simon; except, of course, when Jesus was displeased with him when he reverted to either Simon or Simon Peter or, worst of all, Simon, son of John —but that was much later. Jesus would have asked Peter to use his boat. At that moment a mixture of excitement and dread seemed to fill his wary heart —excitement, because of his feeling that something life-changing was about to happen; dread because he felt curiously out of his depth. Simon got to his feet and, never one to shrink back, ran down to his boat moored at the water's edge. Hitching up his fisherman's clothes, he jumped in and, in an almost casual way, welcomed Jesus aboard.

Jesus gave him one of his long and lingering looks, as if he knew something of which Simon Peter was entirely ignorant. It was a little unnerving at first, but you eventually grew accustomed to it. After a while it made you think, and later—if you were alert—pray! Jesus asked him to put out a little way from the shore, so that he could teach the people —and sat down

17

in the boat. This was the first of many occasions when Jesus would sit in, sleep in and clamber aboard his boat. Peter rowed out a little way from the shore and then Jesus began to speak. So often he began with the words, "The kingdom of God is like...." The theme was practically always the same but it was usually punctuated with stories about landlords, families, farm workers, merchants, greedy people and the self-righteous. Sometimes Simon heard the same story repeated in a slightly different way for a different audience or occasion. Sitting there in the boat, Peter could watch the faces of the people. Their attention was held by the stories; sometimes they added their own comments or interjections. Sometimes you could tell they were moved or provoked or were looking more than a little uncomfortable. Watching their faces was like watching a Galilean sky in autumn with its changing clouds: sometimes cloudy and foreboding, and then bright blue with the sun picking out the sea or shoreline. When it was about midday, and it was plain that the crowd could take in no more and that they were getting hungry, Jesus turned round to Simon, who was himself feeling ready for some lunch and said, "Put out into deep water, and let down the nets for a catch."[10]

He could still remember now what he had felt like and thought when Jesus made that request. It was a preposterous idea! It was midday when the sun was at its hottest. The fish would be at the bottom; what is more they had fished all night and caught nothing! The lake had been stirred up by a sudden storm two nights before and the fish were not back in their normal grounds. He objected slightly, "Master, we've worked hard all night and haven't caught anything. But because you say so, I will let down the nets."[11] The nets were barely dry from the previous night's fruitless fishing, but nevertheless Peter pulled them into the boat. Jesus pointed to the area of the lake where he wanted Simon to go. Peter's eyes followed the direction to which Jesus' arm was pointing, thinking that they would never get anything there at that time of day! He rowed out anyway, putting up a bit of sail when they rounded the lee of the hills. James and John, who had been listening, decided to follow in the other boat. They were inquisitive and had nothing else to do —and it was normally eventful around Jesus! In retrospect, it was a good thing that they had followed. And later they reflected on whether it was all part of the plan!

About twenty minutes later they were in the deep water. Peter tried hard not to look sceptical. Andrew had come along too, and was not saying much but was keeping his own counsel about this fishing trip. He generally let Peter do the talking in the family and he was not going to change now. So having prepared the nets and positioned the boat so that it would drift in the breeze, they threw them over the side and settled down for what Peter thought would be a very long wait, glancing at Jesus every so often to see if there was the tiniest flicker of doubt on his face now that they were out here.

Jesus was impassive and appeared to be enjoying the trip. In the distance Peter could see the other boat catching them up; he remembered thinking they would be here in a few minutes, no doubt hiding their grins behind their hands. Simon thought about Jesus. Who was he? Was he another prophet or teacher —or more than a prophet? And what was he doing in his boat anyhow? His thoughts came to a sudden halt. The boat stopped drifting. It was as though they were anchored to the bottom, except that here the water was deeper than his longest nets could reach. Peter immediately concluded that they were snagged — on an old wreck probably, of which there were several at the bottom of the lake, on account of the fierce storms that blew up when the warm air from the east met the moisture of Galilee. Just as he was thinking what to do, he noticed that the nets were vibrating. He began to pull on them furiously. Everyone pulled with all their strength. They made a good team, Simon thought. He knew from the way the nets were straining even before he saw anything that there were a lot of fish in them. When the catch broke the surface of the water there were hundreds of large, gleaming, writhing fish; tails and heads were spinning over each other as the water drained away through the mesh. In the ten years he had been fishing since he first went out with his father, he had never had a catch like this!

His heart was once again filled with a mixture of excitement and awe; there was something uncanny about this catch! As Simon ladled the fish out of the nets, the hull of the boat filled up so rapidly that it seemed as though the boat was becoming too heavily laden. Seeing James and John in their boat not far away now, Simon signalled to them to come over and help, as there was a serious risk of sinking. They drew alongside, and Peter began to offload the fish into their boat as more and more spewed out of the breaking nets. When all the fish had been loaded, both boats were only just above the waterline.

Then, spontaneously, without any premeditation or artifice, Simon fell to his knees and, amongst all the writhing fish, facing Jesus, he said, "Go away from me, Lord; I am a sinful man!" It seemed to James and John a strange reaction. But Andrew could sense that his brother's heart was overwhelmed by the occasion. Peter always dated his call from that moment; everything else followed on from it!

Maybe it happened something like that. It was certainly an overwhelming moment of revelation and awe. Although, as is obvious from the Gospel accounts, this encounter on the Sea of Galilee was not their first one with Jesus, it was the determinative encounter in Simon Peter's call. Soon afterwards, Andrew, James and John, and Simon Peter stowed away their nets and fishing kit and left everything to follow Jesus.

There was a threefold nature to Peter's call. Firstly, it was a moment of transcendence. It is said that there are four great quests in modern man. They are a search for identity, a search for community and a search for transcendence; which together can all be wrapped into an ultimate search for meaning or significance. Without meaning and significance we cannot make sense of life, nor have satisfaction in living it. This event, which took place in a boat on the Sea of Galilee, brought Peter face to face with something which, at the very least, was greater than his previous experience. As such it was the intersection of the supernatural with the natural, the eternal with the temporal, or the supranormal with the everyday. For sure this was no ordinary catch of fish; it happened in no ordinary manner, and it occurred with a person whom Peter knew to be no ordinary man. Peter, true to character, and as he would so often do in the Gospel stories, responded both suddenly and intuitively to what he felt. He knelt down in a pile of fish, his stock in trade and, in words which showed that he had been overwhelmed by what had happened, he said in effect that he felt vulnerable, weak and unworthy of such a miracle happening in his boat; surely there was someone else more deserving! Or, to put it another way, he felt instinctively that something heavenly had come to his little boat and life, and he did not count himself ready for or worthy of this.

If transcendence is that moment when something heavenly touches something earthly then, in fisherman's terms, this had truly happened. That pile of fish in the boat, which by any normal stretch of a fisherman's imagination should not have been there, was both a testimony and a witness to the fact that something "other" and "different" had happened, and he could not be unchanged by it.

Although most calls may not seem so spectacular or memorable, it is nonetheless vital to effective spiritual leadership to sense a call. It may be a growing conviction spread over time, or it may be the sudden realisation that God is calling you to be a leader in his church. But it was to leadership in the church that Peter was called, and this book is a study of what that meant —then as now.

If that miraculous catch provided the occasion which drew Peter's attention to his call, his immediate response was a sense of real unpreparedness and unworthiness. Nor is this an unusual response on those occasions when the holy intersects with the human.

When Moses was confronted by a strange sight in the desert—of a bush on fire but not being burnt—he said, "I will go over and see this strange sight —why the bush does not burn up."[12] As Moses considered this transcendent event, in which a perfectly normal desert bush was alight but not consumed, he too was both addressed and called by God.

When Abraham, many years earlier, looked up one starry night, he also heard the voice of God speaking into his heart —and he learnt that God would establish with his family a covenant based on faith.[13]

21

When Isaiah found himself in the temple one day, in the year of King Uzziah's death, and had a vision of the holy majesty of God, he likewise was commissioned to go with a message to the people, having had his lips cleansed by a burning coal taken from the altar by a winged seraph. He too felt a profound sense of unworthiness.[14]

Transcendent moments do not come much greater than these! If, on the one hand, they arrest attention like nothing else, they also lead to a sense of awe and wonder, not to say unworthiness.

So the second aspect to Peter's call was his own sense of unworthiness or inability. Like Isaiah and Moses before him, Peter felt profoundly unprepared and innately unworthy. It was the presence of Jesus, disclosed in greater reality through this miraculous catch, that made Peter feel naked, vulnerable and ashamed. It was this sense which must have precipitated Peter's cry, kneeling amongst the fish at the feet of Jesus, "Go away from me, Lord; I am a sinful man!"

However, a sense of inadequacy rather than a sense of our own ability is a better qualification for the task of spiritual leadership. Just as the leader must have a real sense of vocation either precipitated or confirmed by such a moment, so also this call may often be accompanied by an equal sense of inadequacy. Moses, for the best part of Exodus 4, pleads with God that he send someone else to rescue the Israelites from Egypt. Isaiah knows himself to be a "man of unclean lips", unworthy of becoming God's messenger to the people; and, in line with these great predecessors with whom he would never have compared himself, Peter made that confession of his own sinfulness.

But that was never a disqualification for service — otherwise there would be no one capable of serving. A sense of inadequacy is in fact a precondition to effective service of God! In response to our misgivings, innate inadequacy and fearful longings, Jesus says, "Do not be afraid." It is a word which we must constantly hear, in Christian ministry. A spiritual leader had best keep that sense of inadequacy for the task if he or she is to make the most of God's available power.

Recently, a Pentecostal pastor from Malawi, Stanley Ndovie, visited our church. He leads the Living Waters Church in Blantyre, which has some five thousand members and has planted a further five hundred churches in Malawi! He is a compelling preacher and one of the foremost leaders of the church in his country. However, in a conference on leadership, which we held at our church in 2003, Stanley told us the hilarious account of his resistance to God's call to becoming a pastor and to enrolling in a Bible school in Malawi for his training as a pastor. He had questioned his father's decision to send him to Bible school but went anyway.

However, despite a miraculous deliverance from a deadly snake bite through the prayers (and lengthy preaching!) of a very old "man of God", he disobediently decided to pack his bags and leave the Bible school. But on the day of his departure he was called to preach in front of the students at their evening service. Although reassured in a vision that God would remove his fear of others so that he could preach, he still felt totally inadequate for the task. He devised a strategy to use up the time of the service by asking the most garrulous student, well known for his very long prayers, to pray before his preaching so that he would have only a few minutes to speak. However, he need not have feared, as in the moments before speaking he was given such an unprecedented calm as well as the text from which he should speak. He began then what has since been a remarkable ministry of preaching all over the world. But it all began with an acute sense of fear and inadequacy, even though in his own body he had received a remarkable healing miracle.

It seems that repeatedly in the Bible God delights in taking the weak and fearful and turning them into spiritual leaders whether it be Moses, Gideon, Jeremiah —or Peter. Our sense of weakness, nervousness and unworthiness is more a qualification than a disqualification for God's service.

The third strand of Peter's call was the call to leave — "leave", that is, in the context of a new mission ("hence-forward you will be catching men"), but leave nevertheless. It is vividly portrayed in Luke's Gospel account: "So they pulled their boats up on shore, left everything and followed him." There cannot be discipleship of any kind without leaving, and nor can there be effective leadership of the church without sacrifice. Just as in the call of any disciple there is a leaving behind of an old way of life, so in the call of a leader of the church there will be a particular sense of leaving or sacrifice.

There is a danger in my own denomination of so professionalising the call and work of ministry and the work of the clergy that it may sit well with, say, an EU directive for work, but it bears little resemblance to the ministry of the New Testament! Ministerial work may well mean financial sacrifice, sacrifice of privacy, working long and unsociable hours, intermingling family and ministerial life —to name just a few places where "the shoe may pinch". But surely this is all part of the call to leave a lifestyle in which our own comfort is primary; and to take on a new way of life common to all believers but especially to leaders. This does not mean that a leader in the church is to be abused, taken advantage of or exploited, but rather that in being called to ministerial service we are placing our rights second to the call of following Jesus in the service of the gospel. We are in danger of forgetting the word "leaving" in our own call, or having "left" once, expecting to return to all that we once left behind!

Unlike the world of celebrities and politicians, in which they are constantly trying to lay down an enforceable line between public and private life, no such distinction can exist in the life of the spiritual leader. What I am at home must be what I am in the pulpit; a seamless line of existence should run between the two! Or, to put it another way, what your congregation see and hear on Sunday is what your children or spouse get during the week! Of course we all fail but that is the aspiration, nevertheless. A private life, which I can run differently from a public persona, is not a camouflage in which the leader can hide.

So in the call to leadership, perhaps even more than in the call to discipleship, there is a call to leave. For Peter and his companions it was, amongst other things, a call to leave their familiar routine. The disciples had begun the biggest adventure of their lives; and if the Christian life is

24

not an adventure it is nothing. And if leadership is not a continuing adventure you have to ask whether it has become something it was not intended to be.

So Peter began this great adventure, which at times must have seemed like a roller coaster unequalled even by the fierce squalls of Galilee. It was to have moments of almost unbelievable joy and ecstasy alongside others of almost unfathomable pain. It was an adventure in which his horizons of experience were forever widening and deepening. This occurred on two fronts; firstly there was his ever-deepening understanding of Jesus and the kingdom he had come to inaugurate, which continually yielded up new and surprising vistas, and secondly there was a deep and painful journey into his own self-knowledge which at times became almost too painful to bear. Any true spiritual leader will have travelled the same way, and could sit you down and tell of the moments of sheer joy and elation, but alongside that could equally tell you of pain and mistakes. For Peter, these moments came fast and furiously —not least in the episode we shall look at next.

2

GALILEAN MINISTRY
—A Sabbath to Remember
Mark 1

At the start it was just the five of them —Jesus, Simon Peter, Andrew, James and John.[1] Later, Jesus would choose a further eight disciples. Nevertheless there would be times in the future when Jesus would take with him three of the original disciples, an inner circle; for instance at the healing of Jairus' daughter, the transfiguration or the agony in the Garden of Gethsemane. But during these early days before Jesus called the other eight, there was a particular intimacy in their life together. They were the first disciples. The four of them knew each other well. They were fishing partners. They had Jesus to themselves —that is, when the crowds were not pressing in from every side and his attention was not taken up with a multitude of human needs! And of all those early days around Galilee, one was especially memorable. Later, Peter would tell Mark, who recorded it in his Gospel written in Rome many years later. This day was a Sabbath in Capernaum.

Capernaum was Simon's home town; he was well known there, as were James and John and their father, Zebedee. It was a lakeside town, surrounded by highly productive land and a plentiful spring.[2] It had a small garrison and a customs post. It has to this day the best-preserved Galilean synagogue dating from the fourth century. It was here that Jesus settled and made his headquarters for his Galilean ministry. It figured largely in that early period, and he performed many miracles there, one of which happened on a particular Sabbath....

A NEW TEACHING

As was their custom, Jesus and his disciples went to the synagogue for morning worship. It was to be an eventful service, the start of a remarkable day. Perhaps it went something like this, if we can use our imagination around Mark's text....

There was considerable excitement in the synagogue as Jesus was present. News had spread fast in the villages around Galilee. A rumour was circulating that Jesus had been present at a wedding nearby where the wine had run out![3] It had been so embarrassing for the host! But Jesus had given orders to the servants to fill six large water jars with water. He then told the waiters to serve the water to the guests! Naturally they were reluctant; but like Peter—whom Jesus had told to put out into the deep having caught nothing all night—they did what he said —but not without a little encouragement from Mary the mother of Jesus, who was there as well. And then miraculously, when they served from the great stone jars, the water turned to wine, the equivalent of three hundred bottles, and of the very best quality! Those at the wedding feast had remarked on both the quality of the wine and its generous supply.

Understandably, the waiters had talked! So, soon, most of the villages around and about had heard about this miracle —the first of Jesus' ministry. Naturally there was a buzz in the synagogue that morning. Cana was only a few miles away, in the hill country west of Capernaum. To Capernaum, the provincial centre in that area, news had travelled. Indeed, later, a royal official from Capernaum came to Cana where Jesus was then staying and requested that he heal his son, which Jesus did with a word![4] So there were links between Cana and Capernaum.

28

Perhaps those at the synagogue that Sabbath wondered gleefully what the after service refreshments would be like today!

Given that it was Jesus' first miracle, maybe the more censorious people there commented on how unusual this miracle of turning water into wine had been. What a way to begin! What a precedent to set! What misunderstandings it could suggest! It seemed almost self-indulgent to make so much wine, risking excess and drunkenness! After all, you would have thought Jesus would do something more serious, less domestic, and more sensational than relieving the embarrassment of a host at a wedding and supplying the drinking needs of the guests! Understandably, later he would be accused of being a wine-bibber and a glutton.

So there was considerable excitement that Jesus was here in the synagogue that Sabbath morning, along with some of the disciples. And as Jesus already had a reputation as a rabbinic teacher, although he had not studied at a rabbinic school, he was invited to teach from the Scriptures. He stood up and went to the front to teach. There was an expectant silence. What would he say?

Although we do not know exactly what Jesus was teaching about, as we do when he spoke at the synagogue in his home town of Nazareth a few weeks earlier,[5] it is a fair assumption that it was about the kingdom of God, and that it was time for his audience to repent and believe! If we do not know the text, we do know what happened during the service.

Jesus had been teaching for a few minutes when there was a sudden interruption. It was from a man, well known in the community, who was often unwell. Today he was more than usually agitated. Many thought that he had an evil spirit, which oppressed him. During Jesus' address he cried out, "What do you want with us, Jesus of Nazareth? Have you come to destroy us? I know who you are —the Holy One of God!"

Jesus replied sternly and said to the spirit, "Come out of him." The evil spirit shook the man vigorously and came out of him with a shriek. Everyone was amazed. The man was left quiet, prayerful and praising God. Although this was the first time that Peter saw such deliverance, it would by no means be the last. In the coming years there would be countless similar occasions.

Jesus called them signs of the kingdom of heaven being amongst them.[6]

No wonder the people were amazed, as Jesus' teaching and actions were so different from what they normally received at the synagogue. The teaching by the Pharisees was usually designed to show them, the congregation, how they had failed to keep the law and how they were to observe it more strictly, as by keeping it they would become righteous and prepare themselves for the future. By observing the law they would be distinct and maintain a form of independence of spirit from the Romans. But it was so burdensome! It was just as Jesus said in some of his later teaching about the Pharisees, that they would cross seas and continents to make a single convert and then they would make him twice as much a child of hell as before! But the truth was that they never practised what they preached.[7] They loved honour, the best seats, flowing robes, power and especially money,[8] and their religion was only skin deep! As Jesus said, "You are like whitewashed tombs, which look beautiful on the outside but on the inside are full of dead men's bones and everything unclean. In the same way, on the outside you appear to people as righteous but on the inside you are full of hypocrisy and wickedness."[9] For years the people had been burdened by the religious teaching of the Pharisees; it was a heavy load to carry.

But the teaching that day was different! It was new in the sense that it came from a different realm. It was like so much of what Jesus came to bring. He brought a new way of loving, crossing boundaries that had not been crossed before! He brought liberation, not condemnation. He brought a kingdom and not a tyranny. He brought festivity and mirth, not impoverishment and sullenness. Usually, it would take an hour or two before the effects of synagogue wore off and normal human living could be resumed! But that day they burst out onto the streets to tell people what had happened. There was something to say, something to tell, and a teacher like no other they had heard. Here was a spiritual leader to inspire —and to follow.

The most striking testimony to Jesus' teaching was that someone who had been unwell was cured. This was a new kind of teaching which led to a change, rather than a sense of helplessness facing an impossible and unending task. Its essential quality was authority, not in the sense of telling you what you already knew from the Torah but could do nothing about, but in the sense of commanding change where it was needed most. This was an authority which actually brought transformation in its wake. He spoke or commanded —and it happened!

Maybe at the end of the service Peter went over to the man who had been delivered, to have a quiet word. Crowds of neighbours were around him, touching him and pulling him about, as if to test that it was all real. We can imagine Peter asking him to recall what Jesus had said. The man would have remembered those strange words he had uttered: "What do you want with us, Jesus of Nazareth? Have you come to destroy us? I know who you are —the Holy One of God!" For some reason it had been those words which had made Jesus look more sternly at him, as if he did not want anyone to hear them. Peter then embraced the man who had been healed, did not say anything more and moved away from the crowd thoughtfully.

Peter remembered the fish in the lake; the wine at Cana, and now this man completely changed. But it was time to be going; the sun was well overhead, it must be past the usual time for lunch, and time for the usual rest during the afternoon, the hottest part of the day.

He invited Jesus to his home where others would be waiting for them. So the five of them went to his house for the midday Sabbath meal. It was always the most important Jewish family meal of the week.

HEALING AT PETER'S HOME

When they arrived at the house, there was some concern as Peter's mother-in-law, who was living with them, was unwell. She had a very high fever and was unable to help in preparing or serving the meal for the extra guests. There was still a lot to do and fewer hands to do it. They did not often have five hungry men coming for lunch, as well as the family. Andrew, Simon Peter's brother, would be there too, as well as others who wanted to come and meet Jesus. So they needed all hands on deck.

When Jesus learned that Peter's mother-in-law was unwell he asked whether he could go and see her. He was taken through to her room where she was lying down. She was obviously too weak to help, but she was both disappointed and annoyed with herself that she could not cook on such an important occasion. When Jesus came into her room she was embarrassed and a little guilty, although there was no need for either. She, too, had heard about the wedding in Cana, the embarrassment of another host and how Jesus had helped them in their domestic crisis. It was too much to hope for his help again.

When he came into the room she tried to get up, but was too weak. Quickly sinking back onto her couch of cushions piled up on the earthen floor, she muttered an apology at her failure to rise and her inability to cook. Jesus came over to her, took her by the hand and helped her up! Immediately, the fever left her; she was completely cured!

Straight away, she went to the place where they were preparing food and began to help —chattering to the others, telling them that when Jesus took her by the hand and spoke, her fever had left instantly. The meal would be a special one today. Soon they were all relaxing around their simple dining area spread out on the floor. Jesus gave thanks for the food and they ate. They were hungry. There were things they laughed and joked about: the look on the Pharisees' faces when the man shouted out in the synagogue; the hopes of the congregation for more wine after the service; but there were things too which they had all heard (the sound of the possessed man before he was cured) about which they said nothing, as they were more than a little awed.

Peter reflected during the meal, as he watched his mother-in-law serve them, that a moment ago she was too feverish to stand. Who was this man, Jesus, on the other side of the room? Already so much had happened in a few days since he had left his boat at the nearby fishing village. If all this had happened in just a few days, what would lie ahead in the next months and years? And how different this was to everything they were used to. Here was a new teaching with authority and power to change people's lives. Jesus was quite unlike the

Pharisees, who as soon as they left the public gaze, became vengeful and jealous. Jesus remained the same both in the synagogue and in the home; his teaching and actions were as seamless as the robe some of the women had recently given him.

Even as Peter was thinking about all this and the others were having a rest, there was the noise of a crowd outside, shouting for Jesus to help them. The sun had just about gone down, and when Simon Peter opened the door, he could see in the dusky light about a hundred people gathered there. It seemed as though the entire town's sick and oppressed were gathered at his door and they wanted Jesus to come out and heal them. He did. Every one of them was healed. If Peter had not seen it with his own eyes he would have found it unbelievable.

That night Peter went to bed both exhausted and elated. It was to be an almost permanent condition over the next three years. At dawn, when he awoke, there were more shouts for Jesus, but he could not be found.

A SOLITARY PLACE

Although it was exasperating at the time not to be able to find Jesus when so many people wanted him, it was a lesson that Peter would not forget in later life. Word had gone round the rest of the town and surrounding villages of what had happened the night before; consequently—as Peter had told John Mark for his account of the ministry of Jesus for Mark's Gospel—everyone was looking for Jesus. Nor was it surprising, as scores of people had been healed the night before. But Jesus was still not to be found. He had risen early, left the house and gone outside the town to a lonely place.

Peter went out to search for him when the crowd had started banging on his door. As he wandered the streets of Capernaum, he found a man who had risen early to do a household chore. He told Peter that he had seen someone heading out of the town for a lonely spot. Peter followed his directions. After a little more searching around, he eventually found Jesus in a deserted place overlooking the town. Peter said, "Everyone is looking for you!"

Jesus seemed neither surprised nor perturbed. His thoughts

had obviously moved on as he replied, "Let us go somewhere else—to the nearby villages—so that I can preach there also. That is why I have come." For a moment Peter was amazed; surely there was more to do in Capernaum, people who needed healing. But clearly the demands of the people were not paramount; their needs were not the final word. Jesus was marching to a different beat than human need alone. There was some sort of programme to follow, some sort of mission to accomplish, that kept them from settling in one place. He came, Jesus constantly said, to do his Father's will, and whatever he was told to do or saw his Father doing, he would do. There was a task that Jesus had come to do, and nothing would deflect him from that purpose.

Later, Peter asked him what he was doing leaving the house so early and seeking solitude. The answer was that he was praying, and had chosen a solitary place. A pattern would soon emerge in Jesus' life where periods of intense activity, when there was no time even to eat, would be followed by times of rest, reflection and prayer. Sometimes Jesus would slip away by himself to pray to his Father. Sometimes he would take the disciples with him in the boat, as it was the only way of outwitting the crowd from whom they needed some respite. The boat was an essential crowd control mechanism through which they could sometimes escape those relentless demands. Sometimes they sought solitude but the crowds did get the better of them.

After a day which was as long as it was eventful, it was time to move on again to another town or village. On the way, a leper fell at Jesus' feet and asked for healing.

Peter noticed that the atmosphere of their life together was almost imperceptibly changing; soon the five of them would increase to twelve and a new pattern of ministry would begin. Thankfully for Peter there were still occasions when Jesus spent time with the three closest disciples, but increasingly he realised that he would have to share Jesus with others.

That Sabbath in Capernaum had been one to remember, but the events of the next months around Galilee were forming Peter into the leader he would be.

3

GALILEAN MINISTRY
—*Walking on Water*
Matthew 10:1–42, 14:1–36, 15:29–16:12
Mark 6:6b–56, 8:1–21, Luke 9:1–17, John 6:1–70

After their first preaching tour of a number of towns and villages in the district of Galilee, Jesus and his disciples returned to Capernaum.[1] The pattern of ministry had by now been fairly clearly established. Jesus would teach in the synagogues in the towns and villages and in the open air to large crowds. To the crowds he spoke mostly in parables; these he would later explain to his disciples.[2] He would deliver any who were oppressed by the devil. He would heal the sick. He would call the most unlikely people to follow him, like Levi (or Matthew) the tax collector.[3] He would eat cheerfully with all sorts as he did in Levi's house, with tax collectors and other unspecified "sinners". And he was never far from controversy.

Jesus continually offended the Pharisees and teachers of the law by his claim to forgive sins, which he regarded as more indicative of his authority than even curing the sick or maimed.[4] He offended by his failure to fast ostentatiously,[5] by his inadequate washing before meals[6] and by his plucking ears of corn from the fields on a Sabbath.[7] This last accusation was not one of stealing — as gleaning was permitted under the Jewish law — but rather of working on the Sabbath through the simple action of picking ears of corn from the fields. Sabbath breaking was the Pharisees' especial *bête noir*, and they continually accused Jesus of doing it.

In these ways a discernible rhythm of ministry emerged. And everywhere there were crowds, filling every room, doorway, house and field, so that it was hard to get close to Jesus.[8] Even his family despaired of ever seeing him alone, saying that he was "out of his mind".[9] To their chagrin, Jesus redefined his family: "Whoever does God's will is my brother and sister and mother!"[10] The events were overwhelming, exciting, exhilarating all at the same time, but Peter could not see where it was all leading. Would Jesus restore the kingdom to Israel, overthrowing Roman power and putting his followers in positions of influence and authority in this new kingdom about which he was forever speaking? We may well suppose that Peter would have understood Jesus to be building a power base through his winning actions and remarkable teaching in the region of Galilee —the most notoriously volatile area in Israel, where only a few years earlier, in AD 6, there had been a political insurrection against the Romans. It was a hotbed of insurgency, fermenting with discontent. Peter may have imagined that through his extraordinary gifts Jesus was building support in the north of the country before marching triumphantly on Jerusalem.

It did not come as a total surprise therefore to Peter when Jesus began to organise his followers in a more systematic and methodical way for what he thought would be an assault on Jerusalem; although Peter must have thought Jesus' choice of leaders a little suspect. But then Peter found both Jesus' choice of people and his policies for his kingdom continually surprising. He was in essence conservative, a fisherman from a small town who had to continually widen his horizons to keep up with the ever-surprising ways of his master. He shared the widely held view that when the Messiah came he would liberate his people from their Roman overlords.

One day on a mountainside after a prolonged period of prayer, which went on all night,[11] Jesus called out twelve from amongst his much larger group of followers, and in a deliberate and significant way appointed them to a new order in this burgeoning kingdom. He called them apostles.[12] They were a new group, larger than the tightly knit inner circle of three, which included James and John and Peter, but much smaller than the seventy two whom Jesus later identified and sent out.[13]

However, this newly selected cadre of apostles was a vital strategic grouping. Jesus' disciples were formed in three concentric circles around him. There was the small, intimate group; another larger group — the twelve — which could be trained for future leadership; and, finally, a much larger band which would be given a taste of making known God's kingdom, who were the seventy two.[14] Whereas the three were close knit and already related by blood or business, the twelve were very mixed. Although they were all Israelite they had little in common apart from their willingness to follow Jesus. They were certainly not homogeneous in background, outlook or expectation.

Peter and Andrew were brothers, and likewise James and John. These four were the nucleus of the twelve. The others were hardly natural allies. For years Matthew had worked as a stooge for the occupying Roman regime, despised by the Jews from whom he raised deeply unpopular taxes. Contrastingly Simon, known as the Cananaean or the Zealot, followed a party, which was openly hostile to the Romans. Ten or more years previously, a rebel called Judas had incited a revolt against the Romans, urging his countrymen not to pay taxes to the Roman emperor. And later one of Judas' sons would capture the stronghold of Masada from the Romans and hold out against them rather than surrender. Nine hundred and sixty men, women and children resisted to the end, taking their own lives rather than fall into the clutches of the loathed Romans. Masada would become one of the greatest symbols of resistance in Jewish history.[15] No ordinary leader would put Matthew and Simon the Zealot in the same group and at the centre of a new movement for freedom; surely sooner or later they would come into conflict!

Amongst the other disciples chosen to be part of the

twelve were the sophisticated Philip, close to the Greek culture of the Sadducees, and the blunt speaking, sceptical Thomas. They were like the proverbial oil and vinegar—the one suave and assured, the other prickly and doubtful. "Surely", Peter must have thought, "they will rub each other up the wrong way!" But who was he to speak? And then there was Judas —why on earth did Jesus choose him? Surely he knew that he would turn out to be both a thief and a traitor![16] But then, considering who were chosen to be members of the twelve, what was amazing was not that one "messed up" but that the remaining eleven should still have been together in the Upper Room two and a half years later, on the day of Pentecost![17] Only prayer could have achieved that.[18]

But now, a few months into the public ministry of Jesus, a new shape had come into their life together, and a new sense of preparation and focus on training. It was no longer the case that Jesus was content to do everything himself; he now expected his disciples to do the very things that he did, and before long that was exactly what happened.

He summoned the twelve to him and told them that they would go out and do the same things that he had done. They were sent out in pairs. They were told to take nothing for the journey, neither food nor stick, nor money, nor spare clothing, but they were to go to the villages of the area and speak about the kingdom of God. They were to heal the sick, cast out evil spirits and preach the gospel, telling those who would listen that the kingdom of God had come close to them. If they were received they should stay with those people, receiving hospitality from them and not going from house to house, but if a community rejected them, they should shake the dust from their feet as a symbolic act that they had had their opportunity and rejected it.[19] This mission of the twelve was one of the most exciting pieces of ministry that Peter and the other apostles did.

The exercise was to be repeated later by the seventy two, and when they returned from their dramatic and remarkable mission, Jesus had never seemed so animated or excited. Full of joy in the Holy Spirit, he praised his Father.[20] However, on the return of the twelve from their mission, Jesus decided that they should get some peace and quiet, as the crowds were so demanding. What is more, Jesus had just heard some devastating news.

A DAY TO RECALL

Mark in his account, most of which came from Simon Peter's lips, makes it clear that the twenty four hours following the return of the twelve from their mission were tempestuous in more ways than one. Perhaps it was the news that Jesus had just received which made him seem less outwardly ecstatic with the achievements of the twelve than he would later be with the achievements of the seventy two. It was not that he rejoiced any the less in their accomplishment, but that he, as Matthew tells us, had just received a group of John the Baptist's disciples who had told him that John was dead!

He had been cynically executed in gaol —beheaded at the command of Herod, to please Herodias. Her daughter, Salome, had requested John's head after she had so moved Herod by her dancing that he promised her anything she asked. Deferring to her mother's wish, Salome asked for the head of John on a plate and Herod had reluctantly provided the gruesome prize. This news of John's hideous and gratuitous execution came at the same time as the return of the twelve from their missionary exercise.

Naturally, with news of John's death still ringing in his ears, as well as his desire to hear how the twelve had got on, Jesus decided to find some peace and quiet, both to hear what they had done, and to reflect and mourn, following John's death.[21] But they were not to escape the crowds so easily. The people found out where he was going and converged on him, like bees to a hive; even running ahead of his boat to meet him. Jesus, when he saw them, had compassion on them; he taught them many things, healed their sick and then discovered that they were hungry, having spent the whole day with him.[22] In a similar way, Luke tells us in one of the most delightful verses in his Gospel, "He welcomed them

39

and spoke to them about the kingdom of God, and healed those who needed healing."[23] So, far from having a peaceful moment to discuss with the twelve what had happened on their mission, they were launched into the biggest catering operation of their lives to date!

They were in a desolate place and miles from any village. The people had been there for most of the day and had not eaten anything; nightfall was coming soon. The disciples thought Jesus should send the crowd away so that they could find something to eat. But Jesus had other ideas. It was a perfect training opportunity for his disciples, so he said to Philip, "Where shall we buy bread for these people to eat?" John tells us, "He asked this only to test him, for he already had in mind what he was going to do."[24] Andrew, Peter's brother, said that they had found a boy with "five small barley loaves and two small fish, but how far will they go among so many?" How would one packed lunch feed five thousand men and others besides? Jesus made them sit down in groups of fifties and hundreds and, having thanked his Father for the food, he sent the disciples out to feed them —presumably with a small piece of fish and bread each. It seemed absurd, but they knew better than to remonstrate with Jesus at what they thought would be their impending humiliation. For Peter, Jesus' command to feed the huge crowd from the meagre rations provided by the boy must have had echoes of Jesus' command to him to let down the nets for a catch after a fruitless night's fishing.

In their hands the food multiplied. The mathematics of miracle took over: seven into five thousand went more than enough times to satisfy their guests. And the leftovers surpassed the original main course by many hundreds of times. You cannot imagine the astonishment of the disciples and the amazement of the diners! All the way home, they must have been asking how it was done; "Heavenly catering" was in action again: first the wine at Cana, now the food by Galilee!

Satisfied, taught, and with many healed, the crowd began to disperse, but there was more than a whiff of political rebellion in the air, and Jesus, knowing that some wanted then and there to make him their king and rally the people against the Romans, quickly left the scene before there was any disturbance.[25] Although it is only given a cursory mention by John in his Gospel, Jesus' refusal of political power handed to him by a politically intoxicated crowd, and his repudiation of a revolutionary mob bent on the hopeless whim of regime change of the Roman power, is one of the great turning points of his ministry. By this rejection of the crowd's way, he was once again defining the nature of the mission he had come to fulfil.

Towards the end of the day, Jesus told his disciples that he was going up the mountainside behind the lake to pray. He quietly slipped away before the crowd could notice and he told the disciples to get into the boat and return to Bethsaida, which was on the other side of the lake. How he would rejoin them did not cross their minds, as the disciples had taken the only boat; maybe by then they had learnt that Jesus would engineer his own transport —although in the event it must have surpassed their wildest imaginings.[26]

As they rowed, the weather changed and it became hard going to get across to the other side. They had rowed three and a half miles in the rough seas in the dark, and they were beginning to wonder whether they would be able to reach the other side when, through the darkness and above the waves, a figure emerged who appeared to be gaining on them all the while. Terrified, they cried out until they recognised that it was Jesus himself; whereupon Peter, rashly it seemed, shouted out, "Lord, if it's you, tell me to come to you on the water."

Typically, Jesus uttered his favourite word, "Come!" To the astonishment of the others, Peter got out of the boat and began to walk towards Jesus. Initially he walked towards Jesus not more than a few paces, but then the sheer improbability of what he was doing must have crossed his mind: he looked around him and realised the strength and power of the waves. As he did so he began to sink into them, —struggling as he sank. Then he shouted out, "Lord, save me!" —whereupon Jesus, who was by now close to the boat and Peter, reached out a hand, grabbed him and the two of them were seemingly instantaneously in the boat! Jesus, shouting above the storm as they clambered aboard, said, "You of little faith... why did you doubt?" To cap it all, when Jesus was in the boat with them, the wind died down, and within no time they had arrived at the other side. It was not surprising that they fell at his feet and said, "Truly you are the son of God!"

Understandably, the disciples were bewildered by the last twenty four hours; their own mission had barely ended, the news of John's execution in gaol had broken, a chance to debrief with Jesus had been interrupted, a picnic beside the sea had been provided for thousands of men from a lunch made for a single boy, and finally, a night rowing on a stormy sea had been transformed, with Jesus walking over the waves towards their boat! A day is a long time in the company of Jesus! As yet, they could not understand what had happened. And now there followed a further day of teaching by Jesus, in which he said, "I am the living bread that came down from heaven. If anyone eats of this bread, he will live forever. This bread is my flesh, which I will give for the life of the world."[27]

Peter surely must have looked back on these events as a defining moment in his own development as a disciple and future leader. They would mark the end of one stage of Jesus' ministry and the beginning of another. Although it would take hindsight to see this, surely that was the case. There were four vital lessons for him to learn from the events of the past two days.

LESSONS FOR LEADERSHIP

On a few occasions whilst sitting in a church building I have looked closely at some of the memorials. Nowadays it is unfashionable to put up memorials for people, partly because of expense and partly because to some it seems either too ostentatious or too congratulatory —or maybe there are other reasons in our present climate that make such public individual memorials unfashionable. But in former periods of history it was a natural way of showing regard and affection for those who had served God and died.

One memorial in our church is to the wife of a previous vicar. She died just before the Second World War, and he about seven years after it ended. So for twelve years, and during the war, he continued in ministry in the parish as a widower. I occasionally wonder what it must have been like for him. Nor is he alone in suffering bereavement whilst in full time ministry. Others, tragically, have lost children or spouses whilst in the full flow of ministry. But it is less common in the UK for a Christian leader to suffer the loss of a close colleague or relation through deliberate persecution on account of either the message they preach or the life they live. But for Jesus the death of John the Baptist was a critical moment. It comes just before the hinge moment in his ministry when he turned away from Galilee and set his face to go to Jerusalem. It must have reminded him of the sacrifice that he would make, even as John through his preaching had courted the persecution of Herodias and eventual death.

Matthew, in his Gospel, paints the scene most vividly. The death of John the Baptist is recorded in the early verses of chapter fourteen. The story of his death simply ends with those telling words, "John's disciples came and took his body and buried it. Then they went and told Jesus."[28] The next paragraph begins, "When Jesus heard what had happened, he withdrew by boat privately to a solitary place." There was no mistaking what Jesus intended to do in the light of his sudden bereavement brought about by persecution of his cousin John the Baptist. He used the boat to get away from the crowd and, with his disciples, gain privacy and solitude to mourn John. His cousin's death was a stark reminder of the fate that awaited him at the hands of men.

It is impossible for us to know clearly what Jesus felt at the news of John's death, and some will say that it does not matter anyhow (and that discerning the feelings of Jesus is a very modern line of enquiry, too), but what is plain from Matthew's account is that Jesus sought solitude and privacy to reflect with his disciples. But, as so often happened in his ministry, he had to face the expectations of the crowd.

But the lesson that Peter must have seen illustrated here by Jesus was his combination of extraordinary self-discipline together with overwhelming compassion towards the needs of others, so that he continued in ministry when he himself was in need of solitude and privacy to mourn.

If we were asked to tabulate, in order of priority, occasions when people should be left alone, then surely very near the top would come periods of bereavement! We would say, "Don't bother him now; he has just heard tragic news." And most of us would be embarrassed even to ask anything of someone who had recently been bereaved. But although Jesus felt the impact of this sudden bad news, which he probably expected to come sooner or later, his feelings did not prevent him from ministering to the crowd and recognising their need of him.

We recall again Matthew's words, "When Jesus landed and saw a large crowd, he had compassion on them and healed their sick." To put it plainly, their need of him was greater than his need for solitude; and anyhow it seems that Jesus realised he could find that later, as indeed he did.[29] But in the meantime his own self-discipline and compassion for the people enabled one of the great moments of his ministry to take place, which was the feeding of the five thousand.

Perhaps Peter reflected on the way Jesus had handled the conflicting needs of the moment. He must have been conscious on the one hand of Jesus' need for privacy and solitude, both to mourn John's loss and to hear their account of the mission from which they had just returned, and on the other hand he must also have been aware of the crowd's need for Jesus' teaching and help. It was therefore a moment of tension, which is not strange to the ministerial life where private life (or, in this case, specifically grief) and public ministry intermingle, and the one informs and deeply affects the other. Sudden tragic news will affect people differently, depending both on the circumstances and the temperament of the individual. For one person the events may be totally disabling, whilst another may have the temperament and resources to cope.

I remember with great admiration a friend Henry Orombi,

now Archbishop of Uganda, speaking at the funeral and thanksgiving service of his son, who died while he and Phoebe, his wife, were studying years ago at St John's College, Nottingham. I can still picture him standing in front of a small white coffin, saying that although we can never answer the question "Why?", we can answer the question "What?" — "What can we do? What can we learn?" Humanly, I know I could not have done likewise; but unusual grace is given in extraordinary circumstances.

Peter, observing Jesus that day, saw that his compassion for the living was greater than his own grief concerning the dead. For however great was his own grief — whether it was at the tomb of Lazarus or, in this case, at the loss of John the Baptist — it did not constitute a reason for withdrawing from the activity of making known God's kingdom. In this way, Jesus always sets death in a context where it does not leave us powerless or useless, but rather with a further opportunity to proclaim the kingdom of God and the resurrection. Never was this more the case than when later, after Pentecost, the church was suffering persecution. How was Peter later to respond to the outbreak of persecution in Jerusalem, which resulted in his own trial, imprisonment, and the loss of friends like Stephen? Surely the shape of his response then must have been partly formed by observing Jesus' own reaction to the news of John's death, as well as the supreme example of Jesus' own handling of his sufferings and death, to which Peter will return repeatedly in his epistles. In a word, personal grief and pain was not a reason for pulling back from declaring the kingdom, but a platform for making known the hope of resurrection to a world without hope. The very use of such circumstances for such a proclamation is all the more compelling.

The underlying impression of this episode was that Jesus shaped his life by a combination of principles. One was to find the solitude that he needed to pray and reflect on the ever-changing circumstances of ministry; another was a willingness, dictated by his compassion, to respond to the needs of people as they presented themselves, even when emotionally it must have been hard. Undoubtedly there is a tension between the two; the key is to have such trust in the Father that when the former must be deferred to fulfil the latter, there will be time for solitude and privacy later —and to trust that, in the meantime, God will provide the resources to continue until that space is provided. For Jesus, it meant waiting until the evening, when he dismissed his disciples; then, "He went up on the mountainside **by himself** to pray." Meanwhile, the disciples, who had been dismissed by Jesus, were struggling in their boat to get to the other side, and Peter was about to experience his second great lesson of the day.

There is no way of knowing how often Peter was to reflect on what happened. But surely he did! John tells us that the disciples had managed to row three or three and half miles across the lake.[30] As on another occasion when a storm whipped up quickly on the lake, they probably wondered whether their master cared if they perished. After all, he had commanded them to embark. Rowing in a storm at night was no fun! Peter must often have recalled that moment when, through the spray and waves, a figure had appeared, which naturally they thought at first was a ghost until Jesus made himself known to them. His response, "Lord, if it's you, tell me to come to you on the water", was a blend of bravado and circumspection, impetuosity and intuition. After all, he might have simply got out of the boat and headed off towards Jesus, which would have been unalloyed recklessness, as he had no divine mandate to leave the boat. Or he might have never even suggested the idea of joining Jesus on the water, and simply stayed put. In fact his reaction was in between those two responses. He was willing to come, but only at the invitation of Jesus; so he signalled his willingness and sought Jesus' permission. It was then that Jesus said, "Come!"

What followed then is a classic parable of Christian leadership; a parable which is set in history but which has lessons for every spiritual leader. They are threefold. Firstly, at the command of Jesus Peter got out of the boat and onto the stormy water. "Getting out of the boat" has become an essential part both of Christian leadership and discipleship.

It is hardly possible to lead a group of Christians without "getting out of the boat". In essence this means to take some action based on faith, which is both risky and possibly dangerous. Dangerous in the sense that you are no longer in control of what follows and that either your life or part of it —e.g. your reputation—is at stake; and risky, in that there may be a genuine challenge to you in the course of this action. But it is this ingredient of risky action **at the invitation of Jesus**, which lies at the centre of true spiritual leadership.

It could lead to all kinds of activity for God. It might mean, as it did for Abraham, leaving what is familiar to go somewhere which is unknown. It might mean doing something which does not come naturally but which you feel called to nonetheless. This could be speaking in public when it is the last thing you would want to do, or leading a small group, or planting a church, or embarking on a building project to provide more appropriate facilities for the church in the community. "Getting out of the boat" is anything which takes you to a new level of trust, if what you are doing is going to succeed. But whatever it is, it must be done at the invitation of Jesus, who says, "come", if it is to be part of his will for us. Such risk-taking faith creates something new for God where previously there had been nothing.

A verse that has been formative in my own thinking in this context is that the God in whom we trust is "...the God who gives life to the dead and calls things that are not as though they were."[31] It is this expectation that God can call into existence, through our faithful trust, that which had not previously existed, which must lie at the heart of true spiritual leadership. This is rather like having sanctified imagination, in which we imagine something that God has laid on our hearts, and believe that with his power it can come into existence. In response to Jesus' word of command, Peter stepped out of the boat and was able for a few short steps to walk on water. This was daring faith! What Peter did not do was to call a committee meeting in the boat to see whether the conditions were right for walking on water! — which of course they were not! All too often, sadly, this is exactly what my own denomination is prone to do before it ventures out from the security of its institutional existence and believes that once again God can create "out of nothing".

The third lesson, which is as classic as the first, is that having taken the initial step out of the boat we must be careful where we look! It is a truth which most Christians will have imbibed "through their beakers" as infant Christians! But having said that, it is also a lesson which we continually need to learn and re-learn. As Paul said, "We live by faith, not by sight."[32] And this was never more so than when Peter walked on water, at night, during a storm on Galilee! The temptation naturally is to take your eyes off the one person who is able to give you buoyancy, and instead to fix them on the "waves" which threaten your very standing. This was exactly what Peter did. Seeing the wind and waves, he allowed fear to replace faith in his mind, and he immediately began to sink.

There are undoubtedly squalls, some of acute severity, on any Christian journey. Some are common to all human-kind —life's disappointments, bereavements, unfulfilled hopes, injustice and sudden illness to name but a few; others may relate to the path of a Christian leader in particular facing opposition or personal hostility from others. But having embarked on a course of action at the invitation of Jesus, the only way to proceed is to keep our gaze fixed on him until it is completed. To alter our gaze and look alone at the problems that confront us is a sure first step to beginning to sink as Peter then did. But he soon realised that he was looking in the wrong direction.

Peter, and this is the fourth lesson, had the good sense to cry out, when he realised that he was sinking, "Lord, save me!" And we are told that Jesus immediately reached out his hand and caught him.

"You of little faith," he said, "why did you doubt?" We know the origin of Peter's doubt, which was that in the cold spray of the moment on the turbulent sea, he forgot the ability of Jesus to sustain him, and he suddenly realised what he was doing. He saw the forces of nature arraigned against him, and his courage and faith failed. He went back to thinking naturally rather than in the realm of faith. This was a pitfall, which Peter was to experience again in a few days time at

Caesarea Philippi; and in other ways it would dog him for much of his life.

Maintaining our faith focus when facing forces that would destroy our trust is a discipline which is inescapable for the spiritual leader.

In John's Gospel we are told of an almost amusing game of hide and seek which followed Jesus' nocturnal walk across the stormy sea. He arrived back at the Capernaum side of the lake in the early hours of the following day, and left behind bemused crowds. The crowds who had been fed the previous day continued to look for him, but with no success. Others arrived from elsewhere in boats, looking for him, too. But they could not find him. They were intrigued as to how he could have escaped from them, knowing that he had not left with the disciples the previous evening in the only boat. They went back across the sea in the boats which had only recently arrived. Eventually they found him on the other side of the sea, and understandably their first question was, "Rabbi, when did you get here?"[33]

Jesus, as ever, is robust and uncompromising in his teaching. He accused the crowd of only being there for the food: "...you are looking for me....because you ate the loaves and had your fill." He tells them to labour for the food that does not perish.[34] He is understandably tired of their request for a miracle when they have just witnessed a catering miracle of gigantic proportions. He proceeds to challenge them by saying that he is the "bread of life", whereupon they protest that he is from their area, they know his parents —so how can he say, "I have come down from heaven."[35] Jesus, far from making it easier for the crowds, now says that not only is he the bread of life, but that this bread is his flesh which he will give for the life of the world. Grumbling turns to argument,[36] and argument turns to desertion. John tells us, "...from this time many of his disciples turned back and no longer followed him." It was a sudden turn of events. The crowd had wanted to make him king, and he had escaped their ambitions; yet we read now that, "From this time many of his disciples turned back and no longer followed him."[37]

Jesus asked the twelve, "You do not want to leave too, do you?"

It was Peter who replied, "Lord, to whom shall we go? You have the words of eternal life. We believe and know that you are the Holy One of God."[38] At a time of great uncertainty Peter knew that Jesus alone had the words of eternal life; there are times when almost every spiritual leader, buffeted by the squalls of exercising that leadership, must hold onto the fact that Jesus alone has the words of eternal life —all others are hollow, and literally hopeless. This is often the bottom line which leaders reach when experiencing disappointment through the struggles of leading the church.

It is also a rallying point for the future. If Peter was now realising with greater clarity who Jesus was, he had yet to see **what** he had come to do and **how** he would do it. Both his clear-sightedness and blindness would be laid bare at Caesarea Philippi. There Peter would show conviction as to the identity of Jesus, but painful ignorance as to what he had come to do.

4

CONVICTION AND CORRECTION

Matthew 16:13–20, Mark 8:27–32, Luke 9:18–27

It was clear in the days after the feeding of the five thousand and Jesus' teaching in the synagogue the following Sabbath that there was a greater sense of gravity and even foreboding to his ministry. The previous forty eight hours had recorded some pivotal moments: the death of John the Baptist, the mission of the twelve, the feeding of the five thousand, the walking on the water, the attempt to make Jesus king —and, lastly, the desertion by many disciples who wanted something from him which he was not prepared to give. His popularity had plummeted as it dawned on the crowds that he was not about to rally an army against the Romans. No wonder, then, that Jesus determined to travel north where there would be a chance to re-group, and talk seriously with the disciples about what lay ahead.

For Peter, this conversation at Caesarea Philippi would be another roller coaster of revelation and ignorance, elation and humiliation. In a few brief moments, Peter moved from the heights of Jesus' commendation to the depths of his opprobrium. Revelation is followed by remonstration; he moved from being rock-like to becoming something more like a heap of rubble! He enjoyed praise for his conviction and then sharp correction for his wrong assumptions. Although clear about Jesus' identity, Peter was still ignorant of Jesus' true mission.

Most leaders will experience a similar juxtaposition of highs and lows, success followed by failure —even if the stakes are not as high as in this bruising spiritual encounter with Jesus. For a typical pastor today, this height/depth pattern could take the shape of a well-received sermon being followed by a pastoral debacle; or, conversely, hearing praise from a church member who appreciated your pastoral ministry to criticism from another who found your teaching sadly lacking.

The cycle of success and failure may, in broad outline, follow a similar pattern. Nevertheless, the points at issue in this famous conversation between Jesus and Peter were fundamental. One concerned the identity of Jesus; the other a correct understanding of what he had come to do. If Peter's eyes were already opened to the identity of Jesus, they were closed as far as his mission in the world was concerned. Like the blind man in Mark's Gospel who needed two touches from Jesus in order to see, so Peter needed a second touch on his spiritual sight before he understood both the identity and the mission of Jesus.

WHO DO YOU SAY THAT I AM?

Some time had elapsed since Simon Peter's call on the shore of Galilee. Peter had both witnessed and personally experienced events which constantly begged the question, who was this man whom even the winds and sea obeyed, and who was able to cure Peter's own mother-in-law after Sabbath synagogue; and who came walking across a stormy sea, inviting Peter to join him in an adventure which, for a moment, looked like leading to a watery grave? That day in the boat on the stormy sea, when Jesus walked across the water towards them, had already done much to form Peter's understanding of who Jesus was. But there was still a need to affirm—and confirm—his embryonic convictions.

Jesus had been wanting to take the disciples away for some

rest and reflection, but the crowds had previously frustrated him. So now he chose to take them to the far north of Israel, to the region of Caesarea Philippi. Situated well to the north of the Sea of Galilee, it was a frontier town of Israel, on the southern slopes of Mount Hermon. Undoubtedly it was a beautiful place. Caesar Augustus gave the city to Herod. When Herod's son Philip became tetrarch of the region, he rebuilt it and renamed it, after both himself and the emperor, Caesarea Philippi. It was to a place near this city that Jesus withdrew with his disciples.

It was here that Jesus chose to confirm his identity, an identity which the disciples had already guessed at. Luke places the episode at the end of Jesus' Galilean ministry, before the pivotal verse of Luke 9:51 in which Jesus turned towards Jerusalem where he was destined to die: "As the time approached for him to be taken up to heaven, Jesus resolutely set out for Jerusalem." Jesus now confirmed his identity by asking a question, first generally, and then more specifically. Nor did he appear to do this without considered thought and prayer, for Luke tells us that it was in the context of prayer that Jesus asked the disciples the question, "Who do the crowds say I am?"[1]

In their answers, the disciples chime in with what the crowds generally said about Jesus' identity and which had, it seems, become common currency. "Some say John the Baptist" (although that answer defied chronology), "others say Elijah; and still others Jeremiah or one of the prophets."[2] Clearly, they recognised Jesus as a man of God. For the crowd he was either John the Baptist come back to life or he was Elijah, who the Jews believed would return before the coming of the Messiah, or he was one of the prophets.

But Jesus then pressed his question, "But what about you, who do you say that I am?" The question Jesus was asking now was, in essence, how do you regard me —as a man, a prophet, or more than a prophet? No doubt the disciples looked at each other, waiting for one of them to take the lead. They did not have to wait long. Peter, in typical fashion and with real confidence, said, "You are the Christ, the Son of the living God!"[3] His answer signified a turning point for both

Peter and Jesus. But it was not Peter's intellect or intuition alone that brought him to this conclusion; his conviction was founded on revelation.

"Blessed are you, Simon son of Jonah," said Jesus, "for this was not revealed to you by man, but by my Father in heaven." It was this conviction or confession that Jesus was the Messiah, founded on revelation from the Father, which formed the basis for Peter's future leadership. It may seem obvious, but is worth saying, that without this conviction there could be no mission to the world. Establishing the true identity of Jesus is foundational to Christian leadership; without this clear understanding of who Jesus is there can be no clear spiritual and Christian leadership.

It was said some years ago that if Jesus had asked a group of modern theologians who he was, they would have said "You are the eschatological manifestation of the ground of our being, the kerygma in which we find ultimate meaning in our interpersonal relationships"! But Peter's conviction about the identity of Jesus was obviously not formed in terms of modern philosophical categories; it was brought about through an act of revelation in the light of his previously held hopes of the Messiah; hopes that were shaped by the Old Testament. In the months ahead, the shape of those expectations, based as yet on an erroneous understanding of the Scriptures, would have to change —but this would not happen until after the resurrection.

Peter came to this conviction by way of revelation, as Jesus himself said. In keeping with other parts of Scripture, and in particular with the so-called Johannine part of Luke's Gospel,[4] we see that there is a mutual revelation of the Father and Son in the godhead. Luke records Jesus as saying, "I praise you, Father, Lord of heaven and earth, because you have hidden these things from the wise and learned, and revealed them to little children. Yes, Father, for this was your good pleasure. All things have been committed to me by my Father. No one knows who the Son is except the Father, and no-one knows who the Father is except the Son and those to whom the Son chooses to reveal him."[5] This means that the Son reveals the Father and the Father reveals the Son. This is evidently what happened to Peter. The Father revealed the identity of the Son to him. Through the accumulated evidence given to Peter it was revealed to him that Jesus was none other than the long awaited Messiah of whom the prophets had spoken. Peter gladly welcomed this and must have been amazed at this privilege. But in time this conviction that Jesus was the Messiah would be tested to breaking point, and Peter discovered almost immediately that he would have to change his understanding of what the Messiah had come to do.

CONVICTION

At a recent international conference, with around four hundred delegates from right across the world, a youth panel was asked to report on what they hoped for in the church by twenty five years later (which would be the year 2029). The panel comprised one American, one Egyptian, one Ugandan, and one from Brunei; they were led by a young Argentinian pastor. Their hope was for leadership in the church that was based on the authority of Scripture and marked by openness to the Spirit, as well as being rooted in the stream of church history, prophetic and prayerful. Space does not allow a more detailed summary of their hopes for church leadership. But leadership was their number one requirement, with its implicit challenge to the state of leadership in the church now. Their insights were warmly received. Their expectations were the very highest. What was apparent was that leadership in the church should arise from a deep conviction of the lordship of Jesus in all areas of life. (*SOMA* Silver Jubilee Conference, Canterbury, 2004.)

Without conviction there cannot be effective leadership, whether it is the arena of sport, scientific exploration, government or military campaigns. However, Christian leadership begins with the conviction that Jesus is God's Son; or as the centurion said, watching Jesus die on the cross, "Surely this man was the Son of God."[6] It was such inner conviction, which came as a result of revelation, that resulted in Peter's confession of Jesus as the Messiah. It was this conviction that would be tested and strengthened in the years ahead, until becoming both mature and dynamic at the day of Pentecost. It had its moments of sublime confidence and of acute testing. Few Christian leaders get away without experiencing both.

It is important to understand that this conviction had its origin in revelation. Revelation was the forerunner to conviction, just as this conviction was the forerunner to the confession of Jesus as Messiah. This revelation was a God-given event. In the New Testament, revelation is as a result of divine action, and is often compared to the opening of blind eyes. Paul describes in graphic language to the Ephesian Christians what is involved in this process of revelation: "I keep asking that the God of our Lord Jesus Christ, the glorious Father, may give you the Spirit of wisdom and revelation, so that you may know him better. I pray also that the eyes of your heart may be enlightened in order that you may know the hope to which he has called you, the riches of his glorious inheritance in the saints, and his incomparably great power for us who believe...."[7] Here is as clear a statement of the process of revelation as we can find in Scripture. As a result of prayer and through the work of the Spirit, the "eye", which, in this case is located in the heart, can be opened, so that we "know" something spiritually which previously was veiled.

In the case of Peter we can only think that, at some point in his daily observation of Jesus' life and ministry over the last few months or years, he came to the conclusion that this Jesus was the Messiah for whom he and his people had been waiting. When Peter had replied to the question Jesus posed, by saying that he, Jesus, was the Christ, Jesus responded that Peter was the rock upon which he would build the church.

There has been much controversy down the years as to what Jesus meant when he said to Peter, immediately after his confession, the words, "And I tell you that you are Peter, and on this rock I will build my church, and the gates of Hades

will not overcome it."[8] Traditional Roman Catholic interpretation has taken it to mean that Peter himself was the
rock upon which the church would be founded; and that his
rock-like qualities would be the bulwark of the church, so
that nothing would overwhelm it; and that certain declar-
ations of Peter's successors, by virtue of their succession to
Peter, were invested with an infallibility which could not be
questioned. Protestant teaching (partly in reaction to the
Roman Catholic claim that the primacy of the papacy was
based on its succession to Peter rather than conformity to
Scripture) argued that it is not Peter himself who is the rock
upon which the church is built, but it is his *confession* that
Jesus is the Messiah which is the true "rock" on which Jesus
would build. Although that is undoubtedly true, it could be
said that it is not the plain meaning of the text here. Jesus,
addressing Peter himself, did say that *he* was the rock upon
which the church would be built. The fact that Jesus said
this is testimony not so much to what Peter was *then* as to
what he would eventually *become* after Pentecost. Peter was
indeed becoming a spiritual leader, as indeed every leader
in the church is *becoming* —as no one has finally arrived!
Jesus' confirmation of Peter's role and name is also testimony
to the call and gifting of God which, despite Peter's obvious
failures, was, to use Paul's term, irrevocable.[9]

Or to put it another way, we may rejoice that God will fulfil
his purposes in us, even though at times we may fail badly,
and that he will complete in us what he has begun.[10] The
fact that Jesus called Peter a rock is not the same thing as
saying either that he or his successors are infallible, since it
is clear, even after Pentecost as we shall see, Peter was quite
capable of being wrong, as Paul shows us in Galatians
1:14ff. But it is an example of how Jesus takes frail and
mistaken humans and makes them leaders in the church.
Peter was the rock of the church not because he was either
sinless or always right but because God would give him the
grace to become what he was intended to be, although the
path self-evidently went through failure and restoration.

It is also clear that Jesus gave to Peter spiritual authority,
as is indicated by his saying to him, "I will give you the keys

of the kingdom of heaven; whatever you bind on earth will be bound in heaven, and whatever you loose on earth will be loosed in heaven."[11] This binding and loosing refers to the exercise of spiritual authority in the church, as we see in the days of the early church. It was a ministry, described as the ministry of the keys, which leaders in the church (especially in the first four centuries) were to frequently exercise. In effect it was the bishop's authority to permit or prevent activity or teaching in the church.

Although Peter was called the "rock" on which Jesus would build his church, it is also true from the general reading of Scripture, rather than this specific passage, that the confession of Jesus as Lord is the cornerstone of the church, and that Jesus himself is the rock upon which the church is built. The significance of rocks or stones has a special resonance for Peter, and perhaps this is why Peter returns to the metaphor "rock" frequently in his writings. Thus, taking the word "rock" as referring pre-eminently to Christ, he writes, "As you come to him, the living Stone – rejected by men but chosen by God and precious to him – you also, like living stones, are being built into a spiritual house to be a holy priesthood, offering spiritual sacrifices acceptable to God through Jesus Christ"[12]

Peter goes on to say in his letter that it is Jesus who is both the cornerstone of the church and a stumbling block to those who will not believe. So we observe that the metaphor "rock" is common in Peter's thinking and writings. Moreover, the metaphor of the church being a building is powerfully present in Peter's understanding of the church: it is made up of "living stones", shaped together to form a building in which God is present by his Spirit. So we too, like Peter, are rocks added to the building of the church as we make the true confession about Jesus who ultimately is **the** rock upon which the church is founded.

If Jesus, as the Messiah and the Son of the living God, is the foundational rock upon which the church is built, the conviction that lies behind this confession is also the spring or coil for mission. Of course it was not until after the resurrection of Jesus, and Pentecost, that Peter fully took part in this mission or understood what it was about. Peter's conviction that Jesus was the Messiah was to wax and wane in the closing hours of Jesus' life, both before and immediately following the crucifixion. But after Pentecost it would be the spring for evangelism and mission. As Emil Brunner famously said, "The church exists by mission as a fire exists by burning." Christian leadership needs this passion at its heart; the fire of this conviction provides the combustion that drives mission.

David Hume, the famous philosopher and rationalist, was once seen hurrying along a street and was asked by a friend where he was going. "To hear Whitefield preach," came the unexpected reply. His friend was startled. "Surely you don't believe what Whitefield is preaching do you?"

"No," replied Hume, "but Whitefield does!" Such deep inward conviction arising from clear personal experience is essential in all true evangelism, as David Watson and many others have observed.

So Peter, through this gift of revelation, knew who Jesus was, but this conviction was to be sorely tested in the coming months before he could stand up with confidence and preach at Pentecost. This confession would be tested and deepened through the painful experiences that lay ahead. He would become sure, and gain an authority which was far more selfless.

His own self-assurance would be gradually emptied, and in its place a new confidence would come, based on a deeper understanding of the Jesus he followed. This is an important paradox to grasp.

CORRECTION

We probably know the feeling only too well. After a moment of great acclaim, we fall flat on our face. This was Peter's experience. He had been acclaimed by Jesus: "Blessed are you, Simon son of Jonah...." He was no doubt pleased to be so applauded by Jesus, in front of the disciples, for his bold assertion that Jesus was the Christ. But, as was frequently the case, he overstepped the mark. He thought his revelation went further than it did. He presumed to know the actions of the Messiah. He knew only half the story —who Jesus was; but not the other half—what he had come to do. His conviction passed from being based on revelation to being based on the flesh. Indeed he was to be rigorously told that his reproof of Jesus for predicting suffering and death was not simply human thinking but the work of the devil!

As soon as Jesus began to tell them that the Messiah "...must go to Jerusalem and suffer many things at the hands of the elders, chief priests and teachers of the law, and that he must be killed and on the third day be raised to life", then Peter remonstrated, "Never, Lord! This shall never happen to you." No plaudits followed now. Rather than addressing him by name—as he had done with great dignity a moment before—Jesus rebukes the source of Peter's all too human thinking by saying to him, "Get behind me, Satan! You are a stumbling-block to me; you do not have in mind the things of God, but the things of men."[13] It was a dramatic reversal. Previously, Peter's thoughts had been inspired by the revelation from the Father; now they were informed by the wiles of Satan. He had basked in the warm esteem of his fellow disciples, but now he must have been bewildered and humiliated. He had known that Jesus was the Messiah, but he was ignorant of what the Messiah had come to do.

In common with most of his contemporaries, Peter thought he knew the programme that the Messiah would follow. It would involve gaining the popularity of the people and then, at some point, marching on Jerusalem to overwhelm the Romans and restore the kingdom to Israel. The idea of Jesus being killed by the leaders of his own people and suffering a violent death without overthrowing the Romans was an incomprehensible thought; worse, it was defeatist language, which Jesus needed to be talked out of. Peter probably thought that it came from a moment of uncertainty in Jesus' mind as he contemplated the greatness of his task, and Peter, with his new found confidence (as one who had received revelation from God, hitched to his usual bravado) was the very person to put him straight!

Peter moved, in the space of just a few minutes, from being a "rock" to being a "stumbling block", both stone-like words. His confession led him to being described as rock-like; his wrong assumptions about Jesus' Messianic calling were a "stumbling block" to Jesus himself. The former came from divine revelation; the later from demonic interference. As yet, Peter was not able to distinguish between the two; later, he would. Nonetheless, the lesson for all Christian leaders is an important one.

Peter had moved from the solid ground of revelation to the flimsy sand of his own human assumptions, and he had invested those with a certitude they did not merit. So Peter was slapped down, not because Jesus wanted to humiliate him but because what Peter in ignorance had tried to persuade Jesus against was the very thing which Jesus had come to do —and to which he was now setting his face as a flint: towards Jerusalem where these things, of which Jesus spoke, would shortly be accomplished.

It had been a tough day for Peter at Caesarea Philippi, perhaps one he did not care to remember, but it was nevertheless instructive for those who follow behind. There are times when we all need to be corrected, not least the leader. If we put ourselves in positions where correction cannot reach us, then our leadership is liable to malfunction. Ideally, within the teams in which we work as leaders of the church, such correction should be possible. At other times it may be through people we have made ourselves accountable to: a spiritual director or a Christian friend or mentor, or a special prayer group where they have full permission to ask the awkward question or to speak the unwelcome or difficult truth. Peter's experience shows that, however great the revelation we receive, it is possible through either purely human or fleshly standards or demonic disturbance to be taken off course —even at the very moment of our greatest triumph. God disciplines those he loves. He corrects us through his word. The leader is himself to be like Jesus, to teach both positively and negatively, upholding the good but warning us of the wrong. It would be something that Peter himself would come to teach in his own letters of instruction, and this he makes abundantly clear in the opening section of 2 Peter, the provenance and teaching of which we will consider later.

But events never stayed still for long with Jesus. Six days later, the three inner-core disciples were given yet further revelation as to the identity and mission of Jesus, when suddenly he was transfigured before their eyes.

5

THE TRANSFIGURATION
Matthew 17:1–13, Mark 9:2–13, Luke 9:28–36

In the Plaka district of Athens, just below the Acropolis and not far from where Paul addressed the Areopagus when he went to Athens,[1] is a Greek Orthodox church called the Church of Metamorphosis, or transfiguration. It recalls the next great event in Peter's life after his "confession", in which Peter witnessed a sudden physical transformation or metamorphosis of Jesus before his very eyes.

Some thirty years later, in his second letter, Peter recalled the voice of God the Father which he heard on that day: "We ourselves heard this voice that came from heaven when we were with him [Jesus] on the sacred mountain."[2] On that occasion, Peter had an unforgettable mountain top experience that would stay with him for the rest of his life. But what was the purpose of this event in the earthly ministry of Jesus? And what was its significance for Peter? It was a New Testament equivalent of the great theophanies recorded in the Old Testament which two other companions of Jesus on the mountain of transfiguration, Moses and Elijah, had previously experienced.

In 1979, starting early in the morning, my wife and I walked up what is held to be Mount Sinai, near St Catherine's Monastery in Egypt. It is only a few hours' climb. It is now a well-worn pilgrim route, with lavatories at the top! It was here, or somewhere like it, that Moses went up to receive the Ten Commandments at the hand of God. Sinai, we are told in Exodus chapter nineteen, was wreathed in cloud and smoke and there were peals of thunder and lightning. For days Moses was to remain on Sinai with his three companions Aaron, Nadab and Abihu, where he waited to receive the law; and, to the Israelites watching from afar, "...the glory of the LORD looked like a consuming fire...."[3] During this disclosure of God's majesty, Moses was summoned to the top of the mountain, where he received the law or Decalogue, which was to form the centre of God's covenant with his people. It was to be placed in the ark of the covenant and eventually located in the Holy of Holies in Solomon's temple. There the law was to remain at the core of Jewish worship until the eventual destruction of the third temple by the armies of Vespasian in AD 70.

So Moses was no stranger to mountain top experiences, nor was his companion on the mountain of transfiguration, Elijah. Elijah had fled to Mount Horeb in the south of Judah after his famous contest with the prophets of Baal on Mount Carmel. On Mount Carmel, God had answered his prayer and consumed his sacrifice with fire, so being the God who answers by fire![4] But despite this victory in the face of a threat to his life from Queen Jezebel, King Ahab's wife, Elijah fled from Carmel to Horeb. Here he sat down under a broom tree and prayed that he might die! Such was the feeling of anticlimax after the great victory he saw over the prophets of Baal, the sense of depression he felt at further threats to his life from Jezebel, and the real physical exhaustion he suffered after the emotional drain of his struggle on Mount Carmel, that he despaired of life itself, overcome as he was by depression and isolation! In such a condition of depression, not unknown to many spiritual leaders, he was bidden to, "Go out and stand on the mountain in the presence of the LORD, for the LORD is about to pass by."[5] But the Lord was not in the wind that followed, which had shattered the rocks on the mountainside, nor was the Lord in the earthquake, nor in the fire, but in the gentle whisper.

Whereupon Elijah, recognising the presence of the Lord in the whisper, "...pulled his cloak over his face and went out and stood at the mouth of the cave"[6]

Moses and Elijah were familiar with extraordinary mountain experiences after Sinai, Carmel and Horeb, but perhaps none was more amazing than this. Now they were standing with the Messiah on the mountain of transfiguration. Moses, representing the law, and Elijah, representing the prophets, met with Jesus, God's Messiah and Son, for a summit meeting with three further witnesses: Peter, James and John. The purpose of this meeting was essentially threefold: to reveal the true identity of Jesus to the three principal disciples; to afford Jesus the opportunity of talking over his "exodus" that he would accomplish at Jerusalem; and to strengthen Jesus in the task on which he was resolutely set.[7] For soon after the transfiguration Jesus was to move on from his Galilean ministry and begin his approach, through Samaria, to Jerusalem. We shall look at each of these facets of the transfiguration in turn.

THE REVELATION OF JESUS' TRUE IDENTITY

Luke alone tells us that this revelation of Jesus' identity occurred during prayer. "As he was praying," says Luke, "the appearance of his face changed and his clothes became as bright as a flash of lightning."[8] Mark, seeking to describe the change to Jesus' clothes, says that they became whiter than any contemporary detergent could bleach or whiten them! In addition, Matthew tells us, Jesus' face changed, becoming as bright as the sun.[9] The appearance of his face after this metamorphosis is not too dissimilar from John's later description of Christ as he saw him in the revelation he was given whilst in the Spirit on the Lord's day on the island of Patmos. Then John saw Jesus as having "Head and hair... white like wool, as white as snow, and his eyes were like blazing fire."[10] Whatever way the Gospel writers sought to describe what the three disciples saw, there is no mistaking that the appearance of Jesus was both overwhelming and utterly splendid at the same time.

The face of Jesus, thus transformed, became the place where men could see both the glory and salvation of God. As Paul later wrote to the Corinthians, whilst comparing the greater splendour of the new covenant of the Spirit with the fading splendour of the old covenant of the written code which Moses brought down from Sinai, "For God, who said, "Let light shine out of darkness," made his light shine in our hearts to give us the light of the knowledge of the glory of God in the face of Christ."[11]

But the transformation of the appearance of Jesus, whether of his face or clothes, was not the only revelation of his divinity on the mountain; there was also the attestation of his identity given by the heavenly voice coming out of the cloud. There were three occasions when the Father spoke from heaven to attest and confirm the identity of Jesus as his Son during his ministry. The first occasion was at his baptism,[12] the second at the transfiguration, and the third, only recorded in John's Gospel, was when Jesus was about to die, and once again he was speaking about his death. He said, ""Now my heart is troubled, and what shall I say? 'Father, save me from this hour'? No, it was for this very reason I came to this hour. Father, glorify your name!'" Then a voice came from heaven, "I have glorified it, and will glorify it again." The crowd that was there and heard it said it had thundered; others said an angel had spoken to him."[13] Each time the Father spoke of the Son it was both to identify and bear witness to Jesus, as his Son and the Redeemer. But on the third occasion Jesus explicitly says, "This voice was for your benefit, not mine"[14] The heavenly voice both affirmed the identity of Jesus as Son of God, and established that he would suffer on the cross. He was to be both listened to and obeyed.

For the three disciples who had been taken up the mountain, the voice was further confirmation as to the true identity of Jesus. Although Peter had only a few days earlier confessed who Jesus really was, here was remarkable confirmation of his earlier confession. Just as at Caesarea

Philippi, Jesus, after Peter's recognition, began to speak of his death, here, once again, his identity is indissolubly linked to his mission.

THE MISSION OF JESUS

There are two great underlying questions in the Gospels: who was this man that even the winds and waves obeyed? —and, what kind of a kingdom had he come to inaugurate? The answer to this second question was not finally and rightly given until after the crucifixion and resurrection. For the crucifixion of Jesus is the basic clue to the kind of kingdom he had come to bring. If Peter had failed to understand the mission of Jesus at Caesarea Philippi, and had incurred a heavy rebuke from Jesus, he also did not really understand what Jesus had come to do, and what kind of a kingdom he had come to inaugurate until the wind of heaven enveloped him at Pentecost. It is then that we see Peter proclaiming with complete clarity to the crowd what Jesus had come to do. But here on the mountain of transfiguration a further clue was given to Peter and the others that the "departure" or, literally, the "exodus" that Jesus was to "accomplish" at Jerusalem was not waving goodbye to a group of sad and mystified followers, it was an event to be accomplished with every fibre of Jesus' being for the salvation of the world.

It is clear from the accounts of the transfiguration that Peter could not have heard very much of the content of the conversation that occupied Jesus, Moses and Elijah. The reason was that, for most of that conversation, Peter and his companions were asleep. The disciples were fond of sleeping at critical moments of Jesus' ministry! It was to happen again at Gethsemane at a yet more critical time. But either they must have overheard the word "exodus" or they must have asked Jesus what he and Moses and Elijah had been talking about, and he must have told them they were speaking of the exodus "...which he was about to bring to fulfilment at Jerusalem".[15] So they knew at least that the subject for this

67

summit was the "exodus" that Jesus was to accomplish, an idea which lay at the heart of his mission.

For a Jew the term or word "exodus" could not be more redolent of meaning. It was the single most significant event in the Old Testament, and at its heart was a theme of deliverance and salvation, which all the prophets and teachers of Israel continually mined for a deeper understanding of their special relationship with God. The Exodus comprised those mighty acts of God whereby the children of Israel, groaning in their bondage and slavery to the Egyptians, were liberated as a people. These acts began with judgment on the house of Pharaoh, in the form of plagues. The plagues culminated in the destruction of the firstborn, the Israelites' families being protected by the blood of a sacrificial lamb having been smeared on the doorposts and lintels of their homes.[16] The consequent passing over of their homes by the angel of death was to be recalled every year at the feast of Passover, and the ritual slaughter of lambs, in memory of their deliverance.

Following their flight from Egypt, and deliverance from the armies of Pharaoh through the parting of the Red Sea, the nation was formed in the desert. The law was given to Moses and the people from Mount Sinai. Provision of water, manna and quail was made for the people. The Lord's presence was symbolised in the portable ark of the covenant, and the cloud and fiery pillar. The events of the Exodus were thus both salvific and formative, both liberating and binding, and from them the nation gained both significance and hope.

Every Jew knew of these events, as they were re-told annually in the home, prompted by a question from the youngest member of the family present, "What does this ceremony mean to you?"[17]   Peter, James and John would have recalled annually with their families the significance of their nation's deliverance from Egypt.

The questions which must have arisen in their minds, however, were these: what was this exodus, or departure, which Jesus was to accomplish in Jerusalem? And why did it necessitate this extraordinary summit with Moses and Elijah? Could any departure or exodus effected by Jesus in

Jerusalem form a nation, establish a covenant, characterise a people, end slavery, and bring liberation, through an act which was both merciful and judgemental? Of course, we know that this is precisely what Jesus would accomplish through his departure at Jerusalem, but it was probably still too soon for Peter to know that Jesus' teaching about his own suffering at the hands of the leaders of the people (which Peter had so vehemently denounced at Caesarea Philippi), and this "exodus", which Jesus had discussed with Moses and Elijah on the mountain of transfiguration, were inextricably linked. His knowledge of what Jesus would accomplish at Jerusalem was cloudy.

If the transformation of the appearance of Jesus was Peter's greatest clue yet to his divine identity, and the topic of the conversation with Moses and Elijah was a further clue to Jesus' mission, the total effect of the transfiguration on Peter and his companions was one of an overwhelming spiritual experience. It was truly what we have come to call a "mountain top experience", and as such was part of Peter's overall preparation for ministry. It is worth considering the general place of such experiences in the development of a spiritual leader.

THE MOUNTAIN TOP EXPERIENCE

Peter, we are told in the Gospel accounts, was overwhelmed by the immediate experience of the transfiguration, as well he might have been! Anyone putting himself or herself in his position would understand why Peter did not know what he was saying. He and the other disciples had fallen asleep and had woken up to see this extraordinary sight of a transfigured Jesus with Moses and Elijah, as companions whom he recognised. Just as the trio were about to disperse, Peter said, "Rabbi, it is good for us to be here. Let us put up three shelters —one for you, one for Moses and one for Elijah."[18] In case any of the readers of the Gospel were wondering what Peter meant or intended by this remark, Luke adds, "He did not know what he was saying", in the sense that he was speaking words without understanding or meaning.

In essence, Peter was simply overwhelmed and wanting to say something —typically, he said whatever came into his head! Some say he may have been wanting to prolong the experience by building shelters for each of the three; but then what *could* you say when, on waking from sleep, you are confronted by two of the greatest figures in your nation's history, figures of tremendous spiritual significance, together with a person whom you have grown to know well, and who is utterly transformed in your presence! Naturally, you would not know where to begin.

The transfiguration must have had a double effect on Peter. Firstly, in retrospect as with many of the gospel events, it was a further piece of evidence as to the identity and mission of Jesus. Later, Peter would come to understand more fully the true significance of Jesus' "exodus" at Golgotha. He would both preach it in his sermons recorded in Acts, and dwell on it significantly in the teaching in his letters. He would see the change in the appearance of Jesus, the encircling cloud, the exalted company and the heavenly voice as further evidence and confirmation of the divinity of Jesus. Later, in his second epistle, he would use the memory of this event and its historicity as a plank in his case that Jesus was the Christ and that his teaching was not the peddling of cleverly devised myth. As he wrote, "We did not follow cleverly invented stories when we told you about the power and coming of our Lord Jesus Christ, but we were eye-witnesses of his majesty. For he received honour and glory from God the Father when the voice came to him from the Majestic Glory, saying, 'This is my Son, whom I love; with him I am well pleased.'"[19] The transfiguration, therefore, was part of the cumulative evidence given to Peter, which would find its culmination in the resurrection appearances. It would further help Peter to preach as emphatically as he did on the day of Pentecost itself, "God has made this Jesus, whom you crucified, both Lord and Christ."[20]

Although this must have been the lasting value of the

transfiguration, there is another secondary sense in which the event would have been important to Peter. Although in no way can you divorce the **content** of the experience from the numinous and transcendent character of the experience itself, since one is part of the other, there is a sense in which the event of the transfiguration of Jesus was a defining moment in the development of Peter himself. For although he still did not know what the mission of Jesus was, referred to in the word "exodus", he was in no doubt now as to his identity. To put it another way, he had an "undeniable"(a loaded term when we use it in connection with Peter) experience of the glory and majesty of Jesus; a foretaste of the future, a glimpse of heaven, which he could refer back to in his memory, and from which he would gain strength and conviction. This, surely, was part of the benefit of this mountain top experience.

It is clear that uncommon supernatural experiences have been given to God's people in times of great stress or difficulty, at critical points in his salvation plan and when the Spirit of God has been poured out in unusual measure. Sometimes it seems that they are earnestly sought, and sometimes they seem spontaneous, in much the same way as the kingdom of God can be either sought for (like the merchant in search of fine pearls), or stumbled upon (like the farmer hitting gold accidentally in his field). Examples of "mountain top experiences" might include God's appearance to Elijah on mount Horeb, not being in the wind, earthquake or fire but in the still small voice; or Paul's vision, which he was reluctant even to mention, of being carried to the seventh heaven where he saw or heard things too marvellous to mention;[21] or the annunciation by the angel Gabriel to Mary that she was to bear the Christ child. There are many others. The purpose of them is various, but undoubtedly they are defining moments in the lives of the recipients, and in some cases of God's salvation history. Elijah realised that God was both powerful and sensitive on Horeb, something he was in danger of forgetting in his depression after the battle on mount Carmel; Paul realised that although he was the recipient of many remarkable visions and experiences, he would still have in his body the "thorn in the flesh" to keep him from, "...becoming conceited because of these surpassingly great revelations";[22] and the appearance of Gabriel to Mary was none other than a moment on which the history of the world truly turned. These moments are the intersection of the eternal with the earthly. They are too marvellous for words, but each in its own way was formative of discipleship.

Similarly, the moment of the transfiguration was an experience which both informed and overwhelmed Peter and his companions. Mountain top experiences still have the same effect today: they may both add to our understanding and transport us into another, normally hidden, realm which is just as real as our own, but which is normally kept from our senses.

Such experiences may come through the various workings of the Holy Spirit upon our lives. They do overwhelm and, as with Peter, we do not know how to incorporate them into normal rational thought and comprehension. These experiences may be either one-off moments to encourage us in our leadership or our discipleship, or be part of a revival or refreshing which God grants at a particular time, as he has on many occasions down the years. One such "outpouring" took place in New England, in Northampton. Jonathan Edwards, who witnessed and pastored at this time of revival in New England in 1740–1742, observed the effects of such times both critically and spiritually. He wrote of those who were affected in this way: "It is no wonder, when the thoughts are so fixed (on heavenly visions) and the affections so strong — and the whole soul so engaged, ravished, and swallowed up — that all other parts of the body are so affected, as to be deprived of their strength, and the whole frame ready to dissolve."[23]

Such was Daniel's experience. After the visions that he had been given, he wrote that, "I, Daniel, was exhausted and lay ill for several days. Then I got up and went about the king's business. I was appalled by the vision; it was beyond understanding."[24] It is precisely because these revelations are beyond our understanding that they are exhausting, for they have a disorientating effect. But the very experience of them serves to show us that we are caught up in a much larger divine plan in which we are encouraged to play our part. Such "mountain top experiences" cannot and should not be sought for their own sake. The desire for intense personal experiences is a hallmark of our present culture, but our focus is to be on the Lord himself, rather than on experiences as such. But all Christians, including those of us who are leaders, can helpfully put ourselves in the way of such impressions to our soul. Engaging in protracted prayer can do this. My own church, like many others who have done something similar, held last year a ten-day "prayer-athon" (a prayer equivalent of a marathon) from Ascension to Pentecost, when for those 240 hours the church was open for continuous prayer; people came throughout that time to several different stations of prayer around the church. I do not know whether many would testify to mountain top experiences with God, but there was little doubt that many met with him in a profound way.

If we are to become spiritual leaders we must have opportunities for "affective" prayer (which is also effective prayer), which transforms us from one degree of glory to another. Without this, our leadership quickly becomes visionless or dry; we may be going through the motions but not touching the Spirit nor allowing him to touch us. Leadership does need a series of transforming moments if we are to minister in a culture which can quickly squeeze us into its own mould or run us dry of spiritual juices. We all need our moments on the mount of transfiguration, in which our awareness of the love and presence of Jesus is refreshed, our remembrance of his identity renewed, and our involvement with his mission, completed at Calvary and offered to the world in the Spirit, re-invigorated. We should seek out such places and times, and put ourselves in the way of such refreshment. Leaders need to remember to prioritise this, but it applies to all Christians.

On the mountain of transfiguration, Peter was shown that he was a witness to the sweep of God's redemptive plan, which already had involved both Moses and Elijah, and now, through God's grace, was sweeping this untaught fisherman from Galilee into its majestic path. Peter understood more clearly the identity of Jesus. He was to discover through great pain the mission which Jesus had come to accomplish. Jesus was now turning more emphatically towards the conclusion of this mission. Coming down from the mountain, they were soon to head for Jerusalem. On the way, Peter would have three instructive conversations with Jesus, which have been kept for us by the Gospel writers, about rewards, forgiveness and discretion. Each of them is especially instructive for leadership in the church. They were relatively easygoing conversations, before the great test that Jesus and the disciples were to be immersed in once they arrived in Jerusalem.

6

THE QUESTION OF DISCRETION OR VALOUR

Matthew 17:24–27

This story of the coin in the fish's mouth, to pay the temple tax, must rank as one of the strangest incidents and one of the most remarkable miracles in the ministry of Jesus, though, in essence, it is no more remarkable than any of the "nature miracles" in the Gospels.

The principal reason for the miracle in this story is that Jesus might not unnecessarily give offence. In other words, although there are times when offence must be given because what is at stake is the very essence of the gospel or the kingdom of God, there are other times when it is needless. Indeed, it could be that the offence taken will only serve to obscure the gospel which you are preaching.

In my own denomination there is plenty of scope for causing offence and I suspect this is true in most churches where patterns and traditions have been laid down over the years. More ministers have suffered opprobrium for meddling with some cherished tradition of the church, in which people have invested great emotional value, than they have from people in their community who have taken exception to the preaching of the Christian gospel. I do not know many people who have been drummed out of their parish because the people dislike the message, but I know of several who have suffered nervous breakdowns because they had the temerity to introduce change into areas of church life where none was welcome. The areas where ministers generally come unstuck in my own tradition (Anglicanism) are music, church furnishings, clothes – or, technically, vestments – and language (not "bad language" but whether it is suitable language for divine worship!) And this generally means whether the language is suitably old. (I well remember one minister, under whom I trained, wisely telling me that in the prayer for the church militant in the 1662 Communion service it was advisable to change the word "indifferently" – when praying for the implementation of justice – to "impartially"; as indifference was not a quality with which we should beseech the Almighty to clothe the judiciary! Equally he opined that for similar reasons of understanding we should not pray for "concord" as the congregation might think that our prayer had taken a sudden flight of fancy. [Referring to the now-retired supersonic aircraft *Concorde*!]) Although these might be amusing examples of how language changes, they indicate how liturgy needs to change as well.

But such light-hearted illustrations mask the deep attachment people often make to the **outward expression** of their faith rather than to the essence of the Christian faith itself. So the minister must decide, under God, whether it is worth making an issue of getting rid of a robed choir for a modern band; removing the hard old pews for colourful chairs; dressing in jeans and a tee shirt to conduct worship; removing his ear ring because members of the church find it offensive; cutting his shoulder length hair; or, for women ministers, not wearing clothes that are too attractive! To be honest there has probably been more bad blood spilt on such issues than on how the church deals with issues that are banner headlines in the press! In essence we have to recognise that church culture changes, spirituality changes, and increasingly in any one congregation you can have people from four generations present. The effect of this is that differing age groups gravitate to familiar and comfortable ways of worship, but too often one man's comfort is another's irritation. The oldest member of our congregation is 102 and the youngest a few weeks old, and that is probably not all that unusual. How do you lead such worshipping communities without unnecessarily giving offence? Jesus was more than willing to give huge offence to the Pharisees when issues of important principle were at stake, so much so that they were incandescent with rage against him. But on this occasion – admittedly with the help of a miracle – he chose discretion as the better part of valour. So let us study more carefully what happened.

THE ISSUE IN QUESTION

Matthew sets this story soon after the disciples return from the mountain of transfiguration. The three disciples whom Jesus had taken with him up the mountain to see his transfiguration had rejoined the others, who were in some difficulty because they had failed to deliver a young boy from a spirit that frequently damaged him. Jesus upbraided them for their lack of power, which in turn reflected their lack of faith. "Faith as small as a mustard seed", according to Jesus, would have been sufficient to deliver this boy! But Jesus said later, in private conversation with the disciples who wisely asked him why they had failed, that such healing would only come after prayer and fasting.[1] After this incident they returned to Capernaum, the headquarters of their operations in the Galilee region, and almost certainly to Peter's home, where it seems they had stayed many times before. Once again Jesus emphasised that he would soon be betrayed into the hands of men. At this, Matthew tells us, "the disciples were filled with grief."[2]

While they were in Capernaum, the collectors of the temple tax were moving through the town making house-to-house visits. Naturally when they came to Peter's house they spoke to Peter as the head of the household about the payment due each year in the month of Adar (February to March), for the support of the sacrificial system at the temple, and no doubt they had been asked to enquire by the authorities whether Jesus paid this tax as well! Rabbis were apparently exempt from the tax, as were the priests in Jerusalem, and probably there was interest in whether Jesus would claim an exemption too, as a self appointed rabbi. The tax was set at two drachma and every Israelite was expected to pay it for the temple upkeep. Its origin lay with the divine command to Moses for the upkeep of the sanctuary or tent of meeting. Moses was told: "Each one who crosses over to those already counted is to give a half shekel, according to the sanctuary shekel, which weighs twenty gerahs."[3] The tax could be paid in person at the Passover festival and was paid in the Tyrian coinage, which was not in common circulation. The currency could be obtained at the money changing stalls in the temple, where the money changers and the temple authorities, by effectively licensing the money changers, made handsomely on the exchange. It was the custom of the tax collectors to make a sweep of outlying districts a month or so before Passover, so that people could pay the tax at their convenience without joining the crowds in Jerusalem. If this was the case, then the visit of the tax collectors to Capernaum was about a month before Jesus would be crucified.

The temple tax collectors enquired of Peter when calling round for his payment, "Doesn't your teacher pay the temple tax?"

It was a loaded question, like many others that Jesus would be asked in the temple precincts a few weeks later, such as, "Is it right to pay taxes to Caesar or not?";[4] or whose wife in heaven was a woman who married seven brothers;[5] or which was the greatest commandment.[6] Peter replied to the tax collectors' question, maybe with too much confidence and certainty, "Yes, he does". But it was not quite as simple as that.

So when Peter came into the house, Jesus quizzed him with a more searching question, "What do you think, Simon? ...From whom do the kings of the earth collect duty and taxes — from their own sons or from others?" That was a straightforward but probing question. Quite rightly Peter said, "From others"; but what are we to infer from this question of Jesus to Peter?

THE UNDERLYING ISSUES: CHRISTIAN FREEDOM AND DUTY

The attitude of Jesus towards the tax must have been ambivalent at best and hostile at worst. After all, it was of itself a disputed tax; some Jews, like those in the Qumran or Essene community, with their antipathy towards the temple and its governance, paid only once in a lifetime. Although it had originally been implemented as a tax to maintain the tent of meeting in the days of Moses, was it now legitimate to raise the tax for the upkeep of the temple? And then in just a few weeks time Jesus himself would be overthrowing the tables of the money changers, who were, amongst other things as we have said, collecting the tax having exchanged the Israelites' money for the Tyrian currency. So you could argue that, since Jesus certainly opposed the system of which this tax was a constituent part, he might have been expected to be less than positive about the tax itself.

But the question which Jesus asked Peter went to an underlying question of principle for the disciples in relation to the state and other authorities that claimed power over them and placed obligations upon them. Jesus' question of Peter could be taken on two levels. At its simplest it could be taken as an observation about the methods of rulers; that is: from whom do rulers collect tax —their own family, or others (their subjects)? The answer in the ancient world was surely their subjects or "others"; no ruler would tax their own family unless they were perhaps rivals for power and the ruler sought to impoverish them! So, if the children of rulers were generally free in this respect (of having to pay taxes), what did this signify in the spiritual realm of the kingdom of God? And here we come to the deeper level of this question. Jesus, presumably, was comparing his disciples and followers to the "sons" in his question; so he is therefore saying that, in principle, as true members of the family of God – who had himself called for this tax through his servant Moses – they were free of any obligation to pay this ecclesiastical tax, and this was the principle he was seeking to tease out for Peter. Later, Jesus would rule on state taxes with his magisterial reply, "Give to Caesar what is Caesar's and to God what is God's"; but with regard to the upkeep of worship in the temple, was Jesus here anticipating what Paul would later teach, especially the Corinthians, that giving for the upkeep of New Testament ministry was a freewill offering without compulsion, for "God loves a cheerful giver"? The principle that Jesus may have been establishing in the mind of Peter was that his followers are free in this regard, but that freedom does not exonerate us of responsibility.[7] It was a lesson which, as we can see from Peter's later instruction, he learnt well.

In his first letter, Peter teaches a suffering church the principles of Christian freedom and responsibility in the context of a tyrannical and overbearing state. By then he himself had greater experience of living as a Christian under persecution. His instruction to the Christian exiles is trenchant and drew on his own observation of Jesus facing the injustice and persecution of the state in his final days. So Peter writes, "Submit yourselves for the Lord's sake to every authority instituted among men: whether to the king, as the supreme authority, or to governors, who are sent by him to punish those who do wrong and commend those who do right. For it is God's will that by doing good you should silence the ignorant talk of foolish men. Live as free men, but do not use your freedom as a cover-up for evil; live as servants of God. Show proper respect to everyone: Love the brotherhood of believers, fear God, honour the king."[8] The key point here is that the submission of the Christian to the secular state, as well as to "every authority instituted amongst men", is marked by two characteristics: it is a free choice; and it is for the Lord's sake. Both of these motivational forces – which enable the Christian to live as a good citizen – are essential, if the Christian is to be a true disciple in a world where power and authority will almost certainly be exercised corruptly. Although the state rulers have a remit to punish those who do wrong and commend those who do right,[9] their exercise of power in the ancient world, as in many places around the world today, was and is a blunt instrument, and Christians often faced persecution then, as many do today. In such a situation it was vital, if positive discipleship was to exist and be maintained, that firstly a Christian's submission to the state really was for the Lord's sake, and that it was a truly voluntary decision, taken from a fundamental position of freedom.

To return to the question that Jesus asked Peter: "From whom do the kings of the earth collect duty and taxes — from their own sons or from others?"; and Peter's correct reply, "from others", the conclusion is therefore drawn that the sons are exempt! Surely the inference of this conclusion is that the disciple of Jesus – and, even more so, Jesus himself – is free in relation to this particular tax, which was in essence to support what we might call ministry or worship. Nevertheless, for other reasons, they would pay it. Establishing this point about the disciples' freedom was nonetheless vital for a number of reasons: it ensured the dignity of the individual over against the greedy demands of the temple authorities; it gave an overall perspective and understanding of a disciple's freedom; and it put their later agreement to pay in the context of a positive action of discipleship or service so as not to cause offence. As Jesus went on to make clear, they would pay the tax, albeit through an extraordinary procedure and miracle —for a single reason, which was so that they might not offend them.

NO OFFENCE GIVEN

To parody the bard: to offend or not offend? —that is the question. As we have already noted, Jesus gave offence on innumerable occasions. Within a few weeks, if our time structure is right for this account, Jesus would tear into the Pharisees with unrelenting invective summarised in the seven woes found in Matthew 23. But here he chose to pay what would be called a "dodgy tax" today, albeit through roundabout means. Why, on this occasion, did he choose not to offend, when on countless other occasions he chose to do otherwise? Perhaps it was to show Peter, whom he was training for leadership of the church, that we are free both to comply as well as to resist. Jesus' later resistance at his trial and crucifixion would be of a kind which would make a deep impression on Peter, and it would later appear in his epistles. But here was an example of using freedom to comply not because Jesus was necessarily in agreement with the tax – as he could have sent for Judas and paid the tax from the common purse without more ado, rather than sending Peter on another miraculous fishing trip – but because he wanted both to show Peter that there are times when we can choose not to offend, and that it may help the advance of the gospel (or the kingdom) to do so.

When should we stand up, force the issue and take the flack? And when should discretion be the better part of valour? Often, in this context, there are missiological or mission-orientated questions to be asked, in order to arrive at the appropriate course of action. They might be questions such as this: "Will this course of action help the gospel of Christ to be welcomed and understood?" or, "Is this the right time for this action?" or again, "Is this a fundamental matter on which I must insist, or is it an issue of secondary importance, which will only dull the hearing of people to the appeal of the gospel?"

It is always interesting to me that the apostle Paul, who insisted so strongly that churches like those in Galatia and at Colossae should not revert to the teaching of the Judaisers (who insisted on circumcision of the believers), himself took Timothy and circumcised him so that Timothy would be more acceptable to the Jewish community as they knew he had a Greek father.[10] The reason Paul did this was **not** because Timothy's faith was in any way defective, but that it would help the advance of the gospel in the region. Although his circumcision may have had the appearance of colluding with the Judaisers, it was in practice the outworking of Paul's missionary principle that, "To the Jews I became like a Jew ...that by all possible means I might save some."[11] Paul was in fact following the example of Jesus here, who chose not to give offence unnecessarily to the people he sought to reach.

But Peter did not find it easy picking his way between

issues of gospel principle and issues to do with mission. We will look more closely at his own role of taking the gospel to the Gentiles in the second part of the book. But as his actions at one point in the vexed question of Jewish–Gentile relations gave real and needless offence in the early church, resulting in severe criticism from Paul, we should consider how he got it wrong, giving offence where he should have given none!

The situation which is explained in Galatians 2:11ff was that Peter at one stage in Antioch (the chief missionary church in the New Testament days) withdrew from table-fellowship with Gentiles. "Before", says Paul, "certain men came from James, and Peter used to eat with the Gentiles. But when they arrived, he began to draw back and separate himself from the Gentiles because he was afraid of those who belonged to the circumcision group. The other Jews joined him in this hypocrisy, so that by their hypocrisy even Barnabas was led astray." Peter, by not associating or eating with the Gentile Christians, was saying in his body language at the very least that he did not regard the Gentile Christians as genuine unless they were circumcised, thereby undermining the teaching concerning justification through faith. For, as Paul went on to argue, "We who are Jews by birth and not 'Gentile sinners' know that a man is not justified by observing the law, but by faith in Jesus Christ...."[12]

So Peter here gave needless offence to the Gentile Christians, called into question the validity of the gospel, and was in danger of leading astray other influential figures, like Barnabas. The reason for Peter's giving offence was not that he might clarify the meaning of the gospel, which had at its heart the teaching, "...that we may be justified by faith in Christ and not by observing the law, because by observing the law no-one will be justified",[13] but because of his old *bête noir*, namely fear of others which got the better of him. Possibly for this reason he withdrew from fellowship with the Gentiles, risked the essence of the gospel and gave offence to the Gentiles where none was due. In fact you could rightly argue that he offended the wrong people; he should in this instance have been willing to give offence to "the certain men who came from James", but his fear overcame

him. There are times when we should be prepared to give
offence for the sake of the gospel, but as we saw earlier there
are also times when discretion is the better part of valour!
Knowing what to do and when to do it requires both prayer
and wisdom.

I remember a priceless example of someone seeking not
to give offence for the sake of the gospel. I was on a Scripture
Union holiday week for boys where I was a leader in the early
70s. A father came at the beginning of the week to drop off
his son and wandered into the leaders' room, where everyone
was earnestly preparing for the week. Being a friendly man
he offered a cigarette to the somewhat taken aback leaders;
all of whom refused! Looking increasingly rejected, the man
offered a "ciggie" to an elderly schoolmaster called Graham,
who had probably last smoked once fifty years previously,
during the years of the First World War! But, seeing the man's
rising embarrassment, he gladly took a proffered cigarette
and tried to smoke as casually and normally as possible, to
the amazement of all the other leaders present! He chose
by his action not to give offence! He probably did not
approve of smoking nor ever smoked again, but he did not
want this man to leave feeling that an offer meant in kindness
was rejected! —a case again, to use a technical word, of a
missiological reason overriding an ethical one!

Jesus chose to pay the tax so as not to give offence; a few
weeks later he would, in righteous anger, be overthrowing
the tables of those whose work was related to that same tax,
as we have noticed. His method of payment was unique and
memorable, and probably not open to us: Peter was told to
go on another of his miraculous fishing trips, to which, by
now, he must have been becoming accustomed! The reason
for the method of payment adopted was, on the one hand,
so that the payment would in reality be made (so not giving
offence) whilst, on the other hand, the fishing method
distanced Jesus and Peter from the payment itself —so as to
preserve the principle of freedom. A fish with a four-drachma
coin in its mouth is, unfortunately, not a dependable or
typical resolution to a dilemma which we may find ourselves
in, but with prayer it is amazing how a gospel goal may be

achieved without offence being given, if not always. We are not told what the temple tax gatherers made of it all; one imagines they found it "a little fishy"!

7

A QUESTION OF FORGIVENESS

Matthew 18:21–35

Peter must have thought he was being more than generous, even rash, in suggesting to Jesus that he forgive his brother seven times; after all, that was more than the rabbis taught. In some of their teaching they limited forgiveness of a person who has offended or hurt you to three times only! Moreover, some Old Testament passages mention seven times as the perfect or complete number of occasions.[1] So forgiving a person seven times must have seemed like going beyond the full extent of our obligation to pardon another. So how big-hearted Peter must have felt when he offered the suggestion. But imagine Peter's horror and shock when Jesus, who has rightly been called "the model forgiver", looked at him and said, "I tell you not seven times, but seventy times seven." Peter still had much to learn —about his own fragility and the need to forgive, as well as the waywardness of the human heart.

Peter was later to discover personally the truth of what Jesus taught, but at his own expense and through great pain. That lesson would always remain a humbling exper- ience, for the remainder of Peter's life.

Just as Paul would always minister in the knowledge that

he had once persecuted the church – and therefore considered himself "the chief of sinners", so Peter, in the future,
would always minister in the knowledge that he had denied
his Lord. It was part of the scar tissue of his spirituality,
which we will come to later. As a result of his own frailty,
Peter had a sober estimation of the weakness of our ordinary
human "flesh", or self-life.

But here, in this conversation with Jesus, Peter was to learn
in theory what he may have hoped he would never have to
experience in practice, namely both the infinite capacity of
Jesus to forgive the repentant sinner, and his own need to
plumb those depths of forgiveness himself. In our scrutiny
of this conversation, set by Matthew in the final weeks leading
up to Jesus' arrest and crucifixion, we will look at the context
of this teaching, the meaning of forgiveness, and the influence
on Peter and his later teaching of both this conversation and
his own experience of forgiveness.

THE CONTEXT OF FORGIVENESS: COMMUNITY LIVING

Matthew chapter 18 comprises teaching by Jesus about how
the Christian community is to function. So the context of
this conversation with Peter is firmly set by Matthew in the
ordering of the church community's life. If the community
of the church may be compared to an orchestra, in which
the talents and gifts of its members are to be directed in line
with a composition which has been arranged by God, then
some of the notes or the keys to be struck in this community
are to be found in the teaching of this chapter. We recall,
from the New Testament picture of the church as a 'body',
that the necessary gifts are from the Holy Spirit, and that the
members are to be both filled with and directed by the Spirit.

These notes are, in particular, **humility** as exemplified by
a child: "Therefore," Jesus says, "whoever humbles himself
like this child is the greatest in the kingdom of heaven";
ruthlessness in regard to personal holiness: "If your hand or
foot causes you to sin, cut it off and throw it away. It is better
for you to enter life maimed...than have two hands or two

feet and be thrown into eternal fire"; **compassion** in regard to searching for the lost or member of the community who has wandered off (v. 13); and **accountability through listening**, so that the errant brother or sister may be restored. This chapter as a whole would make an excellent vehicle for teaching any church how it should order its life, and surely this was Matthew's purpose in grouping together these paragraphs as he did.

Into this mixture (of fundamental values which should govern the outworking of community life in the church) is added **forgiveness**, which Matthew collects with these other formative values for Christians. From this passage, we learn that as each member of the community aims for humility like that of a child; strives for personal holiness (as a surgeon, removing gangrene from a patient, cuts it out to save the patient's life); undertakes outgoing compassion; practises accountability, which makes members of the community face up to their attitudes and actions; and exercises forgiveness, which prevents those self same failures festering or rankling in or outside the community of the church —so the body of the church grows up healthily.

In short, this chapter in Matthew's gospel is all about values which must be to the fore if the church is to function well. Later, Peter, as we shall see, will incorporate this teaching into his own instructions to the churches of Bithynia, Asia, Cappodocia, Pontus, Asia and Galatia. But now we must see what Jesus meant by forgiveness.

THE MEANING OF FORGIVENESS

No one involved in leadership of a church, as Peter would be, could ignore the ongoing need for forgiveness in personal relationships, both in terms of making sure he did not hold onto bitterness or resentment and in steering the relationships and teaching of the church.

Whereas the previous verses in Matthew 18 have been about the need for the Christian community to hold people to account for their behaviour and ministry – with the hope that the offending parties will listen and change their ways – this conversation with Jesus is principally about the need for personal relationships to be governed by forgiveness and not by bitterness, animosity or revenge. Although, in New Testament teaching, groups of people – the state or particular human institutions – may under certain circumstances have the right to punish, defend their interests or exact retribution, this action is never, it seems, open to the individual, who is encouraged to report a grievance to the appropriate authorities. On a personal level we are encouraged to hold out forgiveness and mercy to another who has offended or hurt us, and not to act in a retaliatory or vengeful manner. In this way both justice may be served as the state enforces laws and personal relations need not descend into recrimination or bitterness.

This is sometimes a fine line to draw, and much harder where there is no fair and equitable recourse to law available for the redress of a grievance. For instance, two Christian neighbours could fall out over a planning application. One neighbour applies for permission for a home extension, to which the other objects. They belong to the same church community. Feelings could run high! The applicant does not feel that it is necessary to withdraw the planning application purely because of the neighbour's objection, as they are using the agreed community planning process. But the objector cannot help feeling aggrieved that the other has not consulted more and taken his wishes into account. Planning permission is granted. It would be easy for the aggrieved party to feel resentful or the successful to feel triumphant. The legal aspect of the planning application may have been settled but there is still the matter of the heart. Hearts cannot be so easily governed, and it is precisely in that area that forgiveness must operate. So what is forgiveness?

There are several words for forgiveness in the Bible. The word most often used in the Old Testament is *nasa*, which means "to have a weight lifted away". Its Greek equivalent *aphiemi* means to "let go" or "send away". In sign language used by the deaf and dumb, forgiveness is indicated by wiping the palm of one hand firmly across the other, as if removing any stain or mess that might be on it. Another word for forgiveness, which occurs five times in the New Testament, is *exaleipho*, and its basic meaning is to wipe away or expiate. The picture here is of an ancient writing slate being wiped clean of the chalk writing on it, with a damp cloth. Older readers will remember a blackboard being cleaned by the teacher with a blackboard rubber that sat on a ledge beneath the board. Wiping the board clean was a daily occurrence in the classroom! God wipes away our daily failings as we pray to him for forgiveness. If he does that for us then we should do the same for others.

If the principal meaning of forgiveness is letting go, Jesus is teaching Peter here that we have to go on letting go of offences caused – even by one individual – if necessary, seventy times seven, and that means endlessly! To reinforce his statement about forgiveness, Jesus goes on to explain our responsibility further with a parable. A servant was forgiven a debt of ten thousand talents, but in turn the servant was unwilling to forgive another a hundred denarii. The sum the master forgave was unbelievably huge, millions of pounds in present day values and "six hundred thousand" times larger than the sum the servant was unwilling to forgive. The obvious lesson that Jesus wishes us to draw is that God has forgiven each of us a vast debt —so how can we not forgive the much smaller debts that we generally owe one another. What right have we to hold on to resentment when we ourselves have been forgiven so much? Major offences against us, which may include abuse, betrayal, desertion, rape, slander, bodily harm or cruelty, may take some time to really forgive, simply because the level of pain and hurt inflicted is so great. The decision to forgive, the act of forgiveness which is an act of the will, may take place in an instant, but it can take years for our thinking and attitude to change accordingly. The important point is that although the reality of complete forgiveness lived out at every level of our being may be difficult to achieve, the question we must answer is: Is forgiveness our hope and target; our final destination? If it is our hope, then our will needs to be engaged in going in that right direction; but we will require spiritual resources from God, who may use others to help us to get there. To help the process forward, there are people who have travelled that hard road which may lie ahead of us, and we should learn from them.

There are a number of well-publicised incidents of remarkable forgiveness which show that forgiveness of even the grossest violation of human dignity is possible. One such is the story of Kim Phuc, a Christian Vietnamese lady. When nine years old she was caught in an American napalm bomb raid on her village. Nick Ut, who later became a close friend, photographed her. She was naked, terrified, burnt by napalm, her skin peeling as she ran away from her village, which can be seen in the background of the photograph. It was without doubt the most powerful photograph to come out of the Vietnam war. Ut drove Kim to hospital and stayed with her until she was treated. But, in an extraordinary sequel, Kim met one of the American airmen responsible for the fateful raid on her village and was able to forgive him. Kim, who subsequently became a Christian and a Goodwill Ambassador for UNESCO, now has a message of reconciliation for communities or individuals at loggerheads with each other. If Kim was able to find the resources through her Christian faith to offer such forgiveness, there is always hope that bitterness and resentment should not imprison us in some tragic incident or event which has deeply damaged us.

Forgiveness (and a willingness to apologise when appropriate), is a *sine qua non* of Christian discipleship. It is essential in leadership. Sometimes leaders have to say, "It is all my fault that such and such went wrong. I am sorry!" If you are a leader of a team in a church, to say those words could not be more helpful to those whom you lead. It demonstrates to them that you are not perfect, you fail and need forgiveness, and that you are well aware of it! It gives permission to others to try and to risk failing. It encourages a culture of risk-taking in church life. It demonstrates that although we preach and teach endlessly that failure is not a reason for exclusion from ministry (or the life of discipleship), we are **not** in fact operating by another (unspoken) standard which, given an opportunity, soon percolates its way into church life, namely: "If you are not fulfilling all the rules then you definitely cannot minister here!"

It is amazing how, in church life, we may teach one thing but, by some strange operating system that can exist within churches or Christian organisations, function in reality by completely different standards. Thus we can teach justification by **faith** alone but can end up modelling that we are justified by **good behaviour** alone. We can speak often about **forgiveness** but find that members hold deep-seated grievances against another. However, if the leader of a church demonstrates his own need for forgiveness by freely admitting his own failures or mistakes, then other members of the team are, in their turn, more likely to be frank about their own mistakes —and to own them, knowing that forgiveness is easily both asked for and received.

It always amazes me that in the church – whose very basis is forgiveness and acceptance – people are so loath to admit that we get it wrong, and that failure is never the last word in God's book! If forgiveness is so freely available between us, as Jesus suggests, it is precisely because it is so frequently needed. But, as the song goes, "Sorry is the hardest word"!

It was said by many church leaders, in the diocese where I work, that when you went to see Jim Thompson, our previous bishop, who died last year, he would first share with you his own difficulties and failings before you had a chance to express your own problems and failings! Naturally, leaders came away refreshed and encouraged! What does that teach us? And what might an interview with the apostle Peter have thrown up, if you had gone to see him to confess to him that you thought that either your own leadership or discipleship was wanting? He might well have told you of the ways he had let his Lord down, and how he had been forgiven. It is precisely because the church should be a forgiving community that it is possible to be honest about our failings and not to cloak them or dissemble. The flip side of forgiveness should be honesty! But sometimes I find churches stilted or laborious about offering the very thing that constitutes its existence, namely the grace and forgiveness of Christ.

Jesus taught Peter that he was to go on forgiving his brother seventy times seven, because God's willingness to forgive our failures is even greater. It was both understanding this teaching and experiencing it in practice, at the acutest moment of his life, that no doubt influenced Peter to write in the way that he did to the suffering church in Asia Minor, present day Turkey, towards the end of his life.

Peter's later teaching about forgiveness is encapsulated in this passage: "Finally, all of you, live in harmony with one another; be sympathetic, love as brothers, be compassionate and humble. Do not repay evil with evil or insult with insult, but with blessing, because to this you were called so that you may inherit a blessing."[2] In these verses Peter summarised his teaching to the whole church community including husbands, wives, slaves and citizens, about how to conduct themselves in the context of an oppressive and repressive state. It is not surprising to find Peter striking the same notes here as Jesus did in his reported instruction to him in Matthew 18, as elsewhere.

Indeed commentators believe that the teaching in Peter's epistle here formed part of traditional catechetical material for converts.[3] The keynotes of this teaching, unsurprisingly, are a call to be humble-minded (the only place where the original Greek word *tapeinophron* is used); to be compassionate, forgiving; blessing rather than returning evil with evil. What Peter himself had learnt from Jesus, seen in Jesus and then received himself from Jesus, he now passed on to other Christians, in testing circumstances, in Asia.

As the narrative of Peter's life moved on toward the unseen crisis ahead, there was one more recorded conversation to be had with Jesus before they entered Jerusalem.[4] It took place in the region of Judea, outside of Galilee, on the east side of Jordan, before the draw of Jerusalem took its full effect on his own and his Master's life. The conversation was about rewards, and to this we turn now.

8

WHAT'S IN IT FOR ME?

Matthew 19:16–30, Mark 10:17–31,
Luke 18:18–29, 1 Peter 5:1–4

It was an all too human and understandable response: "What then will there be for us?" On a number of other occasions the disciples demanded to know what they would get out of being followers of Jesus. On one such occasion, recorded by Matthew in chapter twenty of his Gospel, it was the ambitious mother of James and John who came to Jesus with a breathtaking request. Kneeling, she asked, "Grant that one of these two sons of mine may sit at your right and the other at your left in your kingdom."[1] In the parallel account in Mark it is the twins themselves who make the same request of Jesus, prefacing their demand with the astonishing expectation: "Teacher," they said, "we want you to do for us whatever we ask." Or again, even while Jesus was celebrating the Last Supper, with his mind and spirit full of his impending betrayal and death, the disciples were squabbling over which of them was the greatest.[2] Nor was that a unique occasion, for Mark tells us that earlier, when they were on their way to Capernaum, they were debating the same question —who was the greatest?[3]

The disciples, it seems, were a raw group of men, jostling for position in any impending political structure which Jesus was to build. They wondered, as Peter does in this story, what was in it for them! Peter's question of Jesus had been brought about by an almost shocking encounter with a "rich young ruler", whom Jesus had challenged so severely that it left all the disciples wondering whether they, or anyone for that matter, could be saved!

The encounter between Jesus and the rich young ruler forms the basis for this particular conversation between Peter – as the disciples' spokesman – and Jesus. The rich young ruler is an attractive, self-confident character, assured of his own goodness and secure in his own righteousness. He is looking for eternal life; he is convinced that he has kept the commandments in relation to neighbour, and he assumes an easy relationship with Jesus, calling him, a little airily, "good teacher".[4] He seems personable, with the easy charm born of wealth and the confidence that arises from a good education (in his case mostly religious), which he has seemingly followed. He is moral, intelligent, charming and spiritual, but he is a little too self-assured for his own good.

So Jesus sets about examining the young ruler, both as to his assumptions about who he, Jesus, is, and concerning his own self-understanding. With regard to his understanding of Jesus, he questions whether he really should be calling him (Jesus) "good", not because he is not good but because a Jew could only strictly use that adjective (good) of God. In this way Jesus makes the young ruler examine both his language and assumptions more rigorously than he was prone to do; and, at the same time, no doubt to further evaluate whom he thought Jesus really was. Secondly, with regard to his assessment of his own spirituality, Jesus shows him a spirituality which would be impossible to attain without grace and which, by its very nature, showed his own need for help. "You still lack one thing", said Jesus. "Sell everything you have and give to the poor, and you will have treasure in heaven. Then come, follow me".

As ever, Jesus had correctly diagnosed the spiritual condition of this enquirer, giving him a task which was well beyond his spiritual means, so that he would have to admit his need of grace if he were to implement it. As yet, the rich young ruler did not see that the treasures Jesus would offer him through discipleship were greater than the "treasures" he was being asked to give up in order to follow him. The demand was too great for him —as, having great wealth, which he cherished, he could not find it within himself to even start to do what Jesus had demanded of him. He went away sad; and Jesus, seeing his reaction, used it as another case study of the soul from which to instruct the disciples. The conclusion Jesus drew from his meeting with the young ruler was the famous one about wealth, "How hard it is for the rich to enter the kingdom of God!" and, "Indeed, it is easier for a camel to go through the eye of a needle than for a rich man to enter the kingdom of God."[5]

When Peter heard these conclusions, which Jesus drew from his encounter with the rich young ruler, he and the other disciples were "greatly astonished" and asked, "Who then can be saved?" In their minds, the disciples had concluded from remarks by Jesus that salvation depended on surrender of worldly wealth. But in drawing that conclusion they were confusing the challenge (giving away his wealth) which was designed to show the young ruler his need of God's help, with the only qualification in fact to belonging to the kingdom, which is trust in the king.

Of course, as yet, the rich young ruler did not trust Jesus enough to forgo some or most of his wealth and enter the kingdom. But, as Jesus taught, left to human ingenuity alone it is not possible to prise wealth from the fist of those who hold it, though with God even this miracle is possible!

There are more than enough examples in today's church to show how extraordinarily generous disciples of Jesus can be, for indeed with God all things are possible. I think of numerous churches that have raised millions of pounds for development projects connected to their own church life; even more impressive are those church communities who have given substantial sums away in support of relief or development work in the two thirds world. A leader of any Christian community, by sharing vision, in the context of faith, should be able to see in action what the rich young ruler found difficult to do, namely the giving away of wealth for ministry to the poor and spiritually needy.

Later on, in the early days of the church in Jerusalem, Peter was to see incredible generosity in the church, so that there was no impoverished member. We read that, "Selling their possessions and goods, they gave to anyone as he had need"; and, "No-one claimed that any of his possessions was his own, but they shared everything they had.... There were no needy persons among them. For from time to time those who owned lands or houses sold them, brought the money from the sales and put it at the apostles' feet, and it was distributed to anyone as he had need."[6]

All that lay in the future. But what hitherto would have seemed like impossibility had been made possible by the work of the Holy Spirit in the hearts of the Christian community.

Returning to the conversation between Jesus and his disciples, Jesus' teaching about sacrifice elicited a *crie de coeur* from Peter which also echoed the feelings of the other disciples. They had left everything at the outset, so what was in it for them? That is a question which other disciples or leaders have no doubt asked occasionally ever since. What reward do I get from the sacrifices involved in Christian ministry? On the face of it, this seems like a self-centred question, but Jesus did not dismiss it as such; he gave it a serious answer, which he believed it deserved.

TOWARDS A THEOLOGY OF REWARDS

Christians have normally been rather ambivalent about any theology of rewards. Surely, it is argued, since we have already been redeemed by grace, given eternal life, made children of our heavenly Father, given an inheritance in heaven, what are we doing thinking about some additional reward for service, which may be driven by mixed motives. It tarnishes Christian service with self-interest and thereby diminishes its nobility. But as a matter of fact, neither Jesus nor Paul and Peter are ambivalent about the existence of rewards; the New Testament is spangled with references to rewards! The reason for our ambivalence is that we are probably either more self-effacing or self-denigrating than we should be! Perhaps you can imagine an all too English martyr saying to God, "Oh, no, no, Lord it was really nothing; others are much more deserving and have done far more — look at that lady over there, she was an organist at St Hilda's for fifty years! She is far more deserving than me of any rewards!"

Of course we should be able to serve, sweat and suffer without recognition, but surely it is part of our humanity to give and receive recognition for what is brave, good and so on. Rewards are a celebration of obedience, discipline, fruitfulness and faithfulness amongst other things. God, it seems, loves to celebrate them in style! So Jesus responds to Peter's plaintive cry of "What will there be for us?" not with a rebuke but an answer which recognises the substantial sacrifices that Peter and others had made in their disciple-ship. They had, after all, left everything; will there be something to which they may look forward? Jesus teaches that there will be.

Rewards are connected to the future. I remember listening to an ethical discussion on the radio about the difference between a bribe and a reward, particularly in connection with bringing up children. On the whole, although not exclusively, bribes are given **now** to change someone so that they do something you want. Without the bribe it is unlikely that they would do it, whether the action is good or bad, so the incentive for doing whatever it is is the bribe itself. For instance, a parent may give a child a sweet or pocket money to tidy their room, knowing full well that without the bribe the child would probably never do it; and instances of bribery are not unknown in the adult world of politics and international business! A bribe consists of money or favours given in order to make another do something you want, which sways their actions —sometimes to do something which is illegal or ethically wrong. A reward, on the other hand, is the outcome of achievement.

It so happens that I am writing this chapter on the day a victorious English international rugby team landed back in the UK. Six thousand fans greeted them before dawn at

Heathrow airport. The captain, landing the re-named Boeing 747 *Sweet Chariot*, said, "This is your captain speaking. *Sweet Chariot* has landed and I can confirm that the World Cup is firmly on English soil", to the applause of loud cheers on the plane. On the same day we were told that each player would receive as a reward the sum of £41,000, and for most players that would be only the tip of a very big financial iceberg! The reward is an acknowledgement and celebration of a great achievement. It encourages performance but it does not guarantee it. It celebrates achievement, but it does not itself secure it. If you had been able to ask an English player whether they had done it for the financial reward, they would not have welcomed the question. They played for each other, for their country, for their coach, and for their own personal satisfaction. The reward was a tangible way of the rugby authorities showing appreciation for what they had done.

The reward offered by Jesus in response to Peter's question was both an acknowledgement of what they had done and an incentive and encouragement to continue to the end. Above all, it was reassuring. In particular, they were to be given responsibility and privilege in a future realm, judging the twelve tribes of Israel, "...at the renewal of all things, when the Son of Man sits on his glorious throne..." and their sacrifices would be more than compensated for in this new world.[7] And for their losses or sacrifices in leaving family or property they would receive a hundred times more! There is no doubt that Jesus promised rewards, and Peter was to make this expectation part of his teaching to the leadership of the suffering church in the 1st Century AD.

REWARDS FOR LEADERS

Writing to his fellow leaders (or elders) of churches in the vicinity of Pontus, Galatia, Cappadocia, Asia and Bithynia, Peter gives wise advice about leadership. As he himself was charged by Jesus, as an under-shepherd, with the responsibility of feeding his sheep or lambs, so now Peter charges those who led churches in these areas with the responsibility of tending the flock of God in their charge. "Be shepherds of God's flock that is under your care, serving as overseers —not because you must, but because you are willing, as God wants you to be; not greedy for money, but eager to serve; not lording it over those entrusted to you, but being examples to the flock."[8] We will return to the importance of these charges in respect of pastoral care in the last chapter of this section, but we may now notice how Peter also holds out the prospect of reward for the faithful pastor or church leader. If they fulfil this calling then they can expect that, "...when the Chief Shepherd appears, you will receive the crown of glory that will never fade away." The reward is essentially public recognition of a job well done. The public recognition is the acknowledgement by Christ before others of faithful service given as an overseer. This service of overseeing is acknowledged, celebrated, and rewarded with "an unfading crown of glory" —a visible and permanent accolade.

Overseeing God's flock is not a picnic! It carries with it responsibilities to teach, guide, care for, bring back, reconcile, bear with and correct the sheep. It is ideally based on an extraordinary degree of trust, which is itself a remarkable privilege. But there are undoubtedly, as with all human communities, moments of sharp pain, misunderstanding or rejection, which the pastor must bear as a minor portion of the "sufferings of Christ". At times these difficulties can be almost overwhelming, and it is in such times that it is as well to remember the promise of reward —again, in the sense that the pain does not go finally unnoticed, and the sacrifices made do not go unappreciated. In the reward that is to come, both appreciation and acknowledgement are intertwined. Perhaps all scars are transfigured in heaven, even as the redemptive scars of Jesus are visible for all to see, and there are few pastors without scars of service from sheep-tending! Amy Carmichael put it well in her poem, *Hast thou no scar?*

Peter's question of Jesus may have sounded rather plaintive and pitiful, an almost childish cry of "what about me, Lord"; but then most of us have cried out something similar. The assurance Peter is given is that everything is noticed, even a cup of cold water, and that there will be rewards, not bribes, for all who sacrificed and lost out on the journey of discipleship. As the writer to the Hebrews wrote, "God is not unjust; he will not forget your work and the love you have shown him as you have helped his people and continue to help them."[9]   And if you still doubt that a theology of rewards is integral to our faith, remember that "...he rewards those who earnestly seek him."[10]

9

A VIRTUOUS CYCLE: RECEIVING AND SERVING

John 13:1–7, 1 Peter 5:1–9

Soon after the meeting with the rich young ruler, and the conversation to which it gave rise about riches and rewards, Jesus entered Jerusalem on a donkey, fulfilling the prophecy of Zechariah,

> "Say to the Daughter of Zion,
> See, your king comes to you,
> gentle and riding on a donkey,
> on a colt, the foal of a donkey."[1]

The crowds rapturously received his entry into Jerusalem. They welcomed him as a coming king. It began a period of intense teaching in the precincts of the temple, covering a wide spectrum of subjects including issues relating to taxation, the resurrection, the identity of John the Baptist and the signs surrounding both the return of the Son of Man and the impending judgement of Jerusalem. There is an almost tangible racheting up of tension in those final days of escalating conflict between Jesus and the Jewish author-ities. About a quarter of Matthew's and Luke's Gospels, and a third of Mark's, is taken up with these last days of the earthly ministry of Jesus. But only in John do we have the record of the sustained teaching Jesus gave to the disciples in the upper room. Whereas the other Gospel writers tell us of his ministry in the public places of Jerusalem, with the skirmishes Jesus had with the rulers, teachers of the law and Pharisees, John concentrates almost entirely on the Lord's private preparation of the disciples for the future. And only he gives us one of the most moving and instructive insights into the heart of Jesus' ministry —the washing of the disciples' feet.

We have become familiar with this event, but no action of Jesus could be more illustrative of the very essence of his ministry; and once again Peter is at the centre of its outworking. Initially, Peter is unwilling that Jesus should wash his feet, but after reproof, he lunges to the opposite extreme: "...not just my feet but my hands and my head as well!"[2] Once again, Peter's response in the upper room is not very different to his reaction at either the transfiguration or Caesarea Philippi. He is, on the one hand, shocked by what he sees Jesus doing, and so tries to dissuade him from doing it; and then, on the other hand, to cover any awkwardness or embarrassment, he veers to the opposite extreme as he implores him to wash his hands and feet too. So Peter had to learn, maybe a little painfully, the cardinal lesson that all spiritual leadership involves both receiving and serving.

RECEIVING

There is no doubt that Christian leaders can put themselves into the position of being the ones who must always be giving out. It is a curious but prevalent piece of ministerial behaviour. Some might suggest that clergy or Christian leaders are the kind of people who need to be needed, and that this motivation may draw them to the ministry in the first place. Although there may be some truth in this in some cases, it is an oversimplification to attribute such psychological motives to those who minister. However, the need to be the one who is always giving out can proceed from several states of mind. Sometimes it can result from simply wanting to be in control, and one way of controlling is by always being active and never being in a position of receiving. Sometimes the need to be always giving out proceeds from the false notion that having to receive is a sign of weakness. Thus any admission of need – arising, for instance, from depression; or a sense of inadequacy for the task, or disenchantment with the congregation; or uncertainty as to God's will – or having needs which you have not yet resolved, is thought by some to be an admission of faith-failure. The resulting persona that the minister may adopt is one of being sufficient rather than vulnerable, coping rather than needy, and of being like a fortress rather than an open house.

But such thinking is sometimes a denial of our humanity, and it may result in a suppression of vital issues of "being" which cannot be forever camouflaged beneath an adopted persona of "the coping leader". If that is done – camouflaging our problems – we run the risk, to use a nautical image, of running aground and breaking up in the breakers of those unresolved issues that crash on our over laden hulls! So receiving is a way of offloading the unwanted ballast, so that we can float again!

Of course you might object to this broad interpretation of Jesus' action in John 13, when he washed the disciples' feet. The action of washing in the passage is definitely connected by Jesus with "cleansing". It as though Jesus is teaching at one level, by his action, that by believing in him the disciples have had a "bath" but that they continually need to be "cleansed", as inevitably they (and we) pick up "dirt" through our contact with the world. So we need to be daily cleansed from that dirt; just as feet, exposed as they were then in sandals, needed to be daily washed clean from the grime and dust they picked up on the road. Indeed, it was the general practice to wash or to have your feet washed before a meal; normally such washing in better off homes was done by the household servant. Although this interpretation of the action of Jesus is undoubtedly true, there is no harm in expanding the application of foot washing to include any refreshment of soul or body, which we need to **receive** to restore the **well-being** of our deepest self.

Receiving refreshment, enrichment and nourishment of ourselves, at whatever level, is needful and is a prerequisite of any ongoing spiritual leadership. This is especially the case when spiritual work is full time or remunerated. That is not to say that Christians working in secular employment are not as much full-time Christians as those working directly for churches or Christian agencies, but it is as well as to recognise that those working in the full time pastoral, teaching or evangelistic ministry of the church face a particular set of challenges in which the need "to receive" is immensely important. Having worked with at least seven assistant clergy who have been learning the ropes of spiritual leadership, and as many lay assistants, I have seen that finding access to such refreshment and receiving it is vital to healthy ministry. And in a week in which I learnt of the suicide of one minister and the sudden resignation of another, the urgency of facing this question and putting into place ways of resolving it could not be more urgent.

The ways of finding appropriate refreshment will be as various as the characters that we have, and as diverse as the interests that we enjoy; but undoubtedly there are a few sensible steps that can be taken.

A spouse of a clergy person recently told me that her husband generally worked a 90-hour week! Clearly, balance of work and refreshment had gone out of the window. At the other extreme a newly qualified minister of the Church of England who had entered the ministry from business told his rather astonished vicar that he expected to have Christmas day off! I have met ministers who have previously held senior positions in industry or teaching say how tiring they find the work. It is the mix of self-employment, the feeling that there is always something more to be done, the difficulty of unravelling working life from home life, living over the shop, having your office in your home – as many clergy do – and feeling the pressure of motivating a body of people who may be reluctant to go in the direction in which you wish to lead them, that can be so tiring. One minister who lived by a railway line always rushed off to see passing trains; asked why he repeatedly did this, he said, "It is the only thing in my parish which moves without having to be pushed!" Anyhow, these are just some of the challenges that face those in the ministerial life, especially those with young families at home. If that is not enough, things can turn especially difficult if there is a serious rift with someone who holds an important position in the church or leadership team —few things are more exhausting and debilitating.

If that is a scenario which rings bells with church leaders, then how can we find the refreshment that is needed to see us through? Firstly, we have to accept there are no easy answers. Circumstances vary hugely. But the well-being of the minister will largely depend upon at least four areas of life being healthy, which means sustaining, enriching and nourishing. They are, in order of importance: home life – that is, relations with spouse and children, if married; self-life; team life, and church life.

Beginning with the home, I expect you have heard the story of the minister who found a note on his desk saying, "A parishioner urgently wants a meeting with the Vicar at 6.00 p.m., and will call round then for an appointment", and waited in his study to meet this urgent request for attention. Imagine the minister's horror when his ten-year-old son turned up! His son was the parishioner who never got to see his father although they lived in the same house! It is all too easy for the minister to be at home but "not all there"; instead, he or she can be preoccupied with a pressing church issue which acts like a curtain of impregnability between the family and himself. Finding ways to sustain those relationships must be high on the list of any minister; after all, what is the use of calling others to love and mutual care if this "charity" does not begin at home? Working practices in full-time ministerial life vary greatly. Having been raised in the school of working from 8:30 a.m. through to 10:00 p.m. at least five days a week, I find that older clergy are scandalised at the practice of dividing the day into three sections and then taking one of them off! It is hard to imagine St Paul giving any credence to working directives designed to foster a thirty eight hour working week. However, I am always grateful that some years ago most evenings by 6.00 p.m., when others might have been struggling home from work, I could take a break and play at least half an hour's French cricket with my three daughters (our son had not arrived then) in a small London garden!

The second relationship (some might argue the first) is the nurture of yourself. After all, we are to love our neighbours **as ourselves.** The nurture and love of our own self is not pointless vanity – although in our self-indulgent society we can all too easily worship at the shrine of self-absorption and ego therapy or massage – but a vital necessity. Society at large will argue the need of doing whatever helps me to feel good about myself, but that can quickly turn into a self-centred lifestyle. And the self-life has a voracious appetite! No, we must understand what refreshes our own spiritual, social and personal being, and build that into the rhythm of our lives. Speaking for myself, this will include exercise —spiritual and physical. Physical exercise releases those agents of wellbeing, endorphins, which create the chemical serotonin in the brain, which in turn promotes wellbeing and demotes depression. Spiritual exercise will include the disciplines of prayer and Bible reflection, as well as the possibility of spiritual direction or mentoring. Such things as friendship, reading, company, food, and wine (in moderation!) can also have appropriate parts to play in a well-rounded Christian life. I regard these supports – animate and inanimate as they are – as friends, which have their proper place in sustaining and developing my own self-life the better to serve others. To neglect ourselves is, in the end, to diminish our service.

The third relationship to sustain, in the context of spiritual leadership, is our own team life. I was recently at a meeting in which the principle of "not serving alone" was discussed, and the hope expressed that no minister would serve alone. I cannot imagine being in a situation of church life in which the minister was in solitary leadership —that is, outside a team of people. The team may be part-time or full-time in the Christian ministry, salaried or unsalaried, short-term or long term. But the team creates the context for ongoing support and refreshment. I am fortunate to belong to a ministry team that meets twice a week for prayer, Bible study with reflective reading of the Old and New Testament, as well as sharing mutual concerns. There are shared moments of gladness and sadness, but it is a community of its own, with the power to affect the whole church.

If these three relationships are healthy, then the final relationship of leader to church leadership and congregation is likely to be good as well. In a sense, this relationship is the product of the other three. Of course there may be strains at times, when new ventures are being taken on or changes being made, but if a pastor/church relationship is not mutually refreshing then it might be wise to look at the other three areas.

These are ways of gaining refreshment or receiving ourselves. When Jesus stooped down to take a towel and wash his disciples' feet, he was teaching them to receive from him. Principally, this action was a symbol of forgiveness and incorporation into the Jesus community, but for Peter it was also a lesson in receiving —without which ministry is not possible, either at its beginning or in its sustaining. But more important even than this was the living demonstration that Jesus was among them as a servant, and that this was the key to Christ-like ministry.

SERVING

Peter's initial refusal to have Jesus wash his feet – and so receive the blessing of this ongoing cleansing – was incidental to the main theme of the narrative. That theme was the servanthood of Jesus. Often, as we have already noted, Jesus taught his competitive and ambitious disciples that the greatest amongst them was the one who serves. If they had wanted a visual demonstration of what this meant, they now had it. John puts it in dramatic and unmistakeable terms at the beginning of this event, introducing it with words that still have the power to astonish. There is more than a sense of this scene being a springboard for the greatest days in human history when John writes, "The evening meal was being served, and the devil had already prompted Judas Iscariot, son of Simon, to betray Jesus. Jesus knew that the Father had put all things under his power, and that he had come from God and was returning to God; so he got up from the meal, took off his outer clothing and wrapped a towel round his waist. After that, he poured water into a basin and began to wash his disciples' feet, drying them with the towel that was wrapped round him."[3] At this moment, as John earlier wrote, "Jesus knew that the time had come for him to leave this world and go to the Father. Having loved his own who were in the world, he now showed them the full extent of his love."[4]

In many ways, the foot washing of the disciples marks the beginning of the final descent to the cross. The language is emotive: describing Jesus taking off his outer garment, wrapping around his waist a towel, pouring out water and washing feet. The actions are typically Johannine; at once both simple and redolent of far deeper significance. On the one hand the passage is historical, describing what Jesus did; on the other hand it is allegorical, symbolising far deeper theological truth. They find a natural commentary in the famous Christological hymn of Philippians in which Paul wrote of Jesus,

Who, being in very nature God,
did not consider equality with God something to be
grasped,
but made himself nothing,
taking the very nature of a servant,
being made in human likeness.
And being found in appearance as a man,
he humbled himself
and became obedient to death —even death on a cross![5]

The common themes are easy to follow: the divesting of the outer garment of glory to take instead a towel of servanthood, in order to do for humanity what they could not do themselves, and without which they would have no part of him; the assumption of the role of a servant; and, finally, the ultimate act of sacrifice, the offering of himself in vicarious death. Both Paul and John charted all these actions in their writing. So, having washed their feet, including those of the reluctant Peter, Jesus asks, "Do you understand what I have done for you?" He then goes on to explain: "You call me 'Teacher' and 'Lord', and rightly so, for that is what I am. Now that I, your Lord and Teacher, have washed your feet, you also should wash one another's feet. I have set you an example that you should do as I have done for you. I tell you the truth, no servant is greater than his master, nor is a messenger greater than the one who sent him. Now that you know these things, you will be blessed if you do them."[6] The meaning is unmistakeable: anyone who follows Jesus will be a servant of others. Service is a prerequisite of leadership and, in order to serve (and lead), we ourselves must go on receiving.

It is hard to overestimate the radical nature of Jesus' model of leadership. What other leader exemplifies his leadership by washing his followers' feet? Military, political and expeditionary leadership would eschew such models of leadership in case they were mistaken for weakness. And yet this servant-leadership came to characterise, in theory at least, all forms of leadership in Christendom: politicians of the Crown in the government of the UK are still called ministers; Christian royalty took to itself such mottos as *Ich dien* (I serve); the more traditional aristocrats, like the Duke of Devonshire, lived by the motto *noblesse oblige*; Victorian industrialists, like Titus Salt of Saltaire or Joseph Cadbury of chocolate fame in south Birmingham, saw that their success bred an undoubted duty to serve their workforce with good housing, healthcare programmes and insurance. Today we can still see the vision that inspired them in the communities they left behind. However far short these people may have fallen from their stated mottos, this was, nevertheless, the accepted style of Christian leadership. It surely emanated from the example of Jesus – who came from the Father, and was returning to the Father – who took up a towel to wash his disciples' feet.

111

Contrastingly, there have been plenty of people who took this motto of service but masqueraded behind it, repressing their subordinates all the while. In the past, and some might say in the present, there have been innumerable prince bishops who have been a bane and not a blessing to the church, countless clergy and ministers who have repressed or terrified their people. Roald Dahl could not understand how Fisher, when headmaster of Repton and before becoming Archbishop of Canterbury, could so easily lay aside the morning paper, having checked his financial holdings, and deal out corporal punishment for minor misdemeanours, assuring the miscreant that it would hurt him more![7] However amusing (and they are), the satirical novels of Trollope in the nineteenth century are a testimony to the power politics of the cathedral close, and many shrewd observers of the church today observe similar tendencies at work. Titles, clothes, seating, buildings and processions are fecund ground for continuing these "pecking order" peccadilloes, which can sometimes grow like Topsy into full scale battles of vested and entrenched interests. What possible justification can there be for them in the light of the New Testament?

Peter learnt that day in the upper room that the only form of leadership Jesus was interested in was a servant leadership, which was at complete odds with the style and manner of leadership in the pagan world of his day. Later in his epistles, as well as in the ordering of the early church, Peter shows that this model of leadership was the one to which he aspired and the one he promoted. We shall leave the model of delegated leadership which Peter establishes in the early church in Acts 6 to the next section of the book, when we consider Peter's role as leader of the church in Jerusalem. For now, we will look at the instructions he gave in his letters to the elders or overseers of the church in present day Turkey, as to how they were to lead their flocks over whom they had been appointed "shepherds".

It is not surprising that Peter's favoured word for elders or leaders of the church is "shepherd". Not only had this been a common description of the leaders of Israel in Old

Testament days,[8] but also it was, by inference, the title that Jesus gave to Peter in his famous interview with him on the shore of the Sea of Galilee after the resurrection, when he said to him "feed my sheep", or "lambs". We will look more closely at that interview in the next chapter, but here it is sufficient to see that the Good Shepherd, the chief pastor of the flock, commissions Peter to be himself an under shepherd, with the task of "feeding" the sheep. In turn, Peter and the other apostles appointed other "under shepherds" to serve the flock of God. In appointing them Peter also gives them instructions about **how** they were to exercise this service.

In a beautifully constructed charge which has a timeless application for all pastors, elders, overseers, bishops, church leaders, clergy, ministers and priests – call them what you will – Peter says they are to, "Be shepherds of God's flock that is under your care, serving as overseers —not because you must, but because you are willing, as God wants you to be; not greedy for money, but eager to serve; not lording it over those entrusted to you, but being examples to the flock."[9] It is worth looking more closely at the threefold nature of this charge.

Firstly they are to, "Be shepherds ...not because you must, but because you are willing." This is a check on motivation. Motivation, in all spheres of leadership or performance, is important. We recently had an Olympic gold medallist speak at a church meeting. Amongst other trainers who had worked with her as she prepared for her event was a sports psychologist. Part of his or her function was to check on motivation as well as self-understanding. We know that part of the battle in performing well is in the mind or spirit. If those are in a good and sound state, athletes are likely to perform to the best of their ability. When it comes to spiritual leadership there is a world of difference between being a pastor/leader because of *wanting* to, rather than *having* to.

In fact, Peter begins his charge to these leaders by calling to mind two events, past and future, which had motivated him in his ministry. They are the **sufferings** of Jesus of which he was a witness, albeit at the lowest point of his life, and

113

the future **glory** of Christ, in which he believes by faith that he and all the church will share. Although the believers' sharing in glory lay in the future, so certain was Peter of it that he takes it into account in his own motivation. The suffering of Jesus for the church, to bring it into existence, and the awaiting glory of the church, in accordance with the promise, seem to be the twin engines of Peter's motivation. The sufferings of Jesus remind Peter of the preciousness of God's people for whom Jesus died, and show him that a sincere pastor should also be willing to suffer for the flock of God. Equally, the glory to be revealed reminds Peter that nothing he does for the flock of God will be in vain, nor will it be unrewarded or unrecognised. So he did not pastor because he "had to," out of fear or compulsion, but because he was glad to do so, in the light of Jesus' sufferings for the church and the glory he would share with it. If this was true of Peter's motivation, that poses a challenge to all church leaders to examine how we are serving: are we doing so reluctantly or willingly?

It is as well for all church leaders to take such a reality check on our attitude to pastoral care. If we have moved from the "wanting to" to the "having to", then it could be for any number of reasons. It could be we have lost spiritual vision for what we are doing, as our ministry is overburdened with administration or strained relationships with one or more members of the flock. It could be that we ourselves have become jaded or disillusioned, or tired, and stand in need of refreshment. It could be that we are inadequately resourced through prayer, intellectual stimulation of our faith or opportunities for reflection about our work and own development as pastors and leaders. Once again, it is through some form of real self-examination, accountability to others and guidance in our development that we can prevent the sclerotic effect of moving from the joyful abandonment of "wanting to" to the deadening effect of "having to". Peter makes it clear that God's desire is for us to be willing, free, joyful servants —who do his bidding, but leave the results to his sovereignty.

Secondly, Peter says we should serve as those who are

"not greedy for money, but eager to serve". The same construction is used: a negative followed by a positive. Ironically, serving as a minister is not a quick way to wealth in the UK, but that in itself does not prevent someone from being greedy for money. One bishop in the Church of England was reported to have commented that, "Although the pay was nothing to write home about, the pension was out of this world!" Certainly the current Church of England stipend of £17,800 is somewhat below the average national wage of £24,000 in the UK, but the relative security of the job and housing perhaps compensates for that. Equally, this sum viewed from other denominations (e.g. the Roman Catholic Church, or from other parts of the world) will seem princely! However, it is basically true that clergy are not in it for the money! And in Asia and Africa this must be even more the case. But elsewhere, especially North America, where the church is wealthy in a way that can only be dreamt of elsewhere, Peter's charge may have more obvious application in some denominations. Nevertheless, whether a minister is rewarded with much or little, he or she can find that greed for money or goods can enter in. If church leaders make ministry dependent on getting money for themselves or for their church, then they are already on a slippery slope. It is one of the glorious things about ministry that our teaching, prayer, counselling and time are free at the point of reception, and it comes with no fiscal strings attached.[10]

Thirdly, Peter tells the elders to serve, "...not lording it over those entrusted to you, but being examples to the flock." This could not be a more important charge. For if a minister may not have access to gaining much money in many parts of the worldwide church, that does not mean that they do not have access to status or exercise power. The three main temptations to humanity are sex, money and power, and church leaders are not immune to the temptations common to all. The desire to wield power over people to boost your own self-importance is a real temptation for church ministers, of which we should be aware. However sophisticated we may appear to become in our concepts of ministry – embracing the buzzwords of being consensual and collaborative in style, being enablers and catalysts in role, and being capable of using computer presentations and the other gadgetry of the modern age – such temptations may poke their hydra-head into any area of church or ministerial life. We can have the appearance of modernity, yet be prone to fall into age-old traps set by the age-old enemy who, as Peter says a verse or two later, "...prowls around like a roaring lion looking for someone to devour..."[11] The quest for status, and lording it over others, has been a particular problem in the lives of some church leaders, past and present.

John Stott in a sobering aside, reminded us that we are to be aware that the flock of God is not ours. Leaders are entrusted with it only for a period. In the parish I now serve in, All Saints Weston, there is a list of Rectors on a board at the back of the church. The list begins in 1297, and I reflect that seven hundred years of continuous ministry has been celebrated during my own ministry at All Saints. It is both sobering and humbling to remember that the relatively few years of my ministry here will have been just a comparative "blink of the eye". So, being entrusted with the flock of God, we are instructed by Peter not to lord it over them but to be an example to the flock.

The distinction between leading by example rather than leading by *dictat* could not be more important. Leadership by example leaves people free to follow or not as they choose. Although this may appear to be deeply risky, this approach allows people to mature by freely deciding to emulate an example which they have seen to be both effective and true to the teaching of the gospel. Leading by example does not remove responsibility from a person but allows them to grow in a responsible and healthy way. By contrast, "lording" it over another's faith removes responsibility, makes another dependent, emasculates their sense of living with dignity before God, and often runs the risk of provoking a crisis of faith in later years. Far better, therefore, to live out the Christian faith before the watching eyes of others in the hope that it may inspire another to deeper discipleship. Surely this was the dynamic behind Jesus' example when he washed the disciples' feet.

116

So we return to where we began, with that account in John chapter 13, of Jesus washing his disciples' feet. Peter had first to receive the washing that Jesus offered to him, and humbly receive. As we have seen, every leader must learn to receive in many ways, but then, while receiving, learn to lead by example, not coercing or threatening or frightening the flock of God, but offering them a holy pattern of life to follow. And for a gloss on "holiness" in this context, I would invite you to read my book entitled *Becoming Fully Human*, in which this crucial theme is explored.[12] As you read Peter's instructions to the pastors and elders of the churches in Asia Minor, you cannot help wondering whether, as he wrote, he was reliving the moment when the Messiah washed his feet and said, "I have set you an example that you should do as I have done for you." That is true leadership!

10

FAILURE AND RESTORATION

To be known for your weakest moment seems a harsh legacy for a man who had such a seminal role in the mission of the early church, yet this is true of Peter as for many others. All too often a man or woman who has contributed significantly in their field or chosen profession is remembered, sadly, not so much for that contribution as for their "fall from grace". This is true for Peter partly because the Bible never air-brushes failure from the picture of its "heroes", and partly because the Scriptures seek to teach us as much from the negative example of its characters as from their exemplary deeds of faith and courage. With Peter, as we shall see, it was not so much a "fall from grace" as a headlong dive **into** it, and only by grace could he, or for that matter anyone, be restored.

On the cover of this book is a picture by Rembrandt of Peter at his moment of denial of Jesus —that is, when the cock crew and Peter remembered the prediction of Jesus that he would deny his Lord three times, even though Peter had vigorously protested that he would not! This episode of Peter's denial and restoration falls naturally into three parts: the prediction of Peter's denial, the denial itself and, finally, his restoration. We shall look at each in turn and see what we can learn from each part about spiritual leadership in general.

PETER'S DENIAL PREDICTED
Matthew 26:30–35; Mark 14:26–31; Luke 22:31–34;
John 13:36–38

It was the political philosopher Alexis de Tocqueville who wrote in his study of the causes of the French Revolution that the greatest danger for an authoritarian regime is when it begins to reform. In modern parlance, that moment could be described as a "tipping point". Contrariwise, the moment of greatest danger to the spiritual leader is when he or she thinks that he is managing well, when he assumes God's blessing, when he takes that blessing for granted, when he feels confident of his own ability, when he starts to coast, or finally when he or she grows accustomed to some besetting sins, accommodating them rather than putting them out for collection, like the refuse they are. All such or similar attitudes are dangerous. The Bible has a simple but telling way of summing that up by saying, "So, if you think you are standing firm, be careful that you don't fall."[1] The reason why any of these attitudes are dangerous is because they are based on two false assumptions: the first is an over-estimation of our own spiritual strength, the second is an under-estimation of the struggle and trials we face. In the case of Peter this was exactly true.

Reversing the order of these misapprehensions, Peter did not yet really understand the magnitude of what he and the other disciples faced in the twenty four hours following the Last Supper. That is, he underestimated the struggle and trial that lay ahead. As we saw earlier at Caesarea Philippi, Peter found all the talk of Jesus being handed over to the Jewish authorities and being tried and killed as defeatist. The great Jewish aspiration of the period, ever since the victory of the Maccabaean Rebellion against the Greeks in 165 BC was the overthrow of the Romans and the end of "exile" which had begun with the ending of the monarchy by the Babylonians in 589 BC. Peter was as much a man of his times as anyone else and although not a Zealot, like another of the disciples his namesake Simon the Zealot, nor a Pharisee who fervently practised Torah as a way of establishing Jewish identity over against the occupying Romans, he did nonetheless expect the Messiah to liberate his people from the pagans who occupied the holy land, the holy places and the city of Jerusalem.

So Peter fully expected a bloody confrontation to come, in which victory would offer him an instant reward in the here and now; and defeat, conversely, would mean the loss of his life. Hence Peter said to Jesus, who predicted his denial, "Even if I have to die with you, I will never disown you. And all the other disciples said the same."[2] These were not idle words. Peter probably expected that he might well die in the coming confrontation, but what he may not have expected, although Jesus had repeatedly warned his disciples of this, was that it would be his own people's rulers, the chief priests, who would arrest Jesus and hand him over to the Romans for execution. What is clear is that the disciples expected a fight and, as the disciples on the road to Emmaus said, "...but we had hoped that he was the one who was going to redeem Israel...."[3]

This hope was so strong that even after the resurrection the disciples asked Jesus, "Lord, are you at this time going to restore the kingdom to Israel?"[4] Reading back into these texts, we tend to spiritualise their expectation, but in fact what they hoped from their Messiah was a temporal and national deliverance. Since this was the clear expectation of Peter in the ensuing days, he was ready to draw swords with his and Jesus' opponents, and indeed he did in Gethsemane. However, what he was not ready for was to be part of a revolution that did not depend on the sword, in which the Messiah was tried and punished by Israel's own rulers —and in which Jesus and his followers offered a passive resistance (which was later to make such a marked appearance in his epistles, which he wrote to the suffering churches in Asia Minor.) So Peter was ready, he thought, for one thing, but found himself facing, in the event, a trial of quite a different kind, as we shall see.

Paradoxically, he underestimated the struggle and trial he would face by overestimating the form in which it would come! He expected a fight against Roman soldiers in which the people rose up with him and the Messiah, but instead he got an interrogation from a number of bystanders, including a servant girl, in the context of the Messiah being tried by his own people. There had been a struggle in Gethsemane in which Jesus had forsworn all armed reaction, and in which Jesus had seemed, in their ignorance of what he had come to do, strangely acquiescent.

Later, Peter would understand why Jesus behaved as he did, and make that behaviour one of his cardinal messages to the persecuted church in Asia, but standing in the high priest's courtyard he was in both vulnerable and unfamiliar territory. Peter had imagined one form of revolution and found he was faced by quite another, in which you were expected to fight from a position of having no weapons and seemingly being defenceless.

If Peter had underestimated the nature of the trial ahead, he had also taken to hand the wrong sort of weapons. He had taken up what was familiar, the sword, and had neglected what was still an unfamiliar form of protection, prayer. This became clear in the garden of Gethsemane.

The agony in Gethsemane chiefly portrays Jesus finally and fully embracing, out of his own free will, the way of the cross as his Father's plan for the salvation of the world. The words "not my will but yours" sum up the struggle that Jesus went through in the hour or so in that familiar place of retreat and prayer. If Jesus in his own human flesh shrank from the physical ordeal to come, his divine vision and understanding knew that, "...it was for this very reason I came to this hour."[5] And if Jesus' own prayerful preparation for the crisis of the cross is the major key of this episode in the garden, the minor key is the failure of the disciples, and especially Peter, to prepare for what lay ahead.

While Jesus prayed, in an agony of anticipation and submission, Peter slept! Jesus asked Peter, "Simon... are you asleep? Could you not keep watch for one hour? Watch and pray so that you will not fall into temptation. The spirit is willing, but the body is weak."[6] Prayer was a weapon which Peter had not yet learnt to use in his own defence in the way that Jesus did for him. Three times Jesus came over to where the disciples were sleeping and addressed them, "Are you still sleeping?"; three times Peter was to deny Jesus, and three times Jesus would ask him, "Do you love me?" Prayer was the means whereby temptation could be resisted and the flesh strengthened, but its use was neglected. It was seemingly only as a result of Jesus praying for Peter that his forthcoming failure did not turn into a disaster.

Earlier, Jesus told Peter, as Luke recorded, "Simon, Simon, Satan has asked to sift you as wheat. But I have prayed for you, Simon, that your faith may not fail. And when you have turned back, strengthen your brothers."[7] Presumably it was this prayer of Jesus that enabled Peter later to come out of his bitter despondency and seek restoration from Jesus, on the shore of the Sea of Galilee. Because of his neglect of prayer, Peter was unprepared for the arrest of Jesus when it came, and in the heat of the moment Peter had resorted to violence.

Although Jesus knew that the time of freedom to proclaim the kingdom of God unopposed was passing, and the spiritual environment was rapidly changing – so that whereas before the disciples could go out on their missionary journeys without bag or sandals or purse, now they should take these and even a sword – his disciples nevertheless were **not** to resort to violence or aggression in their mission.[8] For, as Jesus was to tell Pilate, "...My kingdom is not of this world. If it were, my servants would fight to prevent my arrest by the Jews...."[9] But when the temple guards arrived in Gethsemane led by Judas, the unprepared Peter took hold of his sword and sliced off the high priest's slave's right ear! If the synoptic gospels are reticent in naming which disciple used his sword, John had no such scruples, for he tells us it was Peter. "No more of this!" says Jesus, and he heals the man's ear![10]

Peter's response in the circumstances is a classic of its kind. How often the so-called "spiritual leader" fails because we have not done the simplest thing, which is to pray! As a result, we react "in the flesh"; we resort to human methods of building the kingdom of God; we try to compensate for our lack of true spiritual vision by using "what comes naturally!" But we are called to do the harder thing, which is to do what comes supernaturally! And what comes supernaturally does not normally come naturally; it comes as a result of prayer. Peter's natural reaction was to reach for the sword, to stretch his hand for its hilt rather than stretch his body on the ground as Jesus had done in his Gethsemane prayer. The seeds of Peter's downfall were clear: he believed he was up to the task ahead, but in point of fact he did not know what the task would be. He imagined a glorious moment of revolution, manning the barricades and waving the Jewish flag in the face of pagan opposition, but in reality he found himself in very different circumstances. Thinking that he was up to the task of their own imaginings, he and the other disciples slept in Gethsemane, so when the most critical moment in their following of Jesus came, they were not ready. And whereas Jesus was in perfect control, the disciples were in disarray.

FAILURE
Matthew 26:69–75; Mark 14:66–72; Luke 22:56–62; John 18:15–18 & 25–27

Little phrases in the Gospels are often highly charged, and may be open to allegorical or spiritual interpretation. An allegorical style of biblical interpretation is often best resisted rather than deployed, but there are nonetheless phrases in the Gospels which have wound up within them the potential for both literal and spiritual meaning. One such phrase, repeated by all the synoptic Gospel writers, is that "Peter followed him [Jesus] at a distance."[11] Since the original command of Jesus to the disciples was to "follow" him, this descriptive phrase is patient of both literal and spiritual interpretation. The evangelists are probably only telling us that Peter and the disciples followed warily some way behind the arrested Jesus for fear of similar arrest, but you cannot help thinking that "at a distance" also refers to the growing gap between the clear submission of Jesus to the will of his Father and their own lagging and foggy perception of what was going on. The distance between the utter submission of Jesus to his Father's will and the disciples' growing fear was widening by the moment. They were quite simply unprepared for what was about to happen.

Despite their obvious discomfort, Peter and John, whose family was known to the high priest,[12] bravely entered the courtyard of the high priest's house or official residence; John gaining admittance for Peter by virtue of his acquaintance with the high priest and his household. John is quite explicit in his Gospel that it was through his introduction of Peter to the maid on the gate that he (Peter) was able to gain entry to the courtyard: "Because this disciple [John] was known to the high priest, he went with Jesus into the high priest's courtyard, but Peter had to wait outside at the door. The other disciple, who was known to the high priest, came back, spoke to the girl on duty there and brought Peter in."[13] It was an entrance he came to regret bitterly. For it was there in the courtyard, whilst warming himself at a fire with other bystanders, then again while lurking around the porch to the courtyard to which he later in the night retreated, and finally while watching Jesus being "tried" by the high priest, that Peter, the noticeable Galilean, was challenged. This challenge was made twice by a maid in front of a group of bystanders, and then thirdly by a servant who was a relative of Malchus, whose ear he had cut off in the garden.[14] On each occasion Peter denied that he knew Jesus, doing so with increasing vehemence and emphasis.

But it is Luke who, with devastating drama, records most poignantly this awful sequence of events. Precisely at the moment of Peter's third and most emphatic denial, with the cock's doom laden crow splitting the chill night air, the Lord, who was in the midst of his trial, turned to look at Peter. Peter then suddenly realised what he had done, and that what the Lord had predicted, and he had vehemently denied, had happened. At the dreadful realisation of his failure, Peter left the courtyard to weep bitterly outside.

When Peter walked out of the courtyard, rocked with his

own failure, he surely must have felt that it was the end of whatever beautiful dream he had imagined. The revolution he had hoped for had not materialised; the kingdom he had anticipated was not to be established; and the glory he had sought for himself would not come to pass. But not by any stretch of the imagination could he have expected that in a few weeks he would be preaching to thousands in the centre of the same city, in the power of the Spirit of a Lord who forgives and restores. At the time, Peter's life could not have been a more complete mess!

Only those who have been there can imagine the searing quality of such a failure, and leaders of the church are far from immune. It must have been with considerable hindsight that Peter wrote to the leaders and the young men in the churches in Asia, "...Your enemy the devil prowls around like a roaring lion looking for someone to devour."[15] To a church under the pressure of persecution, the temptation for its leaders is to deny the Lord; to the church in the West, facing the pressure of seduction, it is to compromise our faith by either denying Jesus' uniqueness or by accommodating our lifestyle to the standards of our culture. Both are equally powerful challenges, but of different kinds. Denial may come in different forms, but the temptation is there for us all. The preventative medicine prescribed by Jesus twice in the garden was, "Pray that you will not fall into temptation."[16] The simple lesson is that sleeping rather than praying was the precursor to a fall which, in retrospect, Peter would have done anything to avoid. But, despite his failure, Peter did not abandon faith; his restoration was only days away although at the time, when he walked out of the high priest's courtyard weeping, it must have seemed as though there was to be no return.

Failure comes in many guises. For the spiritual leader they can be tragic. The common "hanging offences" are either sexual or financial. The sexual ones are sexual infidelity, abuse, or inappropriate sexual behaviour. The combination of heightened public awareness, fear of a press story, a history of abuse in certain sections of the church, means that even unsubstantiated but reported allegations can lead to suspension of a minister, which itself can be devastating for that person and his family. The need to protect innocent parties, as well as being fair to the "accused", means finding a way of approaching the situation so that people are not pre-judged before the issues are properly examined. There is also a climate of fear that can surround some of these situations in which fear of "trial by tabloid" can precipitate action that has not always been just. Notorious cases, in which it is alleged that incompetence on the part of officials may have allowed people to be placed in positions which they should never have had, understandably fuel more stringent action by officials who are haunted by the idea that failure to act could lead to the abuse of another.

These types of failure are of a very different order to the one that overcame Peter in the high priest's courtyard, but the method of dealing with the causes of failure are similar. Firstly, there needs to be complete honesty about any besetting weakness. For Peter, it meant facing prayerfully his own fear of others, for there is evidence from his denial in the courtyard as well as his withdrawal of fellowship from the Gentile Christians at Antioch that, in both incidents, his actions were driven by a certain kind of fear. Later, facing the opposition of the Jewish Council in a formal head-to-head recorded in Acts, he could not have been more forthright and brave, but in situations where he was challenged in a more ordinary setting, he found that he drew back from what he really knew to be right.

So it is necessary that, by prayer and honesty with those close to us, we guard our besetting weaknesses. For once we collude with them, or even indulge them, then they may prove to have tragic implications for our ministry. The teaching of Jesus is wholly unambivalent: "If your hand causes you to sin, cut it off....And if your eye causes you to sin, pluck it out." It is harsh, but it avoids the pain of bitter tears.

Of course there are many less well-publicised failures in a spiritual leader, in which there is no general interest in the world. These might be quietly giving up the "race" or ministry, going to seed, apparently keeping up appearances but having no or little spiritual fire, neglecting to do ourselves what we constantly encourage in others, and losing spiritual vision. From these, as well as the more sensational pitfalls, restoration is needed. The question that we must now address is: how did that restoration of Peter come about, and what was involved?

RESTORATION
John 20:1 – 21:25

Although John, at the end of his Gospel, gives us the main account of Peter's restoration after the second miraculous catch of fish in Galilee, there are three vital preliminary stages to it. They are: his own tears; his witness of the resurrection; and his keeping fellowship with the disciples. We shall look at each in turn before turning to Jesus' all-important conversation on the shore of the Sea of Galilee, where Peter's reinstatement took place.

The tears that Peter shed on realising that he had denied Jesus three times were, in a real sense, the first stage of his restoration, for although insufficient of themselves to bring restoration, they were the physical indicator of the state of Peter's heart. They were tears of repentance and sorrow — sorrow at his own failure. By contrast, Judas had been given ample opportunity by Jesus to change his course of action but, despite knowing remarks from Jesus during the Last Supper, which indicated that Jesus knew what Judas intended to do, Judas did not change his course or evidence any repentance. He was set on selling Jesus to the high priest for thirty pieces of silver. Peter, by contrast, though previously too confident of himself, having fallen, immediately showed his repentance by shedding bitter tears outside the high priest's house. It was undoubtedly the most painful moment of Peter's discipleship, but his sorrow and tears were the necessary prerequisite to his restoration. Penitence is not a common word today, but it is an essential part of a Christian vocabulary. In medieval theology it became a "work" which merited forgiveness; so that the church would lay on the penitent sinner "works" to perform, which displayed the sinner's repentance, on condition of which the sinner could be offered forgiveness. These penances could be gifts of money, pilgrimages or spiritual exercises supervised by the church. They became a convenient method whereby the church could exercise control over the minds, hearts and purses of people, thereby increasing its own power and prestige. However, such penitential works, which became a plank in the "salvation" offered in medieval church practice, were a corruption of grace and an abuse of power. For just as salvation in the first place is not earned but is a gift of God's grace, so restoration is not a matter of earning it again, but receiving forgiveness through confession and making restitution where that is possible. Penitence is simply shown by sorrow for what we have done wrong, and a willingness to eschew such actions in the future, and provide restitution if possible. If, as is sometimes the case, a failure is caused by an ingrained weakness or habit, then help from a specialist source is advisable. Peter's tears were the first step in the process of restoration because they indicated that he was penitent.

The second stage in the process of restoration was that he kept fellowship with the other disciples. He did not separate off from them. A sudden failure, which in Peter's case was also semi-public since others witnessed it, particularly John who was there in the courtyard of the high priest, can lead to such remorse or shame that an individual cuts himself off from the very fellowship which will be the environment of his restoration. For Peter, his sense of shame may have been lessened by the fact that all the disciples had fled at the arrest of Jesus and had deserted him; all, that is, except for John, who was close to Jesus at his time of trial and who was later at the foot of the cross with Mary, the mother of Jesus. But Peter stayed in touch with the other disciples. The fellowship of a group of people with whom you can share, and who, although knowing the worst about you, continue to support you, is another prerequisite for restoration.

They are true friends who know the worst about us and who are not so prudish that they put fellowship on probation whilst we begin rehabilitation. Peter was content to go back to the fellowship from whence he came, and there to wait on events. He had not long to wait before news from some emotional women came to their locked upper room —that the stone had been rolled away from the tomb where the body of Jesus had been placed, and that the body could not be found. Immediately, Peter and John ran to the tomb to see whether what they said was true!

The third stage of Peter's restoration occurred at the moment when he looked around the empty tomb. John does not tell us in his Gospel that Peter fully understood the reality of the resurrection straightaway. But John says of himself that, looking around the empty tomb, and seeing the neatly folded grave clothes lying in such a way that the body of Jesus had simply left them, passing through their folds to a new existence, he believed. Peter may have had a slowly dawning consciousness that Jesus was alive, but by the evening of the same day there was no doubt, since Jesus himself appeared in the upper room, eating fish and talking to them. For Peter, the reality of the resurrection of Jesus offered the hope of restoration, which was shortly to come on the shore of the Sea of Galilee.

The conversation between Jesus and Peter on the shore of the Sea of Galilee was the centrepiece of his restoration. Jesus, who had put in place a number of circumstances that echoed both Peter's original call and his denial of Jesus, had obviously planned every detail of this meeting. Just as, at Peter's call, Jesus had arranged a miraculous catch of fish, now a similar set of circumstances were to be reproduced. They had caught nothing during their overnight fishing, just as before they had toiled all night and caught nothing. Once again, Jesus gave an instruction which on the face of it may have seemed unlikely to succeed. But once again their nets were full to breaking. Instantly, Peter remembered, and recognised that the stranger on the shore who had shouted out the instruction was none other than the Lord. In a typical Petrine reaction, which obviously stuck in the mind of John, he got dressed properly to jump into the water![17] On arrival at the beach, with the catch counted, they gathered around a charcoal fire, reminiscent of the fire in the high priest's courtyard where Peter, for the third time, had denied Jesus. So the circumstances of this meeting must have reminded Peter both of his call and his denial of Jesus, even before Jesus drew him to one side for a difficult but necessary conversation.

At the end of breakfast, it seems from v. 20 ("Peter turned and saw that the disciple whom Jesus loved was following them…"), Jesus took Peter to one side and walked with him along the shore. It was during this walk that Jesus raised the subject with Peter which he must have both feared and longed for —feared, because it highlighted his failure; longed for, because without it Peter could never move on. But the conversation, while deeply probing, lacked any recrimination. It gave Peter the opportunity to affirm his love for Jesus. Rather than wanting to hear an explanation of what had gone wrong (Jesus knew what had gone wrong only too well, so he needed no explanation), Jesus wanted to give Peter the opportunity to overlay his denials with three affirmations of love and loyalty.

The formality of the questions, addressing Peter as "Simon son of John", was designed to be a re-commissioning. The response of Jesus to Peter's avowal of love was designed to show him that he now had a task to do: that was to care for the sheep, or lambs, of Christ's flock. The probing and persistent nature of the questions, although painful, was also cathartic, cleansing Peter from his failure and allowing him to move on to the future that had been prepared for him. That future, which Jesus briefly outlined to him, was to be deeply costly, but he was to concern himself with what he had chosen to do, and not concern himself with others, like John. To Peter's enquiry, "Lord, what about him?" Peter is told firmly that he was to discharge the renewed commission of feeding Christ's sheep. This was his calling, for which he would be further equipped.

With this interview on the shore of the Sea of Galilee, the first stage of Peter's discipleship was drawing to a close.

"From Galilee to Galilee", given that Peter was called and reinstated after a miraculous catch in that lake, might not be a bad epithet for this first stage of his life. But in a few weeks Jesus would leave his disciples for good, and this was for their good as well as the good of others. He said to them, "But I tell you the truth: It is for your good that I am going away. Unless I go away, the Counsellor will not come to you; but if I go, I will send him to you."[18] Whereas John would go on to write his Gospel after the fall of Jerusalem in AD 70 and then, after exile on Patmos during a period of persecution, would be the father figure of the church in Ephesus, Peter's destiny would be very different. Eventually a martyr in Rome, having led the early church in Jerusalem, Peter would guide the church in its explosive post-Pentecostal phase in Jerusalem. However, if this first stage of development, which we have followed in these first ten chapters, was essentially about understanding the person and mission of Jesus, the next would chart the explosive growth of the early church through the outpouring of God's Spirit.

Peter enters this period of leadership as a mature leader, both a witness to the resurrection and to the sufferings of Christ, convinced that Jesus was Messiah for the whole world, through whom God's covenant promises to Israel had been faithfully fulfilled. If Peter's faith had been formed through not a few tempestuous moments with Jesus, so had his character. Peter now had a greater measure of self-understanding. As Jim Wallis wisely says, in his book entitled *Faith Works*, "Mature leaders are those who not only rely on their strengths but also learn how to deal consciously with their weaknesses. In some safe and secure place, they bring their brokenness into the light and turn toward inner coherence. Thus they guard themselves against their inward life that could finally result in outward paralysis. Dealing with flaws and weaknesses is important for anyone, but especially for those who have responsibility for others."[19]

So the key lesson of this final episode of Peter's pre-Pentecostal life was the need to recognise and deal with his weaknesses as a leader, and it is the same for all spiritual leaders. Tears of repentance, ongoing fellowship, a new

132

experience of the resurrection, and a restorative conversation with Jesus, are still the recipe for restoration
following some denial of our calling. What we must be sure
of is that restoration may follow failure, as surely as Jesus
rose from the tomb.

Part Two
EXPLOSION

11

PENTECOST
Acts 1 & 2

If the three years which Peter spent with Jesus during his earthly ministry were inevitably ones of formation, the months immediately following Pentecost in Jerusalem were characterised by explosive growth for the infant church. Peter emerged from his painful restitution as the undoubted leader of the early church. Those early months following Pentecost were heady indeed, and there appears to be no comparable "revival" during the ministry of Paul who, by and large, founded small but strategic house churches in cities of major influence throughout the Roman Empire, though not in Rome itself. But the church in Jerusalem had a relatively short time to thrive, until the destruction of the city by a Roman army under Titus in AD 70, following the Jewish rebellion of AD 66. The Roman campaign and the virtual annihilation of the city must have severely hindered the church there. It brought to an end Herod's temple, and even led to the renaming of the city. So the church in Jerusalem faced successive waves of difficulty in quick succession in the thirty or so years following the resurrection of Jesus, including persecution, famine, military devastation, and finally almost complete dispersal. Only further north, in Antioch, was there another strong centre of Christian

135

witness, which had become the missionary church for the Roman world. For a few short years the church in Jerusalem thrived, and arguably there has never again been in Jerusalem – or perhaps anywhere else – a church like it!

St Luke tells us that for forty days after his resurrection Jesus appeared to the disciples and spoke to them about the kingdom of God.[1] Another act in the ministry of Jesus was still to come: the giving of the Spirit. This would fulfil the promise of John the Baptist, who said that he came to baptise with water as a symbol of repentance for the forgiveness of sins, but that the Messiah, whose shoes he was unworthy to untie, would baptise his people with the Holy Spirit and with fire.[2] After the twists and turns, the heights and depths of the past three years, a new age was about to begin: the age of the Spirit. Jesus – who had been born as one of us, lived our human life, died for our sins, was raised from the dead and had ascended into heaven – now sent the Holy Spirit to his people, to make them his body. What Jesus had won for his people would be worked out in them. The giving of the Spirit, like all the great events of the ministry of Jesus, was an irreversible one; it would thrust Peter and the widening group of disciples on a course which changed the world.

PRELIMINARIES TO PENTECOST

The forty days in which Jesus remained with the disciples (albeit in his new resurrection body) continued to be ones in which Jesus sought both to convince them of his resurrection and to instruct them. Both on the road to Emmaus and in the upper room, his appearances overlapped with meals; by eating he could convince them that he was not a ghost![3] The disciples showed that they needed both convincing and instruction in those last vital days with Jesus. For, as Matthew says of the disciples after the resurrection, "When they saw him, they worshipped him; but some doubted."[4] —And they were in need, therefore, of the proofs that Jesus offered them.[5] Equally, they needed further instruction since they were still trying to fit the events of the recent weeks into a framework of Jewish expectation which was common to their generation. These two perspectives of a kingdom: the one secret and mysteriously growing which Jesus had taught them about, and the other a kingdom in which a rampant Jewish nation overthrows her oppressors (which was the common Jewish expectation), simply would not harmonise. One must replace the other in their still forming minds. But there were continuing signs of the disciples' mental struggle of trying to force one into the other. "So when they met together," we are told by Luke, they asked him, "Lord, are you at this time going to restore the kingdom to Israel?"[6] Their old expectation that Jesus would restore Israel to national greatness, that her "exile" would be ended and that the Romans would be ejected from their occupation of the holy land, was re-asserting itself, even after the crucifixion and resurrection. They still had more to learn about the nature of the kingdom building they were to be involved with.

However, their speculation about "times and seasons" was precisely that, a speculation that amounted to a diversion from their new mandate: "But you will receive power when the Holy Spirit comes on you; and you will be my witnesses in Jerusalem, and in all Judea and Samaria, and to the ends of the earth."[7] Apparently, according to Luke, these were the last words of Jesus to Peter and the disciples. Their charge now was to wait in the city until they were clothed with power for this task, the power of the Holy Spirit.

In God's timetable there were ten days left before this would happen. Pentecost means "the fiftieth day", recording the fifty days from the feast of Passover. Forty had been spent with the risen Jesus, so ten remained after his ascension until the feast of Pentecost when the Jews traditionally celebrated the first-fruits of the grain harvest. As Jesus had commanded, the disciples returned to the city to prepare for the coming of the Holy Spirit, which would mark the inauguration of the church. But before that event the disciples gave themselves to united and persistent prayer, and attended to the business of making up the number of apostles following the death of Judas.

Just weeks after his reinstatement by Jesus, which took place at the lakeside, Peter once again resumed his position as leader of the apostles. Having committed them to prayer, Peter literally stood up amongst the 120 disciples and initiated an election process for the position of twelfth apostle. It has sometimes been argued that this election was premature since, it is suggested, Paul was meant to be the missing apostle; but there are no real grounds for saying this. Because of the emphasis in the teaching of Jesus that the twelve were a complete number – parallel to the twelve sons of Jacob – and had also been given the mandate of judging the twelve tribes of Israel (see the answer given to Peter when he asked Jesus what was in it for him),[8] it is understandable that Peter should believe that the twelfth apostle should be found. Moreover, he found (in Psalm 109:8, "May another take his place of leadership") biblical support for this action.

The method of the election was that the 120 should nominate two men, and that there should be an election by lot. The one elected should have, "...been with us the whole time the Lord Jesus went in and out among us, beginning from John's baptism to the time when Jesus was taken up from us. For one of these must become a witness with us of his resurrection."[9] After Matthias and Joseph had been nominated, lots were cast, and Matthias was elected to the vacant position amongst the twelve. Peter had thus shown himself to be the accepted leader amongst the disciples, the exegete of the Davidic psalm which led them to this action, and the one who was prepared to take action when it seemed "necessary".[10] This preliminary done with, the membership of the twelve complete, the whole community waited in one place for the event that would transform them forever.

It was also the last time in the New Testament that the old method of selection by lot was used. In future, leaders would be set apart to the work to which God called them during worship and fasting, when the Holy Spirit spoke to the community about who should be chosen. This was the case in the sending of Paul and Barnabas on the first missionary journey by the church at Antioch.[11]

FIRE FROM HEAVEN

The coming of the Holy Spirit upon the disciples was marked by three phemonena: the sound of a rushing, mighty wind; the sight of tongues of fire; and the hearing of strange languages, which were recognised by the pilgrim crowd from the Near East. The disciples were all together and at prayer. Each of these phenomena, which were evident signs of the presence of the Spirit, was powerfully significant.

The mighty wind takes us back to creation, and reminds us of how God had originally breathed life into man so that he became a living being.[12] Just as God's breath gave man the gift of life originally, so now the breath of God, depicted by the wind, gave life to the church. Without his presence and working, the church cannot truly exist. As a wise Archbishop of York once said on visiting a local church, "How much of your work would continue if God withdrew his Holy Spirit?"[13]

The tongues of fire distributed on the heads of the disciples imaged the passion, purity and power of the Spirit which Jesus had come to bring. And the strange languages – strange at least to the speakers, if not the hearers – were a sign that God's great purpose, that through the preaching of the gospel his wisdom would be made known, had at last been inaugurated.[14] The pilgrims from the then known world heard the disciples speaking in their own language.[15] The function of tongues here was both to break down the barrier of language established at Babel and incorporate the by-standers into the promise of salvation that God the Father was offering, in his Son, to the world. It was not simply that a few over-excited disciples were speaking in unknown heavenly languages, but that a new missionary movement had begun at Pentecost which would incorporate into the kingdom people from every tribe, language and nation. And God had put the world on notice that this was his intention, by giving his disciples languages to convey his message of salvation centred on the actions of his Son to all the people groups present in Jerusalem that day. That list of names in

Acts 2:9ff is not just a difficulty for the public reader, but a vital testimony to the fact that this "good news" is for everyone, of whatever race or tribe. Tongues were not simply praise, but evidence that the gospel was now for the entire world.

These three phenomena of wind, fire and languages were unmistakeable signs that the age of the Spirit had begun. But the phenomena by themselves were not enough; it was necessary for Peter to get up and speak. Peter's address on the day of Pentecost, alongside Paul's address to the Athenians, recorded in Acts 17:22–34, are perhaps the two great speeches in Acts; the former to a Jerusalem based but probably mostly Jewish audience, and the latter to an almost exclusively pagan one. They represent the twin axes of mission in the early church: to the Jew first, and then to the Gentile. Peter's speech encompasses three main themes: the declaration that Pentecost marks the beginning of the age of the Spirit; that it also demonstrates the Lordship of the resurrected Christ; and, finally, that it marks the need now for all men and women to respond to what God himself has done for all people. It was a climactic moment, and the pattern of things to come.

THE AGE OF THE SPIRIT

Peter stood up and "raised his voice". Already the phenomena surrounding the disciples had raised a question in the minds of the bystanders: "What does this mean?" It is a classic question, which Peter hoped would often presage the explanation of the gospel.[16] Too often the church is guilty of rushing in with an explanation of a question that has not even suggested itself to the mind or heart of an observer. Too often the church's life does not beg any question, either because its worship is drab, its life uneventful, its fellowship impaired by divisions or bickering, or its welcome tepid or disinterested. Hence, for any or more of these types of reasons, often the bystanders, or observers of the church today, see nothing exciting or provoking in its life. And often

140

its communication is not "in their own language", because Christians insist on talking in ways that only the initiated can understand!

By contrast, Peter had a great advantage. The crowd was astonished, questions about what was happening abounded, and an explanation was required. It was Peter who had the responsibility to explain; he obviously relished the moment. His speech is delivered with utter confidence, humour – "These men are not drunk, as you suppose. It's only nine in the morning!" – and the inner knowledge that a new era of salvation has just begun. He confidently said that what the bystanders had seen was what Joel had predicted; in effect, what Peter was saying was: this is that! It is difficult to effectively preach if there is no evidence around of the life changing power of God, so that the speaker can say, "this is that!" The combination of word and deed is compelling; the absence of either "word" or "deed" in the proclamation of the gospel makes the task of evangelism infinitely harder. The activity of God in another's life begs a question, which the explanation of the gospel answers. Peter, here, was answering the questions which the outpouring of the Spirit had generated. And to Jewish minds the words of the prophet Joel gave just the explanation which was required.

Joel, along with others of the Old Testament prophets, predicted that God would inaugurate a new covenant in which the gift of the Spirit was central. Marks of this new age of the Spirit were that everyone would receive revelatory gifts, whether visions, dreams or prophecy. As Luther put it, "Prophesying, visions and dreams are all one thing." What is meant by this is that they are all revelatory gifts, but use different media: either dream-form, vision-form, or word-form (prophecy). Not surprisingly, the "senior" revelatory gift is prophecy, which is the conveying of a message from God for the, "strengthening, encouragement and comfort" of God's people.[17]

In Old Testament times, prophets spoke to Israel and those prophecies which were included in Scripture were granted universal and timeless authority by virtue of that inclusion, but in New Testament times, and especially after the closure of the canon of Scripture, prophecy had only local and time-framed authority for a particular body of believers, who are able to weigh its importance by virtue of knowing the character of the prophet and discerning the spirit in which it was given. So in the age of the Spirit it is possible for all God's people, young and old, to hear the voice of God and speak in his name. This age has begun, Peter taught, and although there will be signs of God's judgement, "...everyone who calls on the name of the Lord will be saved."[18] It is therefore an age of opportunity and mission, which began with the resurrection of Jesus and continues to his return.

PETER DECLARES THE LORDSHIP OF CHRIST
Acts 2:22–36

The words with which Peter finished this section of his address could not have been more thunderous or epoch making, "Therefore let all Israel be assured of this: God has made this Jesus, whom you crucified, both Lord and Christ."[19] Such words to us sound familiar, but at the time they could not have been more dynamic. What Peter had privately confessed at Caesarea Philippi (to the question Jesus asked his disciples: "Who do you say I am?"), and what he had seen with his own eyes on the mountain of transfiguration, he now fearlessly proclaimed. The man who would not answer the enquiry of a maid in the high priest's courtyard was seemingly a person of the past; here was Peter remade, but nevertheless, as we shall see, still capable like all of us of moments of weakness.

Peter's proclamation of Jesus as the Christ, the anointed one of God, is based on three facts: his accreditation by God during his ministry; his resurrection; and his fulfilment of the covenant promise first made with Abraham but renewed in David. These are the three main strands of Peter's proclamation of Jesus being the Christ whom Israel rejected by crucifying him, but who, in so doing, only fulfilled the "set purpose and foreknowledge" of God. We shall look at each of these three strands before examining Peter's conclusion.

Firstly, Peter, of all people, was in a position to recall the accrediting of Jesus by the Father through the many miracles he performed. Maybe they swept through Peter's mind even as he spoke: the feeding of the five thousand, the walking on the water, the innumerable healings and exorcisms, the raising of Lazarus and Jairus' daughter from the dead, to name but a few. Taken together they were an extraordinary accreditation. They were also incontrovertible, as many in Jerusalem, listening to Peter that day, would either have witnessed those miracles themselves or have known someone who had. These "miracles, wonders and signs" were the first strand to Peter's case that Jesus was the Christ.

The second strand was the resurrection of Jesus. Peter does not dwell on the redemptive power of Jesus' death here, except to record the fact that it was with the help of wicked men that Jesus was put to death by "nailing him to the cross". But he does emphasise the fact of the resurrection. "It was impossible for death to keep its hold on him", says Peter, and, "God has raised this Jesus to life, and we are all witnesses of the fact."[20] Once again Peter must have been more than mindful of the last fifty days, during many of which he must have spoken with the resurrected Jesus. Both those appearances and conversations must have been extraordinarily vivid in his mind. As a primary witness to the resurrection, he had now an utter certainty that Jesus was the Christ.

The third strand was that the resurrection of Jesus, far from being unpredicted in the scriptures, was prophesied in David's writings. Once again, Peter resorts to David, the prophet/king, as his chief source of the Old Testament prediction that the Messiah would rise from death. If he had been unfolding the significance of the sacrificial death of Jesus alone, there is no doubt he would have resorted to the Servant songs of Isaiah, as he later did in his epistles. But since his main purpose in this address was to proclaim Jesus as the Christ who could not be held by death, then the fact of the resurrection, supported by the witness of Old

Testament scriptures was the best way of proclaiming Jesus as Lord. As Tom Wright writes, "David was the new Abraham, the new Moses, through whom Israel's God would complete what was begun earlier."[21]

So from Psalm 16, in which David prophesies of Christ, "...you will not abandon me to the grave, nor will you let your Holy One see decay", and from David's foreknowledge that "God had promised him on oath that he would place one of his [David's] descendants on his throne",[22] Peter concludes that Jesus fulfilled this prophecy. The resurrection is both the proof of the divinity of Jesus and the fulfilment of God's covenant with Abraham, renewed in David. It is therefore only logical that the one who was raised from the grave should then be exalted to the right hand of God, where "...he has received from the Father the promised Holy Spirit...." It is the exalted Jesus who has poured out what the pilgrims could both "see and hear". The presence of the Holy Spirit amongst the disciples at Pentecost was therefore further proof of the exaltation of Jesus, and a further declaration that he is the Christ.

This section of the address therefore moves to its natural crescendo, "...let all Israel be assured of this: God has made this Jesus, whom you crucified, both Lord and Christ." Peter's preaching moves on to its conclusion in response to the crowd's urgent question, "Brothers, what shall we do?"

THE CLASSIC RESPONSE

No sermon or address is worth its salt unless it draws a response. That is part of the preacher's skill, to so hone the message that arising from it comes something that the audience must believe and do. Sermons without that quality are definitely "sermonettes". They may tickle the mind but they do not move the heart or challenge the will. There is the possibility today that preachers lose this sense of being called with authority to do that. Computer projection may add clarity, but it could equally take away challenge. If the response to preaching is not something to believe or something to do, it may be titillating, interesting or debatable but it will not bring about change. Sermons have not much point to them unless they bring about change. Peter's address that day brought about complete change in the lives of three thousand people. The preliminary question was: what must they **do** in the light of what they had heard? Peter gave them a classic statement of what they must do: "Repent and be baptised, every one of you, in the name of Jesus Christ for the forgiveness of your sins. And you will receive the gift of the Holy Spirit"[23] Later we are told, "Those who accepted his message were baptised, and about three thousand were added to their number that day."

There appears to have been no other day like it in the New Testament —not even during the ministry of Jesus; nor was there anything comparable in the rest of the Acts of the Apostles. Peter's explanation of the outpouring of the Holy Spirit as the fulfilment of Joel's prophecy, and his declaration that Jesus was both Lord and Christ, brought about a torrent of new converts. His summary of what they must do to enter the kingdom of God and acknowledge Jesus as Lord remains a classic statement of what any person must do to inherit eternal life.

The response called for was fourfold; each of these four strands was woven into the other, and they created the healthy start of each individual's discipleship. It was also a corporate response, for the crowd asked, "What shall **we** do?" And they addressed the question to each other, "**Brothers**, what shall we do?" These four strands were repentance; baptism in the name of Jesus; reception of forgiveness of sins; and the gift of the Holy Spirit. Each is a vital part of the response of any individual to the preaching of the gospel, which is essentially that Jesus is both Christ and Lord.

Repentance means the turning away from a self-centred way of life and a willingness to live with Jesus as Lord. Baptism in the name of Jesus Christ is an action of faith or trust in Jesus, which symbolically expresses new life in him and the death of an old way of life. It is also a confirmation to the believer of his forgiveness. The fourth strand of their initiation was the reception of the Spirit promised by Joel, offered by the Father and poured out by the Son, and whose presence was now seen and heard amongst the disciples. These four strands may be divided into two pairs: repentance and being baptised; forgiveness and the offer of the Spirit. The first two we must do; the second two God offers and we receive by faith. But as Peter goes on to teach, both what we do and what God offers is enabled totally by God himself. It is of his grace; and man's response is made possible by God's call. Three thousand were baptised that day, and the new church was formed, which has been a model for all other churches ever since.

The health of this new church in Jerusalem depended upon its healthy spiritual beginning. If one of those elements had been missing, then the development of the church would have been lop-sided. This remains true today. If there is no real and tangible break with the past, through repentance and baptism, then our new life in Christ will not get fully underway, it will be hampered by a desire to simply tack onto an unchanged lifestyle a new found religious belief. Equally, if forgiveness of sins is not properly understood, we may be hampered by feeling that our past failures exclude us from being of any use to God. We may see ourselves as spiritual asylum seekers, hoping for residency rights in the kingdom of heaven, rather than full citizens of the kingdom with a right, through grace, to all the benefits of it. Or again, if we do not know that we have received the promised Holy Spirit and his power to help us become what we were intended to be and to witness through word and action to an unbelieving world, we will remain like a shiny new car with no fuel to run.

In short, if we are defective in one of these four areas we will limp along and never reach the potential of which God has made us capable. Sound beginnings make for sound futures; defective births can be followed by real handicap. Peter, through the preaching inspired by the Holy Spirit, was by God's grace able to bring to birth a church which had all the hallmarks of health, as we shall see in the next few verses. But before we turn to Peter's role as the leader of a large and diverse church, with all the challenges that brought to him, we will watch him as a courageous advocate of the faith in a hostile environment.

The day had begun with a group of disciples waiting for the fulfilment of a promise; it ended with a church over three thousand strong, a community whose presence and witness was to forever change the world. It was a remarkable day. Did Peter think back to the words of Jesus at his call (that he would be catching men and not fish in the future) and, like some early-day sportsman, punch the air in delight? It did show what was possible. Though no other day in New Testament times could have been quite like it, since the Holy Spirit's coming to the church was unique, at other times and seasons there have been many days when the Holy Spirit has moved in great power, whether in Wales a hundred years ago, in the eighteenth century revivals in England or North America, or in the Hebrides, when there were further occasions of the Spirit being poured out. Such moments are both the sovereign work of God and involve the united prayer of the church. Peter was the instrument God used; it must have given him a confidence and certainty, that enabled him to face the ordeal of persecution, which was soon to come upon the church.

12

"WE CANNOT HELP SPEAKING"

Acts 3; 4:1–31; 5:17–42; 12:1–19

Looking over these accounts of Peter's ministry in the early days following Pentecost, there can be little doubt that Peter was "on a roll"! There is a heady mixture of miracle, proclamation, defence of the apostolic message and actions before the Sanhedrin, intense prayer, and persecution, which seemed to ratchet up as the days pass. This sequence of events characterised the ministry of the earliest days of the infant church. And such was the compulsion of the Spirit in their lives that they could not help speaking about what they had seen and heard.[1] So a miracle provided a platform for preaching; the preaching brought conflict with the Jewish authorities; the conflict only strengthened their prayer together; and, all the while, the church grew daily. They were remarkable days. We will look at each of these facets of Peter's ministry in turn.

A SUPERNATURAL DEMONSTRATION

A group of five visited our church to talk about Isaiah chapter 58 and its impact on their church life. They are members of

Hope Community Church, Hotwells, Bristol. They have taken seriously that prophecy,

> ...and if you spend yourselves on behalf of the hungry
>   and satisfy the needs of the oppressed,
>   then your light will rise in the darkness,
>   and your night will become like the noonday.

Their church leader literally started their church in Hotwells with himself and one other, a man almost as marginalized as the one whom Jesus healed through Peter at the gate called Beautiful. Although that miracle at the gate was in itself remarkable, it is also worth noticing that the healing was of a man who could not have been more at the margins of their society. Every day he was lifted to his begging position at the the gate called Beautiful, on the way into the temple, where he did the only work available to him, begging. It seems that he no longer looked up at those from whom he begged, watching only the feet of the pilgrims and worshippers intent on reaching the temple. Then, one day, four feet stopped in front of him! He might have been aware of the eyes of Peter trained upon him. He was told to, "Look at us!" He did; and two sentences later he was healed.

The first sentence did not on the face of it sound very promising, "Silver or gold I do not have, but what I have I give to you." After all, what could Peter have, other than money, which would be of any value to the beggar? But the second sentence opened up undreamt horizons: "In the name of Jesus Christ of Nazareth, walk." Peter then lifted him to his feet and he was healed. He accompanied Peter and John into the temple courts, "...walking and jumping, and praising God." The people were filled "with wonder and amazement at what had happened to him."[2]

A double sign was given in this healing. As with other apostolic signs or miracles, this miracle was both a confirmation of the truth and power of the gospel,[3] and a sign that the excluded and marginalized were a special object of God's favour. Just as in the ministry of Jesus so many of his miracles were done to include those who were excluded, to embrace those who were on the margins, so in this, the first notable miracle in the life of the post-Pentecost church, the recipient of God's special grace was a beggar who had spent his whole life outside the temple, excluded from the place to which his benefactors made their way.

The miracle demonstrated the power of the gospel. It was part of the preaching of the gospel —a healing which announced the presence of the kingdom of God. It showed something very important which Peter would proclaim about the nature of God. Its effect was to gather a crowd where the name of Jesus could be made known. That event is, for us, a powerful reminder that "church" is not a place to which we go but an activity in which we engage. The litmus test of "being church" is the manifestation of the presence of Jesus amongst groups of people. These groups could be anything from a crowd assembled around a cured man, previously disabled, to a group of homeless gathered around a soup run with a few of God's people handing out food to them with words of encouragement and hope. Or it could be a group of health care workers in a local hospital praying for the service of their hospital and the care of employees and patients. The church is where the presence of Jesus is both welcomed and active.

Today we may long for miracles as powerful and remarkable as that performed by Peter on the man begging at the the gate called Beautiful, but whether they occur or not we are called to demonstrate the love of God in the care of those who are consistently marginalized by our society. This may be in ways which are not sensational, but which can nevertheless provide security and hope for them. In fact this could be as great a miracle to the watching world, increasingly bent on its own agenda, as the one performed by Peter on the beggar. So, whether it is through a remarkable miracle or through the service of the church for the community, we are to provoke a response, through God's grace, in which there is willingness to listen, and to consider the motivation for the action that has been witnessed. In other words, as we shall later see from Peter's letter, we as Christians should provoke questions in the minds and hearts of outsiders —

151

which we are then ready to answer. In this way we will be a "provocative" church.[4]

A NATURAL EXPLANATION

It was the same dynamic as at Pentecost. The question following the healing of the beggar was implicitly, "What is going on here?" It is **the** question which should ideally precede evangelism. But more often than not our evangelism is not answering a question anyone is asking; or at least the questions are more negative, like, "Why aren't you more united as churches?" or, "Show me what practical difference your church has made to the local community", or, "What quality of life are you exhibiting as a church?" Peter was in the happy position of having a healed beggar hanging onto him while people literally ran to him for an explanation of what had happened! He began his address with a powerful disclaimer: "Men of Israel.... why do you stare at us as if by our own power or godliness we had made this man walk?" In a matter of a few sentences he was telling the onlookers that it was through the name of Jesus Christ that the man had been healed. The incontrovertible evidence of the healed beggar lent both credence and force to his message. His message was an explanation of what had happened. It had happened to someone whom they could now see, and whom they all knew.

So here is a classic piece of evangelism: an event followed by an explanation, rather than an explanation without any event. It was an event which called together a crowd who were waiting for an explanation. In recent years there are many examples of churches engaging with their communities, not necessarily with the blessing of such a remarkable miracle, but with a commitment to pray and work for a gradual transformation of their community. When churches do this, they then speak to a community intrigued by their action.

A number of years ago in Bath, a woman from a local church came across a number of homeless people with next to nothing to eat. She went home to make sandwiches for them; then her church did the same, and finally almost all the churches in the city got together to help out. Now there are around 400 volunteers making sandwiches, running a furniture project, staffing a Sunday Centre and operating a midweek café for anyone wanting a cheap lunch and a chance to talk and be listened to. Many churches have their stories of similar Christian faith works or events which beg for an explanation! However, it is curious to me that churches which are content to work together to offer a "loaf of bread" to the hungry are not equally happy to work together in offering "the bread of life", because another church's ingredients or description of "the bread of life" are not quite *kosher*!

Peter was quite clear that the event or miracle was not due to his own power, but had everything to do with the Lord whom he served. He went on to explain that the God of their fathers had given the highest honour to the Jesus whom they had killed, whom God had raised from the dead. Jesus was the prophet of whom Moses said, "You must listen to him.... The LORD said to me... 'If anyone does not listen to my words that the prophet speaks in my name, I myself will call him to account."[5] Jesus had fulfilled the covenant with Abraham, so that sin could be dealt with and a new humanity brought into existence. They were invited to repent and experience times of refreshing from God. But, as always, there were some who were intent on spoiling the party.

Just as Paul, in his great epistle to the Romans, showed how Jesus was the fulfilment of the covenant made with Abraham, which would reverse the effects of Adam's sin, creating a new humanity to inherit the world, so Peter preaches the same message to the crowd gathered in the temple, that in Jesus God has fulfilled his covenant. The confirmation of this fulfilment was the resurrection. The resurrection was the means of bringing blessing to his people by the means of, "...turning each of you from your wicked ways."[6] But even while he was speaking, opponents were at hand!

MAKING A DEFENCE

On two occasions Peter appeared before the Sanhedrin, firstly in Acts chapter four, following his arrest in the temple while preaching to the crowd and following an overnight stay in prison. He appeared with John before the high priest Annas, Caiaphas, and other members of the high priestly family. Peter and John were anything but cowed by this appearance before the Jewish council. The Sanhedrin noticed their courage and were astonished at their confident and well constructed defence. Moreover, they had the incontrovertible evidence of the healed beggar standing by them when they were speaking. The council's judgement was essentially one of expediency. Since they had closed off the possibility of Jesus being the Messiah through whom this miracle had been performed, they could not expect to win the argument but could only hush up the repercussions by trying to frighten the apostles. But this failed as well. Their attempt to silence Peter and John was challenged by Peter's rhetorical gauntlet, in which he famously stated, "Judge for yourselves whether it is right in God's sight to obey you rather than God. For we cannot help speaking about what we have seen and heard."[7]

Prevented from further punishing them because of their obvious popularity, the Sanhedrin released them. After prayer, they were soon preaching and healing again in the temple, where the new community of believers met in Solomon's Colonnade. But the attention they were receiving aroused the jealousy of the religious authorities. And the stir they were causing precipitated a further arrest, followed by an angelic liberation from gaol and a second appearance before the Sanhedrin.[8]

Once again the high priest himself examined them, "We gave you strict orders not to teach in this name...."[9] Peter's defence is the same and there is complete consistency in his message. He asserts that the God of their fathers raised Jesus from death. He proclaims that the exalted Jesus now offers "repentance and forgiveness of sins to Israel". He affirms that the Spirit who has been poured out is a witness to these things. He began and ended his message with a call to obedience to the God who raises the dead, sends the Spirit and calls for obedience.

The reaction of the council was fury! But Gamaliel assuaged their anger. Gamaliel's speech has been described as either gross expediency or emollient wisdom. There is no doubt that he was one of the leading rabbinic figures of his day. He was a Pharisee. His grandfather was rabbi Hillel, the leading "liberal" rabbi of his day. But in case we read back notions of modern theological liberalism into his teaching, we do well to recall that Paul (or Saul, as he was then) was one of his pupils.[10] And Paul said of himself that he was just as zealous for God as any of his contemporaries. No, Hillel was only more liberal than Shammai. Hillel's grandson Gamaliel was the rabbinic elder statesman of his day. His advice was in fact both patently practical and open to validation, as he suggested. This process of validation was that if a movement succeeded over time (unlike those led by Theudas and Judas the Galilean, which Gamaliel cited in his speech), then it was from God, but if it failed then God was not in it.

Of course, we would need to qualify that pragmatic doctrine. It is not necessarily borne out through history, since false beliefs and paganism have persisted through many centuries. Nevertheless, there may be more than a grain of truth in Gamaliel's dictum, "For if their purpose or activity is of human origin, it will fail. But if it is from God, you will not be able to stop these men; you will only find yourselves fighting against God."[11] Even to have opened the minds of the council – so jealous and prejudiced against Christians – was an indication of Gamaliel's status and persuasive skill.

Peter and John were flogged, but despite their words and lacerations, they counted it a privilege to suffer "disgrace for the Name". They returned to the temple courts "day after day", to teach and proclaim "...the good news that Jesus is the Christ."[12]

By the end of Acts chapter five, Peter had given four major addresses, and one supposes that there were others besides.

There is an emerging pattern to his preaching and defence of the gospel. This pattern is based around the fulfilment of covenant promise made to Abraham. Jesus, Peter preaches, is the fulfilment of what Abraham, Moses and David had been promised. God vindicated his servant Jesus through resurrection and exaltation, and now offers, through faith in his Son, the opportunity for repentance, forgiveness and reception of the Holy Spirit. The necessary response is one of faith and obedience, so that refreshment and blessing may come. But what is remarkable about these addresses, both to the crowds and to the council, is the manner in which they are spoken. What was remarked upon was the boldness and fearlessness with which they were given; a far cry from the cringing of Peter in the high priest's courtyard on the night of the arrest of Jesus in Gethsemane. The reason for this boldness may be sought in various quarters: the time spent with the apostles by Jesus after his resurrection and before his ascension; the gift of the Holy Spirit at Pentecost; and, not least, the saturating prayer which accompanied the life of the early church.

PRAYER

The life of the early church was grounded in prayer. Before the Holy Spirit came at Pentecost, the apostles and others gave themselves to prayer for ten days. When the Spirit came, they were "all together in one place". After their first appearance at the council, Peter and John returned "to their own people", and they prayed together. The result was that they were all once more "filled with the Holy Spirit and spoke the word of God boldly."[13] Indeed, every step forward in the life of the early church was marked by believing prayer, both in relation to their evangelism and in the ordering of their life together. As Michael Marshall has aptly observed, it was prayer which must have raised the spiritual temperature of their life together to apostolic boiling point!

The only glimpse that we are given of the intercession of the early church community is to be found in Acts 4:23–31. It is initiated by the report of Peter and John following their first appearance before the council. Naturally it was a dramatic moment. Their release was followed by a report which itself spilled into prayer. They drew comfort from the fact that rulers had often historically conspired against God's work, whether in the days of King David or, more recently, in the days of Herod, Pilate and their own high priest, who together had conspired against Jesus. But their prayer was anything but shrinking; they asked that they would speak with boldness, and that God would confirm their word with "miraculous signs and wonders".[14] It was not a prayer that they would be spared, but one that would lead to greater courage in the making known of Jesus. The answer to their prayer was indeed that they were filled with the Spirit and spoke the word of God **boldly**.

Boldness was therefore a hallmark of Peter's testimony and it appears to be a hallmark of the church wherever it is true to its credentials. It is a boldness which can easily slip away, especially in a society which prizes maintaining a homogenous uniformity of religious experience. In a culture which continually wants to standardise all forms of religious experience as being valid, and in which to preach Jesus as unique, divine and demanding is not "politically correct", and rocks the religious status quo, the church and all its ministers have special need for boldness. The only way it comes is through prayer linked to the conviction of the Holy Spirit — and the possible response from a culture bent on levelling faiths is persecution of various kinds.

PERSECUTION

Persecution of the church comes and goes. Like many others of my generation I was brought up on books such as *God's Smuggler*, the exciting accounts of Brother Andrew's smuggling of carloads of Bibles across the iron curtain. I knew the look of that iron curtain, having spent some years in Berlin during the height of the cold war, and having often seen the East German border guards patrolling with Alsatians.

The communist authorities had persecuted Christians for decades, and occasionally I met one who had suffered. On one such occasion I met Pastor Josif Ton, who came to the college where I was studying. He was a Romanian pastor who had been imprisoned for his faith, but who exuded a remarkable gentleness and strength in a way I had not come across before. Some eighteen years later, the "curtain" came down, the dictatorships of Eastern Europe fell, and the church was free to worship and act in lands where faith had been proscribed in the pursuit of secular atheism and an all powerful state. The locus of state persecution changed. At the time of writing there are regions of the world where non-registered churches have been harassed, and in some Islamic countries Christian activity, including evangelism, may be prohibited.

But persecution was part of the fare of early Christianity, as we have already seen. Peter soon experienced active persecution from the authorities of the Jewish community. Twice he was imprisoned by the Sanhedrin in the early chapters of Acts, and then, on a third occasion, he was arrested by Herod, following the execution of James the brother of John. The execution of James,[15] which we are told pleased the Jews (presumably meaning the leaders of the council and the hierarchy), must have been another watershed in the life of the early church, on a scale with the stoning of Stephen. James was one of the most senior figures of the church, being one of the inner circle of three whom Jesus had especially groomed for leadership. It is easy to imagine the effect this must have had on Peter, who lost his childhood fishing companion, one of his closest friends, and fellow disciple, who had been with him from the very beginning.

Peter, who had been arrested shortly after the execution of James, was imprisoned by Herod and was guarded around the clock by four squads of soldiers. He was chained and awaiting trial. Herod had planned a show trial after the feast of Passover, which would demonstrate his power to the Jewish people. But, as we know, the show trial never happened. The night before the trial, while the church was praying earnestly, an angel released Peter from gaol.[16] They walked out of the prison in what Peter initially thought was a wishful dream. Eventually, when outside the prison and after the angel had left him, Peter realised that "...the Lord sent his angel and rescued me from Herod's clutches and from everything the Jewish people were anticipating."[17] Having arrived on the doorstep of John Mark's house, where some of the church were praying, and having been left waiting there by an incredulous and overexcited maid, Rhoda, and having also been thought by the Christians who were praying for his release to be an angel, Peter was eventually admitted to the house! It was a deliverance from persecution which both heartened the church at a time when her leaders were deliberately being targeted and also marked a new turn in the development of the church, as Paul's mission to the Gentile world gets fully underway. Peter now disappears from the story with the words, "...he left for another place." Although this has been fancifully interpreted by the apocryphal "Letters of Peter" as referring to Rome, it simply means that he went to a place of hiding in the city.

With the sudden death of Herod, the intense persecution of the church in Jerusalem seems to have abated. As we shall see, Peter was able to stay in Jerusalem for a while, and adjudicated in the Council of Jerusalem in Acts chapter fifteen. At some point he went to Antioch and finally, as tradition has it, to Rome, where he was martyred. Persecution was to play a searing part in Peter's discipleship, and it informed a substantial part of his teaching to the Christian communities in the region north of Syria towards the Black Sea.[18] It is a sobering thought that a church which was so evidently birthed with such excitement at Pentecost, and which enjoyed such remarkable life together in its early days, should have been the focus of such persecution. But coexisting, as it had to, with the centres of Jewish religion – the temple, the priesthood, the council and the teaching of the Pharisees and Sadducees – its life would never be easy. There would be little possibility of a "live and let live" policy emanating from the Jewish authorities, especially since the cardinal tenet of Christian faith is that Jesus is the Messiah. So the church's more than uneasy relationship both with the leadership of the community and with the Jewish faith itself, from which Christianity had sprung, would have continued overtly in Jerusalem until the destruction of the temple and the city by the Roman army under Titus in AD 70.

But to this day, both in Jerusalem and around the world, Jew, Christian and Moslem live in varying degrees of animosity. Although each trace back their roots to their common ancestor Abraham, the action and interaction of these three faiths accounts for a significant portion of the persecution the world has seen: Jew of Christian, Christian of Jew, Christian of Moslem and Moslem of Christian. Although each faith may want to say that it was not a true Christian, Jew or Moslem that undertook such persecution, and that it was conducted by power hungry or vengeful men masquerading as people of faith, all too often it was combination of powerful leaders and naïve or misled "true believers" that conspired to persecute another faith. One recalls the support that Bernard of Clairvaux and many others gave to the crusades.

In recent years in the Western church, there has been much talk of revival, which was especially hyped around the millennium. In certain circles it was preached and predicted as just around the corner. But the lesson of these accounts is that revival was accompanied by persecution. Reading the accounts of the early church, we see that it is much more likely that the church, when most true to itself, will encounter persecution. It seems to be becoming more likely, now that the church is faced by a society in the West which is becoming ever more divergent from Christian faith. Such a secular society will give the church the opportunity either to conform or to remain painfully distinct. If it does the latter then it can only expect to be the object, firstly, of gentle ridicule and then of more obvious persecution. It is therefore much more likely that revival, if it comes, will be in a church which is clearly distinct from its surrounding society, and so facing the real possibility of persecution. If this is the case, then both the experience of Peter and his teaching to the persecuted church of Asia Minor, will become intensely relevant. Both Peter and Paul lived lives which were marked by continual danger of persecution, either from Jewish people or from the Roman civic authorities. Perhaps, rather than simply talking of revival today, we should arm ourselves with the thought that a distinct church courts the possibility of persecution in which revival might take place. Perhaps persecution will precede revival, rather than the other way round. As we shall see, the early church could not have been more distinct from its surroundings, and the consequences were both glorious and painful.

13

THE NEW MODEL CHURCH
Acts 2:42–47; 4:32–37; 5:1–11; 6:1–7

There are few more pressing questions for the church today than how it is to **be** church. "Being church" is one of the buzz phrases of the moment but, as with all buzz words or fashionable ideas, they contain both vital issues to face and hidden dangers to beware of. The issue for the church, particularly in Western Europe, as distinct from North America, where there is a different cultural and intellectual context, is how are we to be church in a society which despite its protestations of belief in God finds attendance at "church" or commitment to the institution of church either un-necessary or distinctly alien. Although the last census in the UK in 2001 produced a figure of 72% of respondents saying that they believe in God, a later poll for a BBC2 programme called "What the world thinks of God", broadcast on 26th February 2004, put belief in God in the UK at 46% —compared with 98% in Nigeria. The poll was from a sample of 10,000 people in each of the countries surveyed. However, in the UK only 8% of the population regularly attend any church, so the gap between those who "believe" and those who attend is huge. This gap between church and secular society has grown since the mid 60s, when the roots of liberal individualism found fertile soil. That is not to say that the roots do not go further back, to the age of the Enlightenment, but that they received substantial doses of fertiliser in the 1960s. In Western Europe, where the church has existed for around eighteen hundred years in one form or another, we live in what has been described as a post-Christendom world. But in fact the situation is more complicated.

To use an analogy or allegory, we live in a world in which the legacy of Christendom remains, but now within its partial ruins many new "buildings" of spirituality, thought, religious practice, paganism and secularism have sprung up. The old ruins of Christendom are visible throughout this cityscape, and in some places they have been assimilated with these modern buildings. In other places these ruins have been distinctively refurbished, creating a vital mixture of ancient and contemporary. Elsewhere, in this picture, just a few of the old stones have been incorporated in entirely new buildings which bear little surface resemblance to ancient Christendom but which are greenhouses of modern Christianity. It is not surprising, therefore, that the builders of contemporary Christian communities should look back to the original and primitive church, which Peter led, to discover patterns of church life to inspire today.

Discovering how to "be church today" involves a form of ecclesial sieving, in which all forms of church are shaken so that those cultural bits which are not appropriate today, or in the situation that a particular church finds itself in, fall through the sieve, and only those essential parts of church remain. It is with these pieces that a new way of being church is put together —experimentally, flexibly and accessibly. It is in just such a process of creating church life that pioneers find themselves looking back to these passages in Acts for both guidance and inspiration.

But I said that in the search of "new ways of being church" there are dangers of which we need to beware. The danger, simply put, is to think that by getting the "form" right we will produce healthy churches which are both attractive and distinct. Of course, this will not necessarily be the case. The irreducible minimum of all church life is healthy relationship with God and one another. This will depend upon teaching, pastoral care, prayerfulness, exemplary leadership, and Spirit-directed activity. If one or more are lacking then, however "accessible" the church may be to modern culture, the church will not become what it should be. Conversely, if these qualities are present, whatever the form, there will probably be a healthy and growing church. Perhaps this explains why smaller, traditional but well-led churches are providing most of the church growth presently. Whatever the form of church adopted – whether, in the jargon, it is "cell", "network", "café" or "congregational"[1] – unless the leadership is founded on the New Testament principles that we see trailed by Peter in the early chapters of Acts, then the form of church, however accessible to modern culture, will not lead to a genuine Christian community. The goal remains for church both to be distinct and attractive, its life revolving around these two poles, which form the axis of its existence, as in its earliest days.

THE EARLIEST CHURCH

The church which was formed at Pentecost and led by Peter was indeed a new model church. Although the family of God's people was first formed when God made the covenant with Abraham,[2] at Pentecost the remnant of God's people became the body of Christ, filled with the Holy Spirit.

The church which was formed at Pentecost was remarkable in a number of ways. It was devoted to a fourfold pattern of teaching, fellowship, sacrament and prayer. These were the four legs of their existence together, the essential spiritual disciplines of their common life. Their devotion to the apostles' teaching showed that their Spirit-filled church was not characterised by anti-intellectualism. The employment of their minds was to help a better conduct of their Christian living. It was not an academic pursuit of knowledge, but rather a practical grasp of the faith which involved their minds as well as their hearts. Alongside this devotion to the apostles' teaching was a devotion to worship expressed in prayer and the breaking of bread. The breaking of bread would continually remind the community that it had been formed through the action of Jesus in dying for them on the cross, while "the prayers" provided the way of expressing their desires, as well as hearing the will of their Lord. The final part of the spiritual quadrilateral was their devotion to fellowship, or *koinonia* —literally meaning what is commonly shared. This fellowship refers to what we share **in** together, as well as what we share **out** together. What the church shares in together is the life of the godhead. What the church shares out together are the resources – spiritual, financial, material and relational – with a needy world around.

This quadrilateral still makes up the foundation of church life; and local church leadership will in part be about providing this ongoing spiritual quadrilateral in the life of the church. The apostles' teaching or, in our terms, the New Testament, will need to be comprehensively taught —not in a dry, academic way, but in such a way as to create an expectation that God will act where he wills, sometimes in "signs and wonders". This intervening grace of God transforms biblical teaching from simply being a record of what once happened a long time ago to an expectation that he will work again in our own day. The church leader will need to teach in such a way as to keep that expectation real. There are few surer ways of doing this than allowing response to the word of God in services of worship. This response has recently been characterised as "prayer ministry", which means the opportunity for a person to respond to the word of God and be prayed for in the context of what they have heard. Alongside this teaching, and various types of prayers, will be times of breaking bread together, in both formal and informal settings. The breaking of bread provides a moment of recall in which the church will remember the origins of its existence through the death and resurrection of Jesus. It provides, repeatedly, the opportunity for the church, and visitors who are present, to hear again the narrative of the events which brought it into existence. Such teaching, prayers and remembrance will constitute a sharing in God's life which in turn should lead to a sharing out of their resources —the *koinonia* of their existence. In fact, in the early church it was their ability to share with those outside their fellowship which appears to have been the most remarkable outcome of their life together.

On two occasions in the early chapters of Acts we are told of their extraordinary generosity on the basis of their pooled resources. "All the believers were together and had everything in common. Selling their possessions and goods, they gave to anyone as he had need."[3] Again, later in Acts, we read, "All the believers were one in heart and mind. No-one claimed that any of his possessions was his own, but they shared everything they had. With great power the apostles continued to testify to the resurrection of the Lord Jesus, and much grace was upon them all. There were no needy persons among them. For from time to time those who owned lands or houses sold them, brought the money from the sales and put it at the apostles' feet, and it was distributed to anyone as he had need."[4] These verses show that at the root of their common life together was this voluntary sacrifice of private belongings for the sake of the whole community. It was, as we shall see from the story of Ananias and Sapphira, a voluntary offering made out of faith and love, but it enabled an extremely dynamic and provocative church life.

Throughout church history there have been movements of renunciation and embraced poverty, in which private possessions were sacrificed, and there continue to be such movements in the church today. The monastic and ascetic tradition, present in the Desert Fathers, in turn gave rise to the monastic communities of the early Middle Ages. The community missionary churches during the period of the Reformation (the Moravians, Huttites and Mennonites) were further examples of churches embracing a fellowship of goods and services, which underlay their mission. Mennonite churches which still exist strongly today in North and South America, with their traditions of pacifism, spiritual discipline and counter culture lifestyle (e.g. no cars, television, radio or internet) continue to exhibit similar traits of renunciation and common ownership. In the United Kingdom, the Jesus Army, with its present emphasis of ministry to refugees and asylum seekers, are able to sustain this ministry through common ownership of property and a sharing of resources. Equally, the programmes of short term mission training conducted by *Youth With A Mission*, albeit for only a few months at a time, are experiences of shared resources in the context of community and training. What is clear is that across the whole church, whether Roman Catholic, Protestant, Orthodox or Pentecostal, there have been and are examples of shared resources made through voluntary sacrifice for the purpose of mission, which often means relieving the material needs of others. What is important to stress is that, in keeping with the grace of God, the embracing of such renunciation must be voluntary, and there must be ways of both joining and leaving without pressure.

It is clear from the description of the life of the early church in Acts chapter two that there was a balance to their church life in one particular respect. We are told that, "Every day they continued to meet together in the temple courts. They broke bread in their homes and ate together with glad and sincere hearts...."[5] So there life together was both public and private, formal and informal, accessible as well as intimate. There was this balance about their existence as a community. They retained their link with Jewish worship at the temple. Presumably a crowd of them was in the colonnades around the temple each day, where they would talk about what was going on —the healings; the teaching of the apostles; perhaps who had sold their property and lain the money at the apostles' feet; the persecution of their leaders by the council; and the conversion of members of the Jewish community. There must have been plenty of godly gossip! But such public exposure in the temple precincts was balanced by the more intimate gatherings in homes, for prayer, food and conversation. The church was in the "market place" as well as in the less public "meeting place". As is emphasised today, worship in the meeting place prepares us for witness in the market place. Its life always needs to be balanced between the intimacy of our own buildings, whether homes, halls or church buildings, and places of public gathering where the church can be identified too. In our own city, one of the most encouraging recent developments has been the running of a lunchtime *Alpha* course in a prominent business in our area. It is held in a non-church environment, a place which is accessible to the public.

There was no question of the early church "planning some evangelism"; it *was* evangelistic! One cannot imagine Peter and the other apostles saying to themselves, "Well, it's time we planned some evangelistic outreach; what about a series of six talks in the temple colonnade, to which we will invite the leading men of the city!" They had not yet got to the point, which we have long since reached, of planning evangelism. Wherever they were, they *were* evangelistic! It was the very nature of their life together as a community. As with so much else, we have compartmentalised our Christian living, but I imagine that, for them, *everything* was evangelistic, whether it was giving away a loaf of bread to a poor person, praying in the street for someone in need, or taking someone along to hear the apostolic teaching. Whereas we are hard pressed to provoke few (or any) questions about our life, I do not suppose there was time to answer all the questions which the Jerusalem people had for the apostles about what was going on, such was the nature of the life of the earliest church. But they were not without their problems too, and it is as well to remember this or we shall have a spiritually romanticised view of the early church and fail to read the lines, let alone between them!

EXEMPLARY DISCIPLINE

You might recall "exemplary discipline" from far off school days. An offender is punished severely in order to deter others from doing the same sort of thing. On a more serious, larger scale, the principle of deterrence is built into most legal codes. The offence committed by Ananias and Sapphira in the days of the early church was one which attracted exemplary discipline.

As we have seen, in the life of the early church there was extraordinary sacrifice and generosity. Many lived in community with others, not owning anything privately but pooling their resources. Others sold their property and brought the proceeds to the apostles, putting the money at their feet, as we are told Barnabas did.[6] There was no compulsion on any to do this; it was a free act of response to the grace of God. In this context, where so many were genuinely sacrificing their assets, one couple sought to give the impression of generosity whilst holding on to some of the money which they were purporting to give away. Their action was one of hypocrisy, and it was treated with exemplary discipline.

If we look a little below the surface of their failing, Ananias and Sapphira wanted to give the appearance of generous faith when in fact they did not have the faith to do what they had pretended to do. Generosity proceeds from faith —that is, actual trust in God. To give away property comes from a faith which both understands that everything we have comes from God – and so we are returning a gift to him – and from a confidence that if we give it away, then God will indeed provide. Whereas Barnabas and others had that kind of faith, Ananias and Sapphira did not. They could not give away all the proceeds because their faith was not so great, so they made (or conspired) to look as though they had given away all the money from the sale. As Peter pointed out later, they need not have done that; the money was theirs. They need only have said that they were giving away some of the money from the sale of land, and that would have been quite acceptable. No one need do more than they have faith for, otherwise our words or actions will simply become strained and insincere.[7] But they wanted the estimation which they thought came with such a public act of sacrifice, without having to exercise trust as a consequence of it because they reserved some of the sale value for themselves. This was hypocrisy and an attempt to deceive both the Holy Spirit and the apostles. As we know, they were both given exemplary punishment.

It has been said that Ananias and Sapphira did in the New Testament what Achan did in the Old Testament. Achan, you will remember, kept for himself some of the treasure which had been captured from Jericho and had been previously devoted to God, hiding it in his tent.[8] He was found out and executed. This punishment, which came near the beginning of the campaign to take the holy land after the Exodus, was exemplary. Indeed, the Greek word for stealing or mis-appropriating is used both to describe Achan's sin and Ananias's "keeping back" part of the proceeds from the sale of land. So there appears to be both a linguistic and a judicial link between these two incidents which occurred when God's people were about to embark on a new stage of their "journey".

If the severity of the judgement was exemplary, it was to show that freedom from hypocrisy was an essential part of the church's mission. If such hypocrisy had entered the church so early on, then its witness would soon have become impaired. Ever since, financial, sexual and "power" irregularities have proved to be the bane of the church's life. If the devil cannot destroy the church by persecution from the outside, he will almost certainly try and destroy internally by one or more of this deadly triumvirate. The means whereby the church can be protected in its life and mission from such an implosion is by the imposition of discipline.

In an age in which standards of behaviour have changed remarkably, the imposition of church discipline is fraught with difficulty. But the church leader cannot shirk his or her responsibility to exercise it, albeit with great caution, and with the intent of bringing reconciliation. If there are cases of notorious immorality in the church when, say, a married partner has "gone off" with another, it may well be right to exercise discipline against the offending pair by barring them from communion or fellowship until such time as they repent. But the church leader will be aware that, if such action is reported to the press, then the "paparazzi" could be encamped around your house for a week until "the story subsides". But Jesus gives clear guidance about church discipline, and I have had cause to follow it on several occasions.

In Matthew 18:15–20, Jesus lays down a method of proceeding which should provide guidance for us in many instances. If a private offence has been caused, then try and resolve the matter privately by going to "show him his fault" on your own. If that does not work, then, "take one or two others along", and if that does not work, tell the whole church, and if that brings no change then treat the person as, "...you would a pagan or a tax collector." Undergirding this process is a spiritual and discerning action of "binding and loosing", which refers to the power of either including or excluding from fellowship. To "bind" is to exclude from fellowship, and to "loose" is to forgive and include; equally, in relation to moral discernment, to bind is to forbid or to enjoin, whereas to "loose" is to permit or allow. In Jesus' day, this procedure of "binding" or "loosing" was common. This is how rabbis decided cases and gave ethical guidance in difficult cases, applying the law by means of "binding" or "loosing", depending how they saw the law applying to each situation.

So Christian leaders, in the context of their own communities, have the authority to bind or loose; that is, to prohibit or permit, forgive or exclude. It is a most important and grave responsibility, which is best exercised in humility and consciousness of weakness, and it should be motivated by a desire to maintain the integrity of the church's mission and guard the holiness of the church's life. Nor is it surprising, therefore, that Jesus, in choosing Peter as leader of the early church, included immediately within that commission the authority to bind and loose —"I will give you the keys of the kingdom of heaven; whatever you bind on earth will be bound in heaven, and whatever you loose on earth will be loosed in heaven."[9] The plain meaning of this statement is that what Peter pronounces on earth will be confirmed in heaven; in other words, he has been given the responsibility of leadership together with the enforcement of discipline.

This incident with Ananias and Sapphira showed the need for church discipline which existed in the early church. It stands as a model to us, not in its severity but in the need to exercise discipline in the church to restore its life and preserve its mission. It is a reminder to church leaders that this is an inescapable part of leadership, not because we leaders are better – we should be more conscious of our shortcomings – but because we are guardians of the life and witness of the church.

STICKING TO PRIORITIES

If one attack upon the life of the early church came through persecution, and another came through the hypocrisy of two of its members, a third came through distraction. These three, persecution, corruption and distraction, still remain in general terms the chief three ways in which the church is threatened. Peter had to counter all three in his leadership of the early church.

The issue, which is recorded in Acts chapter six, arose from a dispute between the two main parties that comprised the early church, namely the Hebrews and the Greeks. The Greek widows were being neglected in the daily food distribution. The very generosity of the church had created expectations which were not being fulfilled. We are not told why the Greek widows were being neglected, but it was not essentially an ethnic discrimination so much as a cultural tension. The reason for this was that the Greek and Hebrew parties were in fact both ethnically Jewish. They were not ethnically divided so much as divided culturally, reflecting the division in Jewish society itself between the Hellenized Jews, who made up much of the then ruling priestly party, and the "purer" Hebraic Jews —a division which was reflected in the Pharisaical traditions of Judaism. They tended to despise the Hellenized Jews as having made a deal with the occupying power and so having diluted the faith.

Perhaps the nearest modern parallel are registered and non-registered churches in some communist countries. Often the non-registered churches (like the Hebraic Jews) despised the registered churches, which correspond to the Hellenized Jews. However, the sad thing was that these attitudes, which were present in Judaism generally, had spilled over into the new church community, and that the Hellenized widows were consequently being neglected. The way out of the problem was for someone to supervise the daily food distribution, so that the murmurings and complaints would cease and both communities in the church would be treated fairly. At this point the apostles had to decide on their priorities, and they came to the important conclusion that, "It would not be right for us to neglect the ministry of the word of God in order to wait on tables."[10] It was not that waiting on tables was in any way inferior to the teaching of the word of God, but that the apostles had been commissioned to teach the word of God. Waiting at tables, though worthy, would have been a distraction from the task they had been given to do.

The issue, I believe, is now even more acute for the contemporary church leader than it was then. If the main functions of a church leader are to teach, pastor and pray for people, then other things need to be done by lay ministers gifted or able to do so. The pressure on ministers to become "managers" or "professionals" has increased and is increasing. In my own denomination there is increasing pressure on church leaders to become managers or enablers of several congregations or groups, so diluting the potency of their ministry by immersing them in a pool of administration. The reason for this is that more and more legislation falls to the minister and church council to fulfil. Thus they find themselves having to implement policies (for instance) relating to health and safety, child and vulnerable people protection, disabled access, and so forth. All of these could not in themselves be more commendable – like the distribution of food to neglected widows – but if these tasks are not properly delegated they can squeeze the time available for teaching the word of God and pastoring those in the flock who are in need. But, if these matters are attended to by people other than the main church ministers then they will be free to pursue their main ministerial calling. In short, the church leader must be wary of being drawn into areas of church life which are either beyond his or her expertise or simply outside his or her remit. For this to be successfully done, close co-operation needs to exist between the lay and ministerial leadership of the church, with a shared understanding of what the lay leadership of the church want from their ministerial leader. Once that is clearly established, it should then be possible for tasks not in the remit of the minister to be attended to by others who are capable in the fellowship. This is what, in effect, happened in the early church.

Having established what he and the other apostles were called to, Peter outlined the way forward: "Brothers, choose seven men from among you who are known to be full of the Spirit and wisdom. We will turn this responsibility over to them and will give our attention to prayer and the ministry of the word."[11] So the fellowship chose the seven men, whose ministry had already been accredited among them, and they were appointed to this task. It was a very successful initiative; the apostles were not distracted, the community as a whole was pleased, the appointment of the seven led to startling development in their own ministries, especially those of Stephen and Philip, as we shall see, and the widows were catered for. Not only that, but Luke tells us that the resolution of this problem in the early church meant, "...the word of God spread. The number of disciples in Jerusalem increased rapidly, and a large number of priests became obedient to the faith."[12]

Peter had successfully piloted the church through its early challenges, the onset of persecution, the corruption from within, and the potential distractions from its growing ministry. Any form of leadership must deal with these issues; from time to time opposition must be met and dealt with, corrupting influences detected and defused, whether in family or corporate life, and distractions from the task in hand eschewed —and, in this regard, the good can be the enemy of the best. In dealing with such issues, great discernment, courage and wisdom will need to be deployed, but these qualities are the stock in trade of leadership. Other challenges were soon to follow which Peter did not find so easy. These challenges came from the widening scope of the church's mission, which had begun in Jerusalem and Judea and was about to expand into Samaria and the Gentile world. In this expansion Peter was to wield "the keys of the kingdom" which Jesus had given him when he was appointed to be the leader of the church.

14

THE KEYS OF THE KINGDOM
Acts 8:1–25; 10:1–11:18

When Jesus commissioned Peter as the leader of the church and the rock on which it would be built, he also gave him the "keys of the kingdom of heaven".[1] From this responsibility of holding the keys come all the apocryphal jokes about Peter being the concierge of heaven, and innumerable ribald stories abound about his supposed guardianship of the entrance to heaven. But this picture, however amusing and consoling, is some way from the reality of what Jesus meant when he entrusted Peter with the keys of the kingdom. What Peter was given was the authority, especially during the expansion of the church, to admit into fellowship ethnic groups which had previously been excluded.

Inclusion of the excluded was a noted part of the ministry of Jesus, whether the excluded was a leper, a sinner, a tax collector or a blind beggar, but now the gospel was to transcend hitherto insurmountable barriers and include those with whom Jews had no dealings. This process was to reach its finale with the admission of the Gentiles. It was Peter who was given the responsibility and privilege of admitting them to the fellowship of the church. Although Peter's was an historic and unique mission of being the instrument through whom the Gentiles were admitted to the kingdom of God, every leader, whether in a family, church, business or corporate organisation, will be involved in including those who have been excluded, or at the very least seeking to make sure that those who might be excluded by virtue of colour, disability, age or sex are made to feel that they too can belong to the community you lead.

When Jesus promised the disciples that they would be his witnesses in Jerusalem, Judea, Samaria and to the ends of the earth, he knew that the kingdom of God would now cross all those boundaries which had previously been impassable.[2] In particular, those who lived in Samaria and in the Gentile world would be included in the kingdom of God; and Peter would be the person who would open the kingdom to them. Having preached the gospel in Jerusalem on the day of Pentecost, from where it would be taken to Judea, Peter was destined both to confirm the inclusion of the Samaritans into the kingdom of God and then the Gentiles themselves, in the biggest cultural shift in the history of God's people. Indeed it is through this action that God's promise to Abraham – that through him God would bless all nations – would come to fruition.

THE SAMARITANS

The precise religious and ethnic background of the Samaritans is hard to pin down. It seems that for a long time since the overthrow of Samaria by the Assyrians in 722 BC and the repopulating of the area of the northern kingdom by the Assyrians subsequently, there had been a diverse ethnic development in this northern region of Israel. It is clear that they were probably ethnically far more mixed than the southern kingdom, Judah. Unlike those who returned to Jerusalem from exile with Nehemiah and Ezra, their Jewish lineage was far more uncertain. It is also quite probable that people in this area were opposed to the rebuilding of Jerusalem after the exile.[3] It is further likely that during the period of Greek rule in the region following the conquests of Alexander the Great, a new cult began in the area around

Shechem, which may have been established by disaffected priests from Jerusalem who may also have entered into mixed marriages.

At any rate, what we have by the time of Jesus is a community which had their own worship on Mount Gerizim and which was defined by a fierce hostility towards Jerusalem. Despite these blemishes on their worship and their mixed ethnic background, the Samaritans got a good press from Jesus. He spent some time in their region after his meeting with the Samaritan woman;[4] he spent further time preaching and teaching in the Samaritan villages where he was well received, except when he showed that it was his intention to go on to the "despised" Jerusalem.[5] And one of his most famous parables has a Samaritan as its hero. Whatever the causes of the division between Jerusalem and the Samaritans, the gospel was to be a way of reconciling them. So, after the outpouring of the Spirit at Pentecost in Jerusalem, the next stage of mission was to be the inclusion of the Samaritans into the kingdom. This was to be achieved through the preaching of one of those appointed by Peter to wait at tables, Philip, and was then to be confirmed by the apostles John and Peter. His keys would unlock the kingdom to them and enable them to receive the Spirit.

Soon after the appointment of the seven, an intense persecution of the church broke out in Jerusalem, which was especially focussed on Stephen. Some members of a particular synagogue called the Freedmen, made up of Jews who originated from North Africa and the Roman provinces of Asia and Cilicia, began a campaign against Stephen, whose preaching and miracles had caused such a stir in the city. The campaign, which was seditious, eventually resulted in his martyrdom through stoning; with the coats of those taking part being laid, famously, at the feet of a young man called Saul. The persecution which claimed Stephen's life soon spread, so that most of the Christians left Jerusalem for Judea and Samaria, and amongst them was Stephen's close colleague and associate Philip.

Philip was a remarkably powerful evangelist, and many believed through his preaching and actions. They were baptised in the name of Jesus but did not immediately receive the Holy Spirit. The reason for this two stage initiation into the Christian faith was not only doctrinal and experiential, but also historical. Pentecostals have traditionally argued that the gift or baptism of the Holy Spirit is a distinct second phase of initiation, as shown in this account of the Samaritans' inclusion in the church —the first stage being their belief in Philip's message and their baptism in the name of Christ; the second being their receiving the gift of the Holy Spirit through the prayer and laying on of hands by the apostles Peter and John. Some Catholics have argued that Acts chapter eight gives a pattern of baptism and confirmation, in which, through the laying on of hands by a bishop who is in the apostolic succession to Peter, the individual will then receive the Holy Spirit. However, such teaching based on this historical episode, which has particular significance in the mission of the early church (and which we shall consider later) is the wrong place to build a comprehensive theology of initiation. The teaching epistles of Paul, especially Romans and Galatians, make it clear that salvation comes by grace through **faith**; this is the "basic law" on the subject of Christian initiation.[6] We then have to recognise that there are varying emphases in different doctrinal streams, concerning the manner and timing of the reception of the Holy Spirit in the personal experience of the believer. Ideally, repentance, faith, baptism and reception should occur close together at the onset of a person's discipleship. In reality some parts of initiation may occur over time.

Nonetheless, the two-stage initiation into the Christian faith which the converts in Samaria experienced served to overcome previous division between Jewish believers and Samaritan believers. The inclusion of the Samaritans in the church was of such importance that it was necessary in God's economy of mission to have the church leaders, Peter and John, include them personally, at the giving of the Spirit. So, "When the apostles in Jerusalem heard that Samaria had accepted the word of God, they sent Peter and John to them. When they arrived, they prayed for them that they might receive the Holy Spirit, because the Holy Spirit had not yet come upon any of them; they had simply been baptised into the name of the Lord Jesus. Then Peter and John placed their hands on them, and they received the Holy Spirit."[7] In this way it was clear that the Samaritan believers were properly and authoritatively included in the church, and that there could be no quibbling that they were in any way second class Christians. They had responded to the good news preached by Philip, they had been baptised into the name of Jesus and they had been included and welcomed by the leading apostles through whom the Spirit had been given to them. Whatever differences and divisions there had previously been between Jewish believer and Samaritan believer had now been overcome in this new age of the kingdom of God.

Peter's role in this was to be the opener of the door of the kingdom to a group long excluded from Judaism. He had turned the key of the kingdom, given to him by Jesus, in a door which had been barred and bolted for many generations. Through the exercise of this ministry, which was confirmed by the gift of the Spirit, a dividing wall had been torn down. The inclusion of the Samaritans demonstrated that the gospel of Jesus was able to bring into being a new humanity which surmounted previously insurmountable barriers, for until then, as we are told, Jews had no dealings with Samaritans, because of their mixed genealogy and impure worship.

From time to time any spiritual leader may be called upon to admit to the church people who would otherwise be excluded by their past, or by the perceptions of others of them, or by prejudice. Often these barriers must be overcome by both example and teaching. Sometimes this might be a costly ministry. In South Africa in the days of apartheid it was costly to welcome into a church or a school those of a different colour. A schoolmaster who had once taught me history at my secondary school, and in particular the American Civil War, subsequently went to South Africa as head of a well-known school. His liberal instincts set him on a collision course with the governors of that school, who opposed his policy of admitting black students. He was forced to resign because he wanted to include those who by virtue of their colour were excluded. To do that was to court the opposition and enmity of those who wanted to preserve the status quo. Nevertheless, his vision eventually came to pass. The leader does in a real sense have the keys to open doors of fellowship, even if such action is not always welcomed. He or she has also the vital function of giving permission for development, or for involvement of people or principles, which otherwise would be excluded. This giving of permission by leaders is a vital function of spiritual leadership in the church; it enables others to participate, frees them to use their gifts, and enables growth into maturity without which an unhealthy culture of dependency grows —which has been too much the hallmark of the church, whether it is "priestly" in its tone or the so called "strong leadership" of the new churches. It is a very courageous thing to do. Peter's action of welcoming the Samaritans may well have raised a few eyebrows in Jerusalem amongst the Christians of pure Jewish stock, but it was just a foretaste of what was to happen next. Indeed, what was to come next, in terms of the spread of the gospel, was the most momentous step that Judaism had seen since the giving of the law some fifteen hundred years earlier.

THE INCLUSION OF THE GENTILES

It had always been God's intention to include the Gentiles in the kingdom of God. The covenant made with Abraham was in time to include all peoples and nations who were outside Israel.[8] Indeed, Israel herself had been called to be a light to the nations, but had failed in her vocation. But now the remnant of Israel, who had believed that the Messiah had come in Jesus, were the ones to take the gospel to the whole world for whom the Christ had died. And Peter, as the leader of the church – with the keys to unlock the kingdom to others – was commissioned to take the gospel to a representative

Gentile household. God chose a Roman centurion who, like others in the Gospels, was a God-fearing individual. In fact, Roman centurions as a profession have the best press in the whole of the New Testament. One had more faith than any Israelite Jesus had met;[9] another was a benefactor of the Jewish people; and yet another, who supervised the crucifixion of Jesus, acknowledged, "Surely this man was the Son of God."[10] And now, finally, God chose a further centurion, Cornelius, to be the first representative Gentile convert.

Luke beautifully tells the story of Peter's going to the home of Cornelius. Reading the story is like seeing a film, as we glimpse two households converging in God's plan. Firstly we focus on the household of Cornelius, a devout, generous man who worshipped God with his whole household. Cornelius has an afternoon vision in which he is told by an angel to send for Simon Peter, who is staying in the house of another Simon, a tanner who lives by the sea at Joppa. Cornelius confides his vision to his more believing servants, who go to fetch Simon Peter. At this point we switch households to that of Simon the tanner, by the sea. Here again we catch a domestic scene, in which a hungry Peter falls asleep and, as the smell of cooking wafts up to the roof where Peter is dozing, he dreams of all kinds of food or animals, which he is bidden to eat. Just as he protests that some of the food is not *kosher*, he is told, "Do not call anything impure that God has made clean."[11] So as to make this lesson unmistakeable, this episode in the vision happened three times. As Peter is puzzling over the meaning of his vision, there is a knock at the door. Cornelius' servants are there inviting him, a Jew, to come to a Gentile's home. The next day Peter, with other members of the local Christian congregation, makes his way to Caesarea to Cornelius' household.

Peter is given a fulsome reception by Cornelius, who throws himself on the ground before him. He protests that he is only a man, and makes him stand up. But from the outset Peter makes it clear how extraordinary it is that he is there at all, saying to the assembled gathering that, "...You are well aware that it is against our law for a Jew to associate with a Gentile or visit him. But God has shown me that I should not call any man impure or unclean. So when I was sent for, I came without raising any objection."[12]

It is clear from this that Peter, although commanded to go to a Gentile house, is hardly free from the strangeness and abnormality of this encounter. He has a clear sense of doing something which had previously been out of the question and prohibited by the commonly accepted interpretation of Jewish law. It is hard for us to appreciate the trauma of this sudden change of perception for Peter and, as we shall see, Peter himself remained somewhat ambivalent toward his own change of attitude.

Nonetheless, having been welcomed and then having asked rather formally, "May I ask why you sent for me?" he gives an account of the gospel of Jesus, which God himself confirms by sending the Spirit upon the gathering. The main elements of Peter's address are the description of the ministry of Jesus, marvellously summarised: "...he went around doing good and healing all who were under the power of the devil, because God was with him";[13] speaking of his death and resurrection, the commission to preach the gospel, and the invitation to receive "...forgiveness of sins through his name." It was then that the Holy Spirit was poured out on all those who heard the message. The external evidence of receiving the Spirit was that they spoke in tongues and praised God.

So, in practice, the Holy Spirit did what Peter had earlier spoken of in theory, which was that, "I now realise how true it is that God does not show favouritism but accepts men [people] from every nation who fear him and do what is right." The inclusion of the Gentiles in the covenant made with Abraham on the grounds of faith alone was the revolutionary concept with which Peter and many in the early church had to wrestle for years to come. Peter had had it vividly explained to him in a triple vision; he had had it confirmed to him by the outpouring of the Spirit upon the Gentiles in the home of Cornelius; and later he would defend his own part in it to the leaders in Jerusalem. But despite all of this, the abandonment of the Jewish law as a qualification for acceptance before God was an insight he would be tempted – if not in theory, then in practice – to row back from.

Peter's account to the leaders of the Jerusalem church is an interesting piece of theological reflection on the revolutionary events in which he had taken a leading role. The inclusion of the Gentiles in the church, and Peter's role in this, were objects of criticism. Their complaint was that "You went into the house of uncircumcised men and ate with them." In fact that was the least of it; not only had he gone to this Gentile home and eaten and stayed with them, but he had included them in the church, baptising them without making any demand upon them with regard to the Jewish law. The question for the Jewish leaders of the church was: on whose authority had this inclusion of the Gentiles taken place? Peter is at pains to show the initiative rested entirely with God himself. The Holy Spirit urged each step of the way. "The Spirit," he says, "told me to have no hesitation about going with them"[14] (the servants of Cornelius who had come to fetch him). Again, Peter tells how, "As I began to speak, the Holy Spirit came on them as he had come on us at the beginning", and then Peter finally and compellingly concludes his testimony with the sentence, "So if God gave them the same gift as he gave us, who believed in the Lord Jesus Christ, who was I to think that I could oppose God?" That was unanswerable!

In reviewing this episode in the life of the church, there are two vital lessons for leadership. The first is to acknowledge that God makes no distinctions of race, colour or education in the new society of the church. It is far too easy to import unthinkingly into the church the attitudes or prejudices of the world, which constantly discriminates between people. Because God does not make these distinctions in his church, neither are we free to make them. But, as we know, the error of discrimination has appeared and reappeared in the church down the years; whether in overt or subtle ways, making people of different colour, race, age or status feel unwelcome. It is the special responsibility of the leadership of the church to be impartial in its style of leadership, showing that all are welcome. On this point it may be necessary to strike a cautionary note, in case the church in the West comes to imitate too closely the consumerist society in which it now ministers. The combination of advertising and mobility will inevitably lead to "branding" in relation to church life, which in turn is a response to the ever increasing desire for choice in all goods and services. Churches will be tempted to present themselves as a particular brand of church in the market place of worship, from which the consumer will make a choice. Although a range of worship is healthy, it can turn church into another consumer choice in which "my own needs" become paramount. The danger is this: that churches catering to particular needs become defined more by their homogeneity than by their locality, so that, unlike the New Testament church, which consisted in the saints in a particular place, now the church is defined ethnically, culturally and professionally.

In "church growth" teaching of recent years, there has been a tendency to encourage what is called homogeneous church growth, in which similar people are banded together in church because this is likely to be more effective evangelistically. In this way we are encouraged to be church in our natural groupings. So, again, there will be church for the thirties, or church for the managers, or church for mums and babies, to caricature it to make the point. Although the first step towards inclusion into the church will often be into a group which is familiar and culturally well known, the church cannot give up its identity as being a community for all. As we shall see, Paul in particular strained every nerve to keep within the church both Jew and Gentile Christian, even to the point of opposing Peter. It would have been easy to acquiesce in the demand for Jew and Gentile to worship separately, but that would have undercut the very basis of the gospel, that in Christ (the covenant made with Abraham had been fulfilled), "There is neither Jew nor Greek, slave nor free, male nor female, for you are all one in Christ Jesus. If you belong to Christ, then you are Abraham's seed, and heirs according to the promise."[15]

So this covenant was for all believers —a single church for all. The temptation we face today is to adopt a missiological process which may well do the business but at the cost of sacrificing the vision of a church for the whole community in a locality. This is clearly put by Michael Moynagh, who suggests that when an "it-must-fit-me-exactly" approach holds sway, churches which are not "my sort of people" may find it hard to survive.[16] But a church which is so finely "encultured" (i.e. embedded in a particular culture) can prove to be discriminatory. This is a tension that church leaders must clearly address, and a dilemma to be faced.

Peter's great revelation was that, "I now realise how true it is that God does not show favouritism." He struggled, as we shall see, to keep the unity of the Spirit, in the multi-cultured church of the first century, in the bond of peace. However, spiritual leadership must be involved in making that a practical reality. The real dilemma here is this: on the one hand there is our drive for mission, which means the enculturation of the church in very specific ways in order to reach different groups, but on the other hand, this may be at the expense of a vision of the church which is truly catholic and non discriminatory. Ironically, Peter realised that the church must break out of its Jewish context and welcome in the Gentiles; only then would it become the church God intended it to be.

The second lesson in spiritual leadership from this episode has to do with dealing with what, in political circles, have been called the forces of conservatism, with a small "c", or to put it in a more churchy way, the forces of Christendom. In a country such as the UK, where the church has been around for over fifteen hundred years, since the mission of Augustine or the Celtic mission to the north of England led by Paulinus, this could not be a more important issue, especially for leaders of historic churches. The issue for Peter and the leaders of the early church in Jerusalem was how were they to regard the previous (also) fifteen hundred years —of Jewish history, since the giving of the law to Moses. It was a deep theological and emotional question. In the next chapter we shall see more of how the early church dealt with it theologically. But here we must note that the inclusion of the Gentiles led to a reappraisal of what constituted membership of the church, or God's people, which is God's new humanity. Leaders of the church are always in the business of evaluating the need for change and how that might be best introduced into the church of which they are part.

In evaluating change, and how or whether to incorporate it into the church, the first step must be to decide whether Scripture warrants the inclusion of whatever it is. In the case of the inclusion of the Gentiles, this was clearly determined by Jesus himself, and was the age old plan since God's covenant with Abraham. There was no question amongst the apostles that this was part of God's will. But nevertheless it met with a critical reaction from Jewish Christians, which would fester in the church for years to come. Peter had to deal with these reactions on several occasions, as we shall see. Likewise, although in far less momentous times, church leaders today must learn to deal with reactions to new styles of ministry and mission. Dealing with those reactions will involve both theological reappraisal and emotional evaluation.

Today we are faced with new issues. For example, can there be such a thing as an internet church, where people are only in virtual but not physical contact? Are our patterns of church worship services, which are broadly based on synagogue worship in the intertestamental period, still valid for today? Are they not too passive, where most people do very little and a few a great deal! Whereas for most people church means going to church on a Sunday, it may increasingly mean belonging to a community which meets midweek for its main spiritual sustenance.

Moulds are being broken rapidly today. The liturgical, architectural and musical changes which have dominated church life in the last thirty years may well prove to be limited, compared with the changes implicit in what it means to be church today. Indeed, I sense in my own constituency of the church that long periods of sung worship followed by say half hour preaching – which might be termed a standard charismatic form of worship – is not necessarily scratching where new entrants to the church now itch. We can be sure that yesterday's revolution will become today's status quo, and new ways of expressing our faith will need to be found which are in touch with our incessantly changing culture. But it is up to leadership to evaluate whatever changes there are on the horizon, by virtue of changing culture and technology, and put them through a process of evaluation, inclusion or exclusion, reappraisal and re-formation. This process will have to deal with the issues of reaction that such changes inevitably bring.

Peter was confronted by a powerful reaction back in Jerusalem to the inclusion of the Gentiles. It did mark the end of Judaism as all Jews had known it. Even Christian Jews had proceeded with a strong sense of continuity with the past, but they were now to face a radical departure from all that had gone before. The observance of the law, circumcision, the Sabbath, and worship in the temple were all to be superseded. Fifteen hundred years of following a certain pattern was to give way to a new, simple but life-changing faith in Jesus Christ. In fact, "The Way" that the Christians would follow would find its origin in Abraham's faith, as expressed in seminal passages in Genesis, notably that moment when looking up at the stars one night he heard the word or promise of God and, as the author says, "Abram believed the LORD, and he credited it to him as righteousness."[17] Here was the key text around which Paul explained "The Way" to the Gentile and Jewish Christians of his day.[18] In our present era in the UK, the legacy of the past fifteen hundred years remains but is gradually passing away, the debris of its existence still subsisting in the collective folk consciousness of some of the people for just one more generation; so it is time for spiritual leaders to both minister to those who have known and loved the manifestation of Christendom, as I do, but at the same time to cut loose of those traditions in order to minister to generations to come who have no allegiance to – or understanding of – those traditions. Peter was the one to carry the church into its new existence, but Paul was the one to explain how the new was always part of God's plan —begun with Abraham and fulfilled and made possible by Jesus.

In the next chapter we will look more closely at how the church of Peter's day handled the great change with which they were faced, which was the admission of the Gentiles, how they went about that process, and the pitfall which Peter himself fell into. It is an instructive process for a church which faces in the West issues that threaten to tear us apart.

15

CHAIRMAN OF THE COUNCIL

Acts 15:1–35; Galatians 2:1–21

The great historic divide in the early church was between Jew and Gentile, and the rapid advance of the church throughout the Empire exacerbated this. The early church grew swiftly. Initially the church was centred on Jerusalem, as we have seen, but with the increase of persecution it spread to the surrounding regions, and more significantly it crossed boundaries which had hitherto been impassable. As we have also seen, the greatest of these boundaries or barriers was the Jew/Gentile one —never before had they mixed!

If growth in membership occurs amongst like minded people, or in the same ethnic group, or amongst those with the same customs or habits, then it may be relatively smooth and uneventful; but if growth occurs in such a way as to throw together people who have little in common outside of Christ then you can be sure that as you travel down the road of fellowship there will be significant hurdles along the way. In this chapter we see how the leadership met – and struggled to meet – one of the greatest tests of the church in its early years.

In chapters eight to thirteen of Acts we see the rapid expansion of the church. It began with the persecution of the church in Jerusalem. We were told, "...all except the apostles were scattered throughout Judea and Samaria."[1] In the next few chapters we hear of the effective mission of Philip to Samaria, the conversion of an Ethiopian official, the remarkable conversion of Saul, the inclusion of the Gentiles into the new covenant of the Spirit with Peter's visit to Cornelius, the growth of the missionary church in Antioch and, finally, the first missionary journey of Paul.

The breathless and dramatic expansion of the church was to continue into the second century AD. In Polycarp's famous address recorded before his martyrdom in Smyrna where he was the Bishop, we are told that, "Polycarp, with a stern countenance looked on all the crowd of lawless heathen in the arena, and waving his hand at them, he groaned and looked up to heaven and said: 'Away with the Atheists'. But when the Pro-Consul pressed him and said: 'Take the oath (to the genius of Caesar) and I will let you go, revile Christ', Polycarp said: 'For eighty and six years have I been his servant, and he has done me no wrong, how can I blaspheme my King who saved me?'"[2]

If Polycarp himself had been baptised as an infant in Smyrna eighty six years previously, which is not an unreasonable supposition, it means that forty years after the death of Christ there was already a settled church in Smyrna in Asia Minor.[3] As Tom Wright says, "The single most striking thing about early Christianity is its speed of growth. In AD 25 there is no such thing as Christianity: merely a young hermit in the Judean wilderness, and his somewhat younger cousin who dreams dreams and sees visions. By AD 125 the Roman emperor has established an official policy in relation to the punishment of Christians; Polycarp has already been a Christian for half a century; Aristides is confronting the emperor Hadrian with news that there are four races in the world —barbarians, Greeks, Jews, and Christians; and a young pagan called Justin is at the beginning of the philosophical quest which will take him through the pagan thinkers and lead him, still unsatisfied, to Christ."[4] All this in ninety years since the resurrection of Jesus; such was the speed of the growth of the church.

It is quite possible that the sheer speed of the growth of the early church around the Roman Empire took the mother church at Jerusalem by surprise. It is also quite probable that the church in Jerusalem was fearful of being over-whelmed by the Gentile converts. There was a need for the apostles and leaders of the church in Jerusalem to define categorically what, if any, of the Jewish Torah the Gentile church must observe. This issue was one of the most pressing for the early church, and indeed continues to be an issue for Christians today. How much of the Old Testament Torah is binding on a Christian nowadays, and if it is not, why not? And if it is, why is it? That remains one of the thorniest hermeneutical problems for us, but the key to understanding how a Gentile Christian is to relate to the laws of the first five books of the Bible is found both in the historical decision of the Council of Jerusalem and in the doctrinal teaching of Paul in the epistles to the Romans and the Galatians. We shall look at both these guides to this issue. Peter was at the centre of the formulation of the decision taken at the Council of Jerusalem, and was also at the centre of the controversy of which Paul speaks in Galatians. We shall look at both these episodes, recorded in Acts and Galatians in turn.

However, in relation to our theme of spiritual leadership, it is worth making the point that the church has always been guided (or misguided) by councils! There are very few churches which do not have a council or something equivalent to guide, develop and discipline the ministry of the local, national or international church. In my own denomination we have our parochial church councils, our synods, whether at deanery, diocesan or national level. Other churches may have their elders' meetings, or their deacons' meetings or boards. Most churches will have their national or international assemblies. Some take to such councils as a duck to the proverbial water; others may drag themselves to their deliberations. Whether we like or dislike such bodies, they are, it seems, a given of church life. It is clear that something similar to them existed in Jerusalem for the ordering of the church, its worship, teaching and mission.

193

Those who lead local or indeed national churches ignore these bodies at their peril!

The wise management of such councils is as much a part of spiritual leadership as the ordering of worship. Failure adequately to prepare for leading them can be as damaging as failing to prepare for a piece of teaching in the Sunday service —perhaps more so! Anyone who has been in church leadership for any length of time will have their stories of stormy or tense leadership meetings, precipitate resignations, or confrontations in them. Unanimous agreement may not be always achievable; there should be space for people healthily to debate or object to issues under discussion, but to do so in a respectful and considerate way. The Council of Jerusalem was called to decide what parts of the Jewish law should be kept by the Gentiles, so that the unity of the church be preserved. If the apostles had not agreed, then the church would have quickly split into a Jewish church and a Gentile church. The Council was needed to prevent schism, to endorse true spirituality, and to enable the mission of the gospel to Jew and Gentile. It is time to turn to its proceedings and learn from its conduct.

THE COUNCIL OF JERUSALEM

What is clear from the deliberations of this Council and their effect on church growth[5] is that the teaching of the church, with its resulting guidance for the conduct of the believers, needs clarification from time to time if the church is to remain healthy and capable of ongoing growth. Just as in our own day there is need for clear teaching on issues relating to sexuality from the councils of the church, so in Peter's day the decisive issue facing the growth of the church was the grounds for justification by faith, and whether those grounds included the need for circumcision or observing the ceremonial of Jewish law.

As we have noticed, the growth of the church in the Gentile world was fast. The conversions of Cornelius, Philip's mission to Samaria, the conversion of the apostle Paul and the mission to Antioch were the original building blocks of this growth. The mission to Antioch recorded in Acts 11:20f was a sign of the vigour of the evangelism taking place, so to speak, "from everywhere to everywhere". The reason for pointing this out here is that those who first took the gospel to Antioch did not come from Jerusalem but from Cyprus and Cyrene. They, we are told, "...began to speak to Greeks [Gentiles] also, telling them the good news about the Lord Jesus." Further, we are told that, "The Lord's hand was with them, and a great number of people believed and turned to the Lord."[6] Barnabas, who was then sent down by the Jerusalem church to see what was going on, was "glad" with what he saw, and, "...encouraged them all to remain true to the Lord with all their hearts." Again, it was Barnabas who went and fetched Paul from Tarsus, and took him to Antioch where they remained for a year, and taught large numbers of people at Antioch who first took the name Christians. This mission to the Gentiles was not initiated by the mother church at Jerusalem but was confirmed as authentic both by Barnabas, a delegate presumably sent because of his open and encouraging nature, and Paul, the apostle appointed by God to minister to the Gentiles.

So what we have is an axis opening up in early Christianity between Jerusalem and Antioch. The former was deferred to as the mother church, with most of the apostles connected to it but not seemingly initiating evangelism, whilst the church at Antioch rapidly became the missionary church to the Gentiles. A division between the two churches would have been disastrous to the early church, setting apostle against apostle and also dividing the early church on Jewish/Gentile lines.

But what we see in the period of the New Testament is strenuous efforts being made by Peter, Paul and James to maintain "...the unity of the Spirit through the bond of peace", by agreeing doctrine at issue between the Judaisers and the Gentiles at the Council of Jerusalem, to cement the fellowship between the Jerusalem church and the Gentile church, by means of the collection which Paul took up for them and personally delivered; in this way, personal differences or misunderstandings between individual church leaders were worked through. So we see the considerable efforts which Christian leaders must make in maintaining the unity of the church through clarifying teaching, sharing resources and resolving differences. It is an arduous process and will continue as much today as it did then.

The trigger for the Council of Jerusalem was that some men had come down to Antioch from Judea and were teaching, "...Unless you are circumcised, according to the custom taught by Moses, you cannot be saved."[7] By this time, Paul had completed his first missionary journey to the cities of southern Galatia, and his church planting work in these towns was threatened by the teaching of the Judaisers which stated that the converts had to observe the Torah and needed to be circumcised, hence his impassioned plea to them, "I am astonished that you are so quickly deserting the one who called you by the grace of Christ and are turning to a different gospel—which is really no gospel at all."[8] This same teaching was infiltrating the church at Antioch itself, precipitating a major crisis in the early church. Paul had already told us in an important autobiographical section in Galatians 2:1–10 that he had previously, together with Barnabas, gone up to Jerusalem to confer with the leading apostles, Peter, John and James, the brother of Jesus. Together they had considered the question of the grounds on which a person could be justified (or set to rights) with God, and whether or not those grounds included circumcision. Having agreed this teaching previously, Paul is astonished to find that Peter in particular did not appear to be living it out, as we shall see. He therefore looked for a definitive ruling from a public council in Jerusalem.

The Council of Jerusalem divides into four parts; the speech of Peter; the account of their work amongst the Gentiles by Paul and Barnabas; the speech of James, and the sending of a letter to the churches with a delegation from Jerusalem. The issue they faced was the conviction of some Christians who were also Pharisees, as Paul had been, that, "The Gentiles **must** be circumcised and required to obey the law of Moses." (My emphasis). This teaching struck at the very heart of the gospel for, as Paul wrote, "Clearly no-one is justified before God by the law, because, 'The righteous will live by faith'."[9] It was essential, therefore, to have an authoritative ruling on this subject so that the mission to the Gentiles could go ahead and the distinctiveness of the gospel be preserved. It was a pivotal moment.

After open discussion, Peter stood to speak. Peter recounted the inclusion of the Gentiles during his preaching to Cornelius and his household. His basic point was that "God, who knows the heart, showed that he accepted them by giving the Holy Spirit to them, just as he did to us. He made no distinction between us and them, for he purified their hearts by faith."[10] He concluded emphatically, "We believe it is through the grace of our Lord Jesus that we are saved, just as they are!"[11] Paul and Barnabas gave flesh to this teaching by recounting the way in which the Gentiles had received the gospel, and the extraordinary way in which their ministry had been accompanied by "signs and wonders".

Finally, James, the brother of Jesus and author of the New Testament epistle bearing his name, stood to speak. He first made plain – through a quotation from Amos – that it had always been God's plan to call out from amongst the Gentiles a people for himself. However, to make the teaching that only by grace can we enter the covenant – made to Abraham and fulfilled by Jesus – more palatable to the Jews, he enjoined on the believers four concessions to the scruples of Jewish believers, which seem to have had only temporary significance. These concessions, sometimes termed the "Jerusalem Quadrilateral", are most probably ceremonial parts of the Torah which included abstaining from food which had been offered to idols, from meat that had not been butchered correctly by the draining of blood, from eating blood, and observing the rules of marriage set out in the tables of kindred and affinity in Leviticus 18. Although the first three of this quadrilateral have temporary significance, any good Anglican will tell you from reading the 1662 Book of Common Prayer that the rules of marriage, rules of kindred and affinity, still apply in church law! I can remember well in my youth whiling away time in boring services reading about those whom I was not permitted to marry, and being greatly relieved!

The Council's conclusions were, then, a combination of laying down the essence of the gospel as issuing from grace and depending on faith alone in God's promise, with a number of concessions to the Jewish church to make the decision more acceptable. Such was the wisdom exhibited by James. And we note that in his epistle he characterises the "wisdom that comes from heaven" as being, "...first of all pure; then peace-loving, considerate, submissive, full of mercy and good fruit, impartial and sincere. Peacemakers who sow in peace raise a harvest of righteousness."[12]

The example of James could not be more instructive for spiritual leadership, which is to be **clear on the essential principles and compassionate in application**. As a *modus vivendi* for leading the church, this could not be more helpful. When it comes to sexual ethics, or questions of marriage and divorce, to name but two contentious areas, this seems to be what the spiritual leader should aim for. We cannot discuss here the range of ethics involved, as each is probably worthy of a book on its own, so much as observe how the Council did its work and what lessons can be learnt.

The resulting letter, which was sent around the churches together with a well-chosen delegation from the Council, of Judas and Silas (who were themselves New Testament prophets) had the gratifying effect of building up the church. The Council could be judged a success. It debated the issues. Both sides of the argument were put. The apostles agreed together. The decision was neither too onerous for the Gentile Christians nor able to be seen as an inappropriate concession to the Jewish-minded Christians. It was clearly expressed, and important members of the Jerusalem church who were clearly filled with the Spirit took the letter to the churches. It also drew a line under an incident which had been painful to Peter when Paul himself had opposed him at Antioch.

THE DISPUTE AT ANTIOCH

The chronology around which we are working here, as you may have already have noticed, is that the dispute, which occurred between Peter and Paul at Antioch, took place **before** the Council of Jerusalem. This helps to make sense of Acts 15 and Galatians 2:11–16. As John Stott writes in his commentary on Acts 15, "I need to share with my readers that I hold to the so-called "South Galatian" view, namely that Paul's letters to the Galatians were written to the South Galatian churches of Pisidian Antioch, Iconium, Lystra and Derbe, which he and Barnabas had just visited on their first missionary journey; that he dictated it during the height of his theological crisis before the Council settled it (for he does not refer in his letter to the "apostolic decree"); that he was writing it probably on his way up to Jerusalem for the Council, which would be his third visit to the city, although he does not mention it in Galatians because it has not yet taken place; and therefore the situation that Luke describes at the beginning of Acts 15 is the same that Paul refers to in Galatians 2:11–16".[13]

However, not every scholar nor even every "conservative" scholar shares this view. Walter Hansen, in his recent commentary on Galatians, takes another widely held view, that Galatians 2:1–10 is Paul's own account of the Jerusalem Council.[14] Although it is true that both accounts do cover similar ground, and they both make mention of the leaders of the Council of Jerusalem, namely Peter, James and John, it is hard to conceive if these two accounts record the same event, namely the Council of Jerusalem, that so soon after the Council in which both James and Peter had played such a leading role, they **both** reneged on it! —James in sending a message to Peter at Antioch of the offence his fellowship with Gentiles was having on the Judean Christians back home; and Peter in withdrawing from fellowship with Gentile Christians in Antioch.

It is surely more probable that Paul, having gained an informal understanding that his teaching had the support of the leading apostles in Jerusalem, was dismayed and horrified that Peter, James and Barnabas had, subsequent to their agreement, given in to the pressure from the Judaisers, withdrawing from fellowship with the Gentile Christians in Antioch.[15] He had then asked for clarification from those apostles as to exactly what they did teach about the need for observing the Torah and this resulted in the Council of Jerusalem, for which Paul returned to Jerusalem. If this chronology is right, then it shows the development of Paul's relationship with Peter, who with James, and to a lesser extent John, were the pillars of the early church.

Paul tells us that he visited Jerusalem on three occasions prior to his second missionary journey, and on each occasion, either privately or in public, he meets with Peter.[16] On the first occasion it is just three years after his conversion that Paul first meets with Peter, staying with him fifteen days.[17] Secondly, he went to Jerusalem fourteen years later as a result of a "revelation".[18] It was necessitated by the fear that a bad report would be given of his ministry by those whom he called "spies", who wanted to denigrate the "freedom" with which he preached the gospel (not insisting on the necessity of circumcision for his Gentile converts). And thirdly, he went to Jerusalem for the Council.

On the second occasion he went privately to the leaders of the church in Jerusalem, both to lay before them the essence of the gospel he was preaching and to get their agreement as to where and to whom he could preach. On both these points he was reassured with their approval and support —not that Paul believed he needed human approval, since he was preaching the gospel of God with the commission of God to go to the Gentiles. So Paul concluded, "...they saw that I had been entrusted with the task of preaching the gospel to the Gentiles, just as Peter had been to the Jews. For God, who was at work in the ministry of Peter as an apostle to the Jews, was also at work in my ministry as an apostle to the Gentiles."[19]

But somewhere between this second visit to Jerusalem, which occurred around seventeen years after his conversion (possibly around AD 49 and when he went with Agabus from

Antioch to bring aid to the church in Judea during the years of the famine under Claudius), and the third visit to Jerusalem for the Council, Peter and Paul had this sharp altercation at Antioch.

It seems that Peter, who was quite frequently at Antioch, had normally had table fellowship with the Gentile Christians, but after a visit from Jerusalem of "certain men" who "came from James" (James the brother of Jesus and leader of the church in Jerusalem), Peter withdrew from fellowship from the Gentile Christians and persuaded others to do likewise; even the big hearted Barnabas followed his lead. The reason that Paul gives for Peter doing this was because, "He was afraid of those who belonged to the circumcision group."[20] This may or may not be the whole story, but the reasons for Peter's actions were either a fear of the Judaisers or an ill-conceived attempt not to cause offence to the Jewish Christians in Judea, who had been scandalised by reports of him eating with uncircumcised Gentile Christians of which James had been informed. Whatever the exact motive for this withdrawal of fellowship, it seems to have been a blend of fear of the Judaisers and a desire to placate his fellow Jews back home in Judea. For these reasons, he and Barnabas withdrew from eating with Gentiles, and in so doing giving the idea that Gentile Christians who were not keeping the Torah were unacceptable to God and not worthy of fellowship with the apostle. In turn this was a slight on the gospel that Paul was preaching, which was that by faith alone in God's grace a person is justified, or becomes a member of that covenant made originally with Abraham and becomes an heir of all God's promises. Paul confronted Peter and accused him bluntly of betraying the gospel and being hypocritical —that is, doing what he knew was wrong.

LESSONS IN LEADERSHIP FROM THE ANTIOCH DISPUTE

So what had gone wrong here, and what lessons for spiritual leadership can be drawn from this incident which, if we are right, led to the Council of Jerusalem? At first sight it seems like a failure of nerve on the part of Peter, but this may be an over-simplification. Nevertheless, both in the high priest's courtyard and in the "dining room" of the church in Antioch he found it difficult to be distinct. Perhaps his natural personal leadership style, despite all his impetuous and forceful actions, was to lead by consensus and not by confrontation; to be more concerned about breaking with people rather than with breaking with principle. Because of this trait, he may have muddied the principle of "justification by faith alone" in Antioch rather than break with the custom of his own people. However, there could have been another good and stronger motivating force for his actions in Antioch, even though the "good" was the enemy of the "best" —in this case as in many!

Peter, being the apostle to the Jews, was pre-eminently concerned with winning them, the Jews, to Christ. He, therefore, wanted to put no obstacle in their path to faith in Christ nor inflame the opinions of the Jews back in Judea. To this end, he withdrew from fellowship with the Gentiles. If this was his reason for withdrawing from fellowship from the Gentiles, it was the case of a well-motivated action leading to confusion and hurt. It is unlikely that it would have placated the Judaisers and, if it had lasted, it would have led to the establishment of two quite separate churches for Jews and Gentiles, and it severely risked undermining the gospel principle of justification by faith through God's grace alone. So as a well-intentioned action, designed for missionary purposes, it had the effect of both splitting the church and undermining the gospel. Such are the pitfalls that spiritual leadership in the church must surmount. As we noticed earlier, we must have the wisdom to know which are the battles to fight and where lines must be drawn. There are few more important issues in spiritual leadership; and if we are sure that we do have a battle to fight, the next thing must be the manner in which the fight is conducted!

By contrast, Paul was all the other way about. He saw the issues and principles very clearly, as well as the possibility of offending his fellow countrymen – and, indeed, fellow Pharisees – but this would never prevent him from teaching and living out the way of grace. However, it shows that Paul was able to put principles before people, in the sense of not allowing personal relationship to govern his pursuit of making the gospel known. Nowhere was this tendency more clearly seen than in Paul's break with Barnabas over whether or not they should take with them John Mark on the second missionary journey, which was started immediately after the Council of Jerusalem, because John Mark had previously deserted Paul and so he was not prepared to give him a second chance.[21]

So in Peter and Paul we have two leadership styles which perhaps reflected different personalities and different outlook or training. There are many styles of leadership, which management schools are quick to label, as well as many personality types, but it would be anachronistic to read back such things upon either Peter or Paul. It is clear that they are quite different. After all, Paul was in his own right a considerable intellectual, trained as a Pharisee under Gamaliel, with an awesome intellectual grasp of the teaching he was giving. He was governed by his apprehension of the gospel, and had been given the commission of preaching this gospel to the Gentiles. Peter, on the other hand, was called an ignorant and uneducated man by the Sanhedrin; he was by instinct more conservative than Paul, and was perhaps not as fearless as him either. This is not to say that Peter was unaware or insensible of the issues he was dealing with, but that the training he received was very different from Paul's. Yes, he had spent three years in the company of Jesus as the Sanhedrin had also noted, but he was not destined to become (nor equipped to be) the supreme teacher and expositor of the faith that Paul was.

Equally, their missionary orientation and constituency was different. Paul, although by no means neglecting the Jews or his desire for their salvation,[22] was primarily focussed on the Gentiles, while Peter was principally dedicated to the mission to the Jews. The incident at Antioch shows up these differing priorities, and their various understandings of the issues at stake. The lessons for leaders of churches or groups today is to consider how our actions may be interpreted, and what signals are given off by what we "do", as much as what we "say". There are many aspects to leadership, but one is consistency between what we say and do; and where a gap occurs between the two, it is an opportunity for a devilish coach and horses to be driven through. We should mind the gap! Peter, at Antioch, did not! But the Council set the record straight and, in its albeit provisional conclusions, gave a basis for moving forward unitedly in mission together. No more could have been expected.

****

At this point we are about to leave Peter struggling once again with the issues related to preaching the gospel in the context of the Gentile/Jewish divide. Peter does not re-appear in Acts after the Council of Jerusalem, generally thought to be around AD 51. Soon after the Council was over, Paul begins his second missionary journey, re-visiting those churches in southern Galatia to whom he had written such a blistering letter. Of Peter, on the other hand, we hear no more in the history of the growth of the early church. He has been at the forefront of the explosion of Christian faith in the Jerusalem church. But we hear nothing more about him until his letters, written to the Christian churches in Asia, churches that he may well have visited. In around AD 65 he wrote his first epistle from Rome.[23] By now the church was threatened in three main ways. Firstly, there was persecution, which had broken out against the church through much of the Roman Empire, and was taking its toll on church life. This persecution was to wax and wane for the next 250 years, until Constantine embraced the faith. Secondly, there were the Judaisers, about whom we have already heard. They were not content with the gospel of grace that the apostles had agreed to preach, and wanted to add the observance of the Torah (either more or less of it) to this gospel of grace. They took their dispute to cities in the Roman Empire, not least the city of Rome, where disturbances in the reign of

Claudius led to the expulsion of both Christians and Jews. And thirdly, towards the end of the first century, we see the growth of Gnosticism, a belief system that denigrated according to Greek culture the importance of the body. This led in turn to a denial of the humanity of Jesus, that he came in the body, and the importance of a discipleship which was worked out in our human flesh. Signs of combating this are already evident in the teaching of Paul to the Romans, Colossians and Philippians, but the chief defender of the faith in relation to this false teaching was the apostle John. Between them, Paul, Peter, John and James (the leader of the church in Jerusalem) were to write in defence and encouragement of the church, when it faced these three kinds of assault.

It is tempting to say that little has changed in terms of the threats that the church faces. The church in some parts of the world faces intense persecution. Elsewhere, the temptation is to either add things to the faith, which are unnecessary, or to suggest that our discipleship can by-pass what we do in our bodies. This latter is now the chief threat to holy or fully-human living that we face in the post-modern, individualistic, pluralistic and existential society in which we live! Peter is one of the New Testament voices that call us to be both truly human and distinct in the light of these contemporary pressures. In this final section we turn to a Peter who, in his final years, had become a chief instructor of the church, both then and now. So from formation of Peter as a disciple by Jesus, to the explosive growth of the early church in which Peter had a pivotal role, we move to Peter now instructing the church from the insights he has gained from thirty and more years of discipleship in the cauldron of the first century Christian life.

Part Three
INSTRUCTION

16

THE CALL TO HOLINESS
1 Peter 1–2:3 and 2 Peter1:1–11

In AD 64, just six years before the destruction of Jerusalem by the armies of Titus, Rome herself suffered a devastating fire. Large sections of the city were burned while, as the saying has it, Nero fiddled. If he had done little to prevent it, he did even less to put it out. If his tenure as emperor was to be secure following the fire, he must find someone to blame for this tragedy. So a small Jewish sect was blamed, whom the emperor Claudius some sixteen years earlier had sent packing from the capital for supposedly causing riots with other Jews over someone called "Chrestus"![1] They were the Christians of Rome.

Nero's persecution of the Christians would be followed by further persecutions that would go on sporadically until AD 313, following the Edict of Milan enacted by Constantine. Successive Roman emperors, like Domitian and Trajan, continued the persecution of the Christians mainly because their exclusive worship of Christ prevented them from giving the emperors or the pagan deities the worship that Rome demanded. Just as the Jews in their fierce monotheism were horrified by Roman standards in the temple precincts, so Christians in their devotion to Jesus Christ would never proclaim the emperor a deity; there was only one Lord and he was in heaven, not in Rome.

It is quite probable that Peter's two epistles were written in Rome after the great fire. This would fix the date of their writing some time soon after AD 64. This meant that they were written some fifteen years after the Council of Jerusalem, which was Peter's last appearance in the book of Acts. What had Peter been doing in the intervening years? Fifteen years is a long period of time. During this time Judea had become increasingly restless, until it broke into a full-scale rebellion against Rome in AD 68. Perhaps Peter had spent his time outside of Judea, going between Jerusalem, Antioch – of which he was the first bishop – and the provinces of Asia in present day Turkey.

These provinces which Peter addressed in his first epistle, namely Galatia, Cappadocia, Pontus and Bithynia, all lay to the north of Antioch and would have formed a natural missionary hinterland to which Peter may have personally travelled. Although Paul had spent time in Galatia, he had not been further north to Cappadocia and Pontus, which bordered the Black Sea. Whatever Peter may have done in the intervening fifteen years, it seems that he was in Rome (which he calls in his first epistle, Babylon) around AD 64.[2] John Mark was with him. He was Peter's close associate, although previously he had been spurned by Paul, who felt him to be unreliable.[3] However unreliable John Mark was in Paul's eyes, he was nevertheless to write down the record of Peter's account of the ministry of Jesus, and publish it first in Rome as the Gospel according to Mark. It was a racy account of the life of Jesus for the citizens of Rome! And it has lost none of its pace and immediacy with the passing of years.

So in this last stage of Peter's life before his martyrdom, which took place during the waves of persecution that now swept over the Christian communities in the Roman Empire, we find Peter a relatively old man, giving instruction to the faith communities which he had probably played a part in founding. Peter addresses them twice as "strangers" in the world.[4] Curiously, the Greek word for stranger or exile is *paroikia*, from which we get our word parish. So the original concept in naming a local Christian community "parish" was to remind the people there that they were a group of Christians exiled in a place journeying to heaven; this gives a whole new meaning to the idea of parishioner! But in one of those ironic reversal of meanings that can take place over time, parish or parishioner now means something or someone who is either a settled member of a community (parishioner) or an historically defined area (parish), because the parish system was set up in England by Archbishop Theodore over a thousand years ago, in the seventh century AD! So what was meant to describe something passing and pilgrim-like, by a strange transmutation of history, has come to mean something or someone who is comfortably settled in existence in the here and now. But when Peter looked out from Rome in AD 64 he saw nothing but an unsettled present and a certain future, and this is very much the flavour of his epistles.

The instruction that Peter gave to these scattered communities was to help them become what they were called to be; that is, holy —or fully human, fully equipped, able to suffer in the present in their imitation of Christ who suffered for them once for all, submissive to government and to one another, attractive to the onlooker, confident of the future and prepared to defend their faith from the corrosion of false teaching. What follows in the final section of this book is a presentation of this unique blend of teaching, which was Peter's for the church both then and now. He probably would be surprised to see, two thousand years on, the church still waiting today for the return of the Lord, but he would not have been surprised to learn that his teaching is as much needed now around the world as it was then. In this, the first of these final five chapters, we shall look at God's provision for our holy living or, as I put it in the first of this trilogy, the quest to become fully human.[5] To do this we will use the opening chapters of his two epistles.

A SURE DESTINY

If we are correct in putting the writing of the first of Peter's epistles at or around AD 64, with the second epistle written by Peter to a similar collection of churches a few years later (and we shall return briefly to the question of authorship when we consider 2 Peter), then it is worth considering the events that may have shaped his consciousness at the time of his writing. For surely the expression of our theology is in part shaped by the times in which we write —especially if you are writing advice to small Christian communities in far off parts of the Roman Empire at a time of great danger. Peter would either himself have witnessed or heard about the conflagration that engulfed large parts of the city of Rome. And if so, it is unsurprising that refining fire should be mentioned in his teaching about a new heaven and a new earth, as well as being shown to be the means of strengthening our faith.[6] For it was fire that destroyed the old city before a new one could be built.

Equally, since persecution of Christians would have begun again in Rome soon after the fire in the city, as well as in far flung parts of the Empire, it is not surprising to see that the theme of undergoing unjust suffering as a result of persecution is one of the major themes of the epistle. Christians were easy targets wherever they were, because of their unwillingness to toe the line or worship the emperor. And Nero was at a point in his reign when he needed all the adulation he could get. Judea was descending into civil war and outright rebellion against Rome, as recorded by the Jewish turncoat historian Josephus. The merchant classes were alienated because of the high cost of rebuilding Rome. A costly revolt led by a warrior-woman called Boudica, in far off Britain, had also strained the imperial coffers! But Peter's sights were on a heavenly city that could not be destroyed, and of this he wrote, "...In his great mercy he has given us new birth into a living hope through the resurrection of Jesus Christ from the dead, and into an inheritance that can never perish, spoil or fade — kept in heaven for you, who through faith are shielded by God's power until the coming of the salvation that is ready to be revealed in the last time."[7] It is quite clear that the final destiny of the Christian was uppermost in his mind, in a way that is not generally the case nowadays. The reason for this was that it contrasted with the uncertainty of the present.

As with Paul, so with Peter: hope dominated their Christian thinking! Paul, writing to the self-same Roman Christians some six or seven years earlier – amongst whom Peter must now have been living – said, "For in this hope we were saved. But hope that is seen is no hope at all. Who hopes for what he already has? But if we hope for what we do not yet have, we wait for it patiently."[8] As Peter taught, it is a living hope based on the resurrection, of which he was a witness on numerous occasions, and which looked forward to the inheritance which is kept in heaven for every disciple. Paul's great teaching in Romans chapter eight explains that we can never expect bliss in this life; that must come later. Here we may experience trouble, hardship, persecution, famine, nakedness, danger or sword, but none of these will separate the believer from the love of God. Such perils would have been all too familiar to those to whom Peter and Paul ministered.

But because of the difficulty of living as a Christian in a world which, Peter later says, is subject to all the forces of corruption from which we need to escape,[9] he begins his teaching in this, his earlier epistle, with a call to look heavenwards. This is the destiny to which we are called! It is commonly said that we can be so heavenly minded that we are of no earthly good, but in fact that need not be true; the reverse could be, that is to say we may be so earthly minded that we are of no heavenly good! A notable example of the heavenly minded being of great earthly good was the Victorian reformer Shaftesbury, who said of the second coming that scarcely a half hour passed without him being conscious of the return of Christ, and that the effect of this was to spur him in his endeavours to improve conditions in the factories for minors and others. Equally, it was the Puritan Richard Baxter who in his book *The Saints' Everlasting Rest* wrote of the necessity of meditating on the reality both of heaven and the judgement seat of Christ, in order to put our discipleship in proper perspective.

So Peter begins where we might, in our society of ease in the West, have ended, namely in directing his readers to their great living hope based on the resurrection of Jesus, of which he was one of the chief witnesses. It is this inheritance, which is kept in heaven and will be revealed, which was the lodestar of their first century faith, and which enabled them, in part, to face the trials of persecution as well as the uncertainties of their earthly existence.

It seems like a provable formula, arising from Christian history, that the greater the uncertainty of life in the present the more the certainty of heaven is marked, and the greater the certainty of life in the here and now, the more shadowy the hope of heaven becomes. Whereas in Peter's day the believers were anything but comfortable with the times in which they lived, we in the West are now, for the most part, so comfortable in our world today that many are uncertain whether an inheritance in heaven can really be an improvement! At any rate, Peter's first epistle to the scattered Christian communities in the provinces of Asia, who knew themselves to be strangers in this world and vulnerable to persecution, begins, as we noticed above, with that wonderful affirmation of the eventual outcome of their faith, including the assurance of, "...an inheritance that can never perish, spoil or fade —kept in heaven for you...."[10] This inheritance is kept in heaven for every believer by God's power, which has been once and for all demonstrated by the resurrection of Jesus from the dead, which Peter himself had the privilege of witnessing on the first Easter day. Not surprisingly, the thought of this incorruptible inheritance in heaven moves Peter to consider the outcome of such a confidence, namely joy, faith and love.

JOY, FAITH AND LOVE

It is one of the paradoxes of Christian living that hardship can produce the exact opposite of what you would expect. Faced by trials, persecution and uncertainty, you might have expected that the Christians then, in the first century AD, would have been depressed, timorous and fearful. Of course, from reading these early Christian documents, we know better. Peter said that they exulted in their hope. Equally, I can recall Christians whose radiant faith in trials is testimony to the same unwavering faith.

I think of an elderly Christian widow, Mabel, whose husband had suddenly died some years earlier. Living in council accommodation in south London, she had been mugged by a youth while returning to her flat. When I visited her she was bruised and battered on her face and arm, but she was full of gratitude for her deliverance from anything worse, and irrepressibly joyful in her faith! She was a modern example of the kind of thing that Peter wrote about when he said, "In this you greatly rejoice, though now for a little while you may have had to suffer grief in all kinds of trials. These have come so that your faith – of greater worth than gold, which perishes even though refined by fire – may be proved genuine and may result in praise, glory and honour when Jesus Christ is revealed."[11] The ground of their rejoicing was the living hope, the incorruptible inheritance, and the coming salvation. In these things they exulted, despite the trials that were coming upon them.

Not only did these trials not quench their rejoicing —for, as Peter goes on to say, they are "...filled with an inexpressible and glorious joy"[12] but they could look at the trials they faced as opportunities for the strengthening of their faith. Just as gold is purified through fire, so their faith was proved through trials. If our world view is that trials of all kinds are bound to come, and that we are bound to be faced with one kind of problem or another, then we will not be too surprised that they do lie in our path. Moreover, we will regard these things as opportunities for proving our faith and seeing fruits of the Spirit grow in us as a result. What is unrealistic is to think that we will not face many or any kinds of trials. The effect of thinking that, in some way, we are immune from the proving ground of trials is to wonder, when they do come along, whether God does not truly care for us —when, in fact, they are the means of testing both our faith in him and our love for him. So let us start from the premise that life is difficult, and that we will face all kinds of trials, and we shall be in a far more healthy position.

The way of facing trials, says Peter, is to rejoice in what **cannot** be taken away, to see these selfsame trials as the testing place of our faith, and finally to affirm our love for him in them. What Peter must have thought remarkable was the love that these Christians felt for Jesus although they had never met him. Peter, by contrast, loved Jesus as he had protested at the Sea of Galilee after the resurrection, but did so having known Jesus intimately for three years previously, sharing extraordinary experiences with him.

You cannot help but sense a slight marvelling in Peter's statement, "Though you have not seen him, you love him." It was, of course, through the work of the Holy Spirit that such love was possible; who, as Peter taught in vv. 10–12, inspired the authors of the Old Testament to predict the redemptive sufferings of Christ for them. To know the reality of the Messianic age was the greatest privilege. Many in late Judaism had longed for it, but it had been revealed to Christians through Spirit–inspired preaching.

So trials would come but joy, faith and love could be the product of fruitfully facing them. But, as Peter goes on to say, the chief aim of God in their lives was their holiness or, as I argued elsewhere, the call to become fully human.

THE CALL TO HOLINESS

The Scottish minister Robert Murray McCheyne was once asked what the greatest need of his congregation was. He replied that their greatest need was **his** holiness. It was a reply which was both pious and perceptive. Today we might well be tempted to reply differently, and say their need is for us, if we are a minister or a pastor, to be a brilliant expositor of the Bible, to be a skilled enabler of others, to be a charismatic and visionary leader, or to be an efficient manager. All of those are useful, but I dare to say not essential; but holiness, in its truest sense, is. In my book entitled *Becoming Fully Human* I suggest a description of holiness. To be holy is to be like Jesus, who is the perfect human, so to be holy is to be fully human in the way that Jesus was. That makes holiness an all-encompassing prospect, touching every aspect of living. To help us to be that "fully human" person, we need the power and guidance of the word of God. As Peter wonderfully says, "For you have been born again, not of perishable seed, but of imperishable, through the living and enduring word of God. For.....the word of the Lord stands for ever."[13]   Without the help of the word and the Spirit we are on a hiding to nothing!

Irenaeus, one of my favourite Patristic theologians, wrote in the first half of the second century, "The glory of God is a man fully alive." The apostle Paul would have agreed whole-heartedly. He wrote in a seminal passage in Romans, "For what the law was powerless to do in that it was weakened by the sinful nature, **God did** by sending his own Son in the likeness of sinful man to be a sin offering. And so he condemned sin in sinful man, in order that the righteous requirements of the law might be fully met in us, who do not live according to the sinful nature [flesh] but according to the Spirit."[14] Likewise, as Peter explains so clearly in his opening sentences of his first epistle, it is only through the sacrificial death of Jesus or, "...the precious blood of Christ"[15] that such a thing is possible. Irenaeus again wrote, "Christ became what we are in order that we might become what he is." At the heart of Christian vocation is this call to holiness, to become like him, for it is a call to become like God, having been made like him. So Peter puts it, quoting the Old Testament, "Be holy, because I am holy."[16]

As Peter makes clear here, holiness involves a combination of things: a realisation of our destiny: "...set your hope fully on the grace to be given you when Jesus Christ is revealed",[17] girding up our minds so that they are focussed both on the objectives and resources of our call, not conforming to a previous way of life which we have left behind, and purifying our lives through obedience.[18] These will be the means to this overall objective of becoming what God has made us — which is holy! Nor need this holiness be unattractive or prohibitive, but something beautiful and lively which manifests the presence of God. Indeed it was this holiness in Christians which eventually proved the undoing of the imperial cult, undermining the previous religion of Rome. Edward Gibbon, in his famous if now little read, *Decline and Fall of the Roman Empire*, wrote that the "pure morals of the Christians" was the fourth of five reasons for why Christianity overtook the established religious practice of Rome. Another was the "doctrine of a future life."[19] It is therefore no surprise to see that these are twin themes of Peter's opening chapter in his first epistle. The holiness to which Peter called the early Christians was not only distinctive but also was attractive. Holiness is supposed to help us to glimpse God, as the writer to the Hebrews showed, rather than to either camouflage or obscure him by a host of rules. It seems that both licence and legalism serve to hide God, whereas the love of God and others reveal his presence and reality. It is this love for God and for others which Peter extols as the outcome of truly purifying ourselves.[20]

There is no doubt that Peter made this theme of a call to holiness a central one in his writing. Not only does he begin his first epistle with it, but the second letter also begins on a similar note. Once again, grace and effort are the two sides of the discipleship coin! There is no concept of cheap grace here, but rather a combination of God's grace with our effort, which is the formula Peter advances.

MAKE EVERY EFFORT

The first few paragraphs of Peter's second letter are not dissimilar in content to the opening chapter of his first epistle. Although there has been considerable doubt expressed as to whether this epistle was in fact written by Peter, there seems sufficient evidence, both of style and content, in both epistles, as well as personal reminiscence by Peter (see his recollection of the transfiguration in 1:16–18), to make the case that Peter did either dictate or write the second epistle bearing his name, too. As well as that, we can be sure that the early church, in its formulation of the canon of Scripture, took much care in excluding forgeries or works of uncertain provenance. However, it is fair to say that 2 Peter was one of the New Testament epistles, along with Jude, 3 John and others, which were only included much later in the New Testament canon. Neither of the letters of Peter, nor that of James, etc., were included in a compilation of scriptures called the Muratorian Canon. J.N.D. Kelly noted that there was a long, tough struggle for 2 Peter to win acceptance. In the Western church, notwithstanding the illustrious name it bore, it seems to have been relatively unknown amongst the Early Fathers, or at any rate ignored until the second half of the fourth century, and even then Jerome reported that many had discarded it because of its stylistic divergence from 1 Peter. However, a clear connection of subject can be drawn between different parts of each epistle; for instance, between 2 Peter 1:3–11 and the opening teaching of the first epistle.

There is a plain threefold argument in the opening teaching of 2 Peter, after the initial greeting. Each stage of this unfolding argument is presented in the three developing paragraphs. The first concerns the call of God to share in the promise he has given his people. The second stage is the need to make the most of this calling by adding qualities of discipleship which will keep us from being unfruitful. And the third stage of the argument is that the addition of these qualities to our divine calling will only make the outcome more certain: "...a rich welcome into the eternal kingdom of our Lord and Saviour Jesus Christ."[21] We shall look briefly at each in turn.

These opening verses of the argument remind me of a human embryo, or a seed. In both, everything is present, in terms of genetic information, for the proper development of their life form. In the case of the embryo, provided stable conditions for development are maintained within the womb, then the embryo will develop into a fully functioning child. Equally, if a seed is planted in the right conditions, it too will germinate and develop; so, too, with the God given gift of spiritual life. The opening verse of this argument could not be more encouraging and complete: "His divine power has given us everything we need for life and godliness through our knowledge of him who called us by his own glory and goodness."[22] Here is the divine seed implanted in any who will receive it, through which a whole new life is possible. And consider again how similar this is to the statement in Peter's first epistle that we noticed above: "For you have been born again, not of perishable seed, but of imperishable, through the living and enduring word of God"[23]

The word is the means whereby everything we need is given for life and godliness. This word of promise, as Peter teaches in his second letter, enables two things: participation in the divine nature, and escape from the corruption of the world brought about by evil desires.[24] God's power, expressed through his word, brings this double benefit. Once again, we are back to the observation of Ireneaus that, "Christ became what we are in order that we might become what he is."

But it does not end there. For a child to become a mature person there are many struggles to face; for a seed to become a fruitful plant there are many dangers to overcome. Likewise, for any disciple to participate in the divine nature and escape corruption there is much to do. So Peter gives a breathtaking summary of the disciplines that we must adopt if we are to realise our potential. The armoury of Christian development is paraded: goodness, knowledge, self-control, perseverance, godliness, brotherly kindness, and love. "For if you possess these qualities in increasing measure", Peter teaches, you will not be "ineffective" and "unproductive".[25] These qualities are the tools for the job; without them the potential described earlier will not be realised. Once again, this list of qualities is an echo of the earlier encouragement in the first epistle, "Now that you have purified yourselves by obeying the truth so that you have a sincere love for your brothers, love one another deeply, from the heart."[26] Peter put a high premium on brotherly love. Through it, productive living and ministry will follow.

Peter's teaching in these opening chapters of both his epistles could not be more instructive for the Christian leader. For the Christian leader to be both productive and effective she or he has only to follow the pithy advice of Peter, gleaned from a lifetime's experience of discipleship, and forged in the fire of his own peculiar trials, which we have looked at earlier. In the opening teaching of both epistles, as we have seen, he is providing reassurance for Christian communities facing difficult times. In the context of these trials, Peter encourages his readers to look beyond the present troubles to their glorious and eternal destiny and to understand that their trials are not without purpose (the proving of their faith). In this teaching, Peter equips the church for handling their present experience, which is a vital task of any leader. Secondly, in these two opening chapters, Peter shows that although they have been given the potential for their new life, being born into it by the imperishable seed, they must still aim at holiness, both because that is their destiny and for that Christ died.[27] Likewise, Peter says at the opening of his second epistle, "His divine power has given us everything we need..." but, nevertheless, "...make every effort...." From his own experience, both in Gethsemane and in the high priest's courtyard, he is instructing churches to keep in mind their eternal destiny at times of trial, and to be assured that, although God's divine power is available and effective, they must still make every effort to add to their lives qualities which will keep them from being unproductive or ineffective. To provide such encouragement and vision is a vital part of leadership, setting the difficulties of the present in the context of the whole, to draw from others the will to persevere. It is instruction informed by both personal suffering and unqualified hope.

Finally, Peter argues that, "If you do these things", not only will you confirm your own calling, but also, "...you will never fall."[28] The outcome is rich indeed but, as with so many other

219

things, it involves taking the wonderful potential offered, "...in his very great and precious promises", and working them out fruitfully with the tools of discipline given to us. Peter knew this well in his own life; he also knew that such a process was inescapable if the church was to be the attractive beacon it was created to be. It is to this subject that we must now turn.

17

AN ATTRACTIVE CHURCH

1 Peter 2:4–12; 3:8–15a; 4:7–11; 5:1–11

It was the influential writer and church leader Lesslie Newbigin who reminded us that it is people who live by the good news that make it credible, and that, rather than writing a book, Jesus formed a community. And William Temple famously made the point that the church exists for those outside it. Though there are people with a particular calling to be evangelists, there is a vital sense in which the church community collectively preaches the gospel, both in its relationships and in the message the church conveys. Those perceptions expressed by Newbigin and Temple continue to reverberate down the years. Both contain true insights: the church must be a community; and it exists for people other than its own members, in that it has a gospel to make known to all mankind. The need to belong to a community, in an age in which many geographical communities are being replaced by other networks, is as strong as ever, but the communities that people now join are determined by a matrix of interests.

If this is true, then we are confronted by the question: how are we to be the church or that community for today? Peter gives us some vital insights into what it means to be church, or the people of God, in any age.

JOINING THE COMMUNITY
1 Peter 2:1–10

It is one of the delights of living in the West Country that here, as elsewhere in the British countryside, many of our fields are surrounded by drystone walls. Constructed of local materials, in our case honey coloured stone, they provide barriers which are totally in keeping with the environment. They look beautiful and they do the job of keeping animals in, and forming a boundary to land. The art of building a drystone wall without any infilling cement or mortar is a greatly admired rural skill. It requires the ability to look at a heap of stones with a discerning eye and see how they could fit together. Only a hammer can be used to knock off a corner, the better to fit them together. It is a skill not much different from being a pastor! Rather than being confronted by a heap of stones, you are met by a pile of what Peter calls "living stones" – people – who need to be built together into a "spiritual house". I find it helpful to think of this in terms of a beautiful drystone wall which used to be just a heap of rubble! And hopefully the use of a "spiritual hammer" is rare!

The way of joining the community of the church is simply stated by Peter: "...come to him, the living Stone —rejected by men but chosen by God and precious to him...."[1] The only criterion for being part of this living community, compared by Peter to a spiritual building, is to come to Jesus —the Stone that was rejected by Israel but has become the cornerstone of the new Israel. Peter himself witnessed that rejection on many occasions, not least in the trial and handing over of Jesus to the Roman authority for execution, as well as in the later refusals of the high priest and the Sanhedrin to accept that Jesus, whom they had condemned, was the Christ.[2] But if we come to Jesus with faith, then we become part of this spiritual community.

The process of how people join the Christian community has been well researched in recent years. It is often a process of belonging, believing and then behaving. That is why we do not say, for instance, at the door of the Nag's Head, or the ancient medieval "church" building, or the school hall, or wherever your church community happens to meet, that you must behave properly before you can become part of us; nor that you must believe certain things before you can enter. NO! Rather we say, "We welcome you to belong with us here since we are here for your benefit, and we will try and explain what we believe, not just with words but with our lives, too." Change will follow on from believing, just as surely as day follows night. For that, surely, is the argument of the New Testament (see Romans 5–8). But joining the community is all about coming to him.

It is not surprising that Peter, in this epistle, favoured all this "rock talk"; after all, Jesus gave him the name Cephas, which means rock and, as we saw earlier, despite all his failure. He was called to be the rock upon which the early church would be built. The master builder had a discerning eye as to where Peter would fit into the edifice, even if his setting in the building would involve a couple or three sharp taps with the hammer to knock off any awkward excrescences.

Joining this community formed around Jesus is a simple description of being church. Or, to put it the other way round, church is wherever Jesus is active drawing people around him in community. Peter then gives us a veritable cascade of descriptions for this new community: the church is a chosen race —in fact, the new chosen race, inheriting all the privileges of the old one and replacing it as the means of transforming the human race; a royal priesthood, for what the descendants of Aaron were to Israel the church is now to be to the world; a dedicated nation, which is a nation to include all ethnic groups on equal terms, a reversal of Babel; and, finally, a people claimed by God, that is brought together as a people by his infinite grace, having previously had no defining characteristics except belonging to the human family. The function of the church is twofold: to offer, "...spiritual sacrifices acceptable to God through Jesus Christ";[3] and to, "...declare the praises of him who called you out of darkness into his wonderful light."[4] If the first calling means offering sacrificial service to the world, the second is the prophetic and evangelistic task of making known the saving power of God, and especially in our worship together.

What an extraordinary description that is! You might think that the church, in order to fulfil its calling, would need to be a powerful institution, but in fact its authentic vocation is to be a pilgrim people who are like aliens in a foreign land. The church is called to travel light.

TRAVELLING LIGHT

There is a thread running through the whole story of the people of God, which is that they were always intended to be a pilgrim people, and once again Peter reminds his readers of this fact: "Dear friends, I urge you, as aliens (*paroikos*) and strangers (*parepidemos*) in the world, to abstain from sinful desires, which war against your soul."[5] The origins of pilgrimage lie in the call God gave to the father of all God's people, Abraham. The Israelites were the descendants of this wandering Aramaean.[6] The new Israel consisted of the body of Christ, the people called into being by Jesus, who also had nowhere to lay his head.

But, just as in the old covenant so in the new covenant, there is a tendency to replace the provisional way of life for God's people on earth with a more settled and secure existence. Originally, God gave his people a tabernacle in which to worship him, but they wanted a temple.[7] Originally, God gave his people God-appointed leaders and prophets to rule over them, but they wanted an established monarchy, like that of other countries.[8] Originally, God gave them three great festivals of Passover, Firstfruits and Tabernacles, in which every male Jew was to journey to Jerusalem in order to recall their exodus and journeying in the wilderness, but later they wanted a shrine on every hilltop. In fact, throughout the old covenant we can see that there was a tendency to move on from being the pilgrim people of God, bearing the salvation of the world, to being indistinguishable from other peoples —with a temple, a monarchy and a similar cult. It was against such a movement that the prophets continuously inveighed with words like those of Jeremiah, who lamented their lost first love:

> "I remember the devotion of your youth,
>   how as a bride you loved me
> and followed me through the desert,
>   through a land not sown.
> Israel was holy to the LORD,
>   the firstfruits of his harvest;
> all who devoured her were held guilty,
>   and disaster overtook them"

But,

> "My people have committed two sins:
>   They have forsaken me,
>   the spring of living water,
>   and have dug their cisterns,
> broken cisterns that cannot hold water."[9]

Israel had spurned its early days of pilgrimage for broken cisterns that brought no refreshment either to her or others. At the last, both monarchy and temple would find their literal end and fulfilment in the Messiah. Ironically, the pilgrim vocation of God's people would endure, but their hope of finding satisfaction in human institutions, albeit permitted by God, would fade. The reason for this is that in founding these institutions they gradually shifted their confidence from being in the God who called them to be pilgrims, to having confidence in the institutions themselves, which they had created to cushion their pilgrimage. In the end, those very institutions, in which they had come to place their trust, became a snare and pitfall. So the monarchy was overthrown by the Babylonians, never to be replaced, and the three temples were successively replaced or destroyed.

But the call to pilgrimage endured as an essential and irreplaceable part of the call. Peter tells his readers that they should live as pilgrims and sojourners, not looking for stability here. It is a calling which is hard to fulfil precisely because everything in our "flesh" cries out against it. Our flesh desires permanence rather pilgrimage, pleasure rather than sacrifice, and stability rather than change. The church has found it hard to travel light, to live as pilgrims and sojourners in the world, but there can be little doubt that such a way of life is the one to which God's people are called.

The people of God would be all the more attractive if they lived "...such good lives among the pagans...", that they, "...may see your good deeds and glorify God on the day he visits us." Too often, the church has sought to impress with its good words, neglecting the good deeds, but latterly perhaps we are rediscovering that the word must be incarnated in flesh; love must be expressed in good deeds, and people need to see as well as to hear. The church's attractiveness lies in travelling light and toiling hard in the production of those good deeds which will speak louder than words. The words should be provoked by the good deeds, as Peter teaches us.

THE PROVOCATIVE CHURCH
1 Peter 3:8–16

In the next chapter we will look at another of the chief themes of Peter's teaching about suffering and submission which further illustrates his teaching about how to be church. But in this section he returns to the issue of how relationships in the church should beg the question of what we believe. In his stimulating book *The Provocative Church*, Graham Tomlin opens the issue of how the church can provoke questions of interest in the Christian faith. Using a quotation from Pascal who said, "Make it attractive, make good men [i.e. men and women of goodwill] wish it were true and then show them that it is", Tomlin shows the need of the church to provoke questions about Jesus by the quality of our corporate life together. Too often in the past the church has assumed knowledge where there is none, offering an experience of church which is not child friendly, comfortable or accessible, nor well presented; it has presented a message in authoritarian language, has lacked any sense of mystery or awe,

226

and has displayed little semblance of harmonious community. One is reminded of the character David, in Nick Hornby's *How to be Good*, who has an experience of attending a church that is dreadfully dreary.[10] A major feature of the service is a notice about a bring and buy sale, and a sense of extreme dullness is extremely cleverly depicted. Many will have suffered such unhappy experiences, and have felt the absence of any real sense of the presence of the living God, still less any expectation that he might move in power.

Small wonder, then, that many in Western societies are disinclined to look to the historic churches with real questions about the Christian faith. Tomlin invites ministers to ask themselves the penetrating question: if they did not *have* to go to the church they lead, would they still choose to attend there? If not, it is hardly likely to be of much help to others!

A "provocative" church is one which raises questions in the mind of the onlooker —not concerning how one might tolerate something deadly dull, rather the opposite! Peter encourages the scattered Christian communities to whom he is writing to "...live in harmony with one another; be sympathetic, love as brothers, be compassionate and humble. Do not repay evil with evil or insult with insult, but with blessing, because to this you were called so that you may inherit a blessing." [11] A community of people with this quality evident in their relationships would be bound to raise questions in the onlooker's mind, even if those questions were initially unspoken. Equally, as Tomlin points out, church situations which lead people to expect transforming experiences, and that are marked by good teaching and a real fellowship, are attractive, and people want to invite others along.[12]

The quality of our corporate life together is the touchstone of whether we live by what we teach and say. As James, Peter's fellow early church leader, says in his epistle, "Do not merely listen to the word, and so deceive yourselves. Do what it says."[13] Peter would have given a hefty "amen" to that.

If this quality of relationship which Peter calls for exists in our churches, then the questions of enquiry should flow fast. Then it is essential that we follow the precept, "But in your hearts set apart Christ as Lord. Always be prepared to give an answer to everyone who asks you to give the reason for the hope that you have. But do this with gentleness and respect."[14]

Church leaders should therefore aim at church health which should in turn produce church growth. They should aim at ensuring a quality of life together which elicits questions, which then can be answered —with the understanding that one volunteered question that has been provoked by the life of the church is better than hundreds of words addressed to questions that no one is asking! What questions is our church provoking?

COMMUNITY LIFE
1 Peter 4:7–11

Peter proceeds to make four points about the community life of the church in the light of what he thought would be their final days. The fact that the final days have gone on for two thousand more years in no way invalidates the truth of his advice to these early Christian communities. It just means that we have longer to put these instructions into practice.

His first piece of advice (or even command) to them was that they should be prayerful. "Therefore be clear minded and self-controlled so that you can pray", he said. Prayer benefits from clarity of mind and spiritual perception, as well as from the self-discipline or church discipline to do it. As the wayside pulpit slogan says, "Seven prayer-less days makes one weak!" In recent years there has been renewed appreciation of the importance of prayer that is not simply to "twist God's arm" to support our worthy church programmes, but to listen and align our wills with his desires. So it is common for churches to have intercession groups alongside the other corporate groupings for prayer. More churches are committing to prayer vigils, or 24/7 prayer-athons, the prayer equivalent of running full or half-marathons. The church overseas, especially in Africa and Asia, shames our paltry attempts in the UK to pray, with their prayer mountains on which church members give themselves to pray day and night. The African church has given us their acrostic, PUSH: that is, "pray until something happens"! In our technological society it is all too easy to depend on method, and allow that to replace the prayer and fasting which often lies at the root of any work of God. Fraser of the Lisu was one of many missionaries who have stressed the crucial importance of intercession, as well as the need to devote one's best energies to it. He likened it to the way a businessman might invest in an unlimited supply of goods which will be to supply a virtually limitless need. The need is amongst those whose harrassed and helpless condition can be changed with the gospel, given perseverance and prayer on the part of Christians.[15]

Peter encourages us to remain both clear minded and self disciplined so that we might pray, by which human need and God's grace may be brought together.

Secondly, and alongside prayer, Peter places the importance of love. It is a theme that Peter cannot keep away from for long. Earlier in the epistle he has written, "Love one another deeply, from the heart," or, as some manuscripts have it, "from a pure heart."[16] Many commentators have noted that this theme is very prevalent in Peter's, Paul's and John's writings, and reflects the commandment that Jesus gave the disciples that they should, "...Love each other as I have loved you."[17] In the same way, Paul says to the Galatian Christians, "The only thing that counts is faith expressing itself through love."[18] The reason for loving each other deeply is that love covers a multitude of sins. In my student days (and my wife might say now still), I was never an assiduous bed maker; admittedly, the advent of the duvet made nurses' corners a thing of the past, but a well drawn-up bedspread could nevertheless cover a multitude of wrinkles or creases! Equally, love in the fellowship can cover a multitude of niggling or irritating sins, foibles or idiosyncrasies, which otherwise might be a cause of division. Love is therefore like a blanket or cover which hides a multitude of indiscretions.

229

Thirdly, Peter almost suggests that the most important person on your church staff team is the cook! No, he does not actually! —but he does draws attention to the importance of hospitality. "Offer hospitality to one other without grumbling."[19] Hospitality can be either offered in a home or in church premises. There is no doubt that the sharing of a meal creates community, and a community is an excellent place for the claims of Christianity to be considered. Undoubtedly the meal together and (invariably) the small group discussion are what those doing an *Alpha* course most appreciate; the talks generally get a lower mark in our church's end-of-course evaluation sheet than the discussion group and shared meal. But that is probably because they are given by me! But in a society in which shared meals are rarer than they used to be, and a real sense of community is at a premium, we cannot overemphasise the importance of eating together. One recent enquirer said at a local event in which the claims of Christianity were explained, "I cannot work it all out for myself; I need to belong to a group of people who believe and, however imperfectly, seek to follow Christ." Belonging to a group in which there is a shared spiritual journey is something that contemporary people can understand.

Lastly, Peter calls the church to be participative. Peter acknowledges, "Each one should use whatever gift he has received to serve others, faithfully administering God's grace in its varied forms."[20] This could not be a more succinct statement of how to be church. The teaching says that each has received a gift. These gifts are various and they are to be used faithfully for the purpose of serving others. If each church member were to follow this instruction, what a difference that would make. Too often the cry of churches is that most of the work done and the money given is from 20% of the membership, with the result either that exhaustion sets in or the overworked become unnatural wastage. An attractive church is one in which the ministry is shared, where responsibilities are assumed,[21] where the pastor does not look continually exhausted, and the elders or leaders are not looking for the first opportunity to escape. Not only does each have a gift but also, Peter teaches, God supplies the strength with which to use it. Then the reader might consider what is his or her gift, and how it is being put to use in the fellowship of the church. The successful deployment of people's gifts is largely the result of effective leadership. An attractive and provocative church will have certain qualities to its leadership.

FOLLOW MY LEADER
1 Peter 5:1–11

The Bible provides many different "pictures" of leadership. There is the helmsman steering the ship around dangers, guiding it to port. There is the shepherd with his flock, taking the sheep to pasture, seeking the lost, tending the injured, gathering the scattered and protecting them from marauders. There is the visionary, urging his people to possess God's future for themselves. There is the reconciler, bringing people together with various "axes to grind" and helping them to put their hands to a common task. There is the action manager, getting and applying human and other resources to a common objective. Each of these distinctive types of leadership requires special qualities, and one leader may be more suited to one role or style than another. Finding out and developing your own particular leadership style is a necessary part of maturing as a person.[22] However, if no-one is following then leadership is not being exercised. It is said that General Eisenhower, the Supreme Allied Commander in Europe at the time of D Day, would often demonstrate this to his officers. Taking a piece of string, he would show that people follow by seeing an example to follow. If one holds the string, it follows wherever the hand goes, but if one attempts to push the string, there is quite a different result! Here in this section, Peter chooses the pastoral model of leadership as the one to present to the "elders" or leaders of the church communities to whom he is writing. So he encourages them to be "...shepherds of God's flock that is under your care...."

231

This section of teaching, as we have earlier noted, recalls Peter's own experience. He introduces himself as a colleague, "a fellow-elder", who shares the same vocation as them; as a witness of Christ's sufferings, who knew first hand the cost to Jesus of purchasing this flock, and as one who will share in the glory to be revealed. Charles Cranfield has remarked on the way in which Peter exhibits a humble, gentle, intimate quality, without impetuosity or domination.[23] He encourages his fellow elders, conscious both of the difficulty and the privilege of their task. Their calling was to lead in such a way that they are willing overseers, not merely dutiful, sincere in their care and not greedy for material preferment, and leading through the authority of example rather than the exertion of office. On each of these leadership counts, so richly and well expressed by Peter, the church has habitually fallen down (and continues to do so). Too often there is a reversion to a form of leadership which is motivated either by money or (especially) power and status.

In our society, however, leadership by community figures, whether clergy, doctors, teachers or politicians, is open to great discouragement. As Graham Tomlin writes, "Denied the financial rewards of business or financial management, seldom thanked when they do well, they feel under constant suspicion, waiting for the ton of bricks to land on their heads when they make a mistake. You cannot build a society on suspicion and mistrust."[24] Perhaps the temptation to discouragement is exactly why Peter both introduces himself to the leaders as one who also will share in the glory to be revealed, and encourages his fellow elders to be mindful of the fact that, "...when the Chief Shepherd appears, you will receive the crown of glory that will never fade away."[25] Leaders must not be so wrapped up in the immediate task of pastoring or leading that its pains and difficulties cloud the prospect of a final glorious future. One eye must be on the grand finale.

Rob Parsons tells the moving story of a missionary who returned to New York after many years in the mission field. He had never before had a furlough. Saddened that he was not met by anyone (the more poignant as the US President,

Roosevelt, returned, at the same time, with a dramatic welcome) back at his hotel he cried out to the Lord. The Lord reminded him that his true homecoming was yet to happen![26]

Having briefly instructed the "young men" to be submissive (which command we shall look at in more detail when we come to the next chapter of the epistle), Peter gives to both groups some general instructions. They fall into three categories: a call to humility, a call to alertness and a call to perspective. Each quality is essential to leadership as it is in discipleship.

Humility was hard won by Peter, as we have seen. Moments like those at Caesarea Philippi, on the stormy Sea of Galilee, in the upper room, in the chief priest's courtyard, and on the shore of the lake after the resurrection of Jesus were like blows by a metal worker, beating out humility of heart. No wonder he writes, "Humble yourselves, therefore, under God's mighty hand, that he may lift you up in due time."[27] Anxiety, too, was to be cast onto God, for he cares. If leaders and church members treat each other with humility, and genuinely give their anxieties over to God rather than blame each other for them, then here is a recipe for an attractive church. That is not to say that all will be plain sailing as, "Your enemy the devil prowls around like a roaring lion looking for someone to devour."[28]

Leaders will find themselves in a context of spiritual warfare; it is part of the warp and weft of leadership in the church. There will be temptations to face, messages to give, issues to confront and weaknesses to defend —that is both personal weaknesses, and weak points in the relational network of the church, which may well have to be protected. These and many other things make up the spiritual warfare of church leadership. In this context it is therefore wise to have a strategy of strengthening yourself. During the last world war, military planners planned in rest. It was found that interspersing frequent rest periods of a few days quite frequently, when possible, enabled the troops to operate far more effectively than with continuous duty. There is a valid application for that in terms of church activity, even though, at a deeper level, no Christian is ever "off combat duty"!

Lastly, Peter urges the church and elders to keep perspective, with these majestic words: "And the God of all grace, who called you to his eternal glory in Christ, after you have suffered a little while, will himself restore you and make you strong, firm and steadfast."[29] The perspective is always the same in the New Testament —it is that the troubles of the *now* are nothing to be compared to the glory of the *not yet*. Hope does literally spring eternal, because God is in charge, and although there are many vicissitudes and trials along the way, the destiny is assured, and as the Psalmist says, "...rejoicing comes in the morning."[30]

So these qualities of humility, alertness to the devil's wiles, and perspective, are part of the framework in which discipleship is found, and they will help the church to remain attractive —even in a situation like that of the first century, when there was so much unjust suffering. It is to that theme of unjust suffering and its consequences that we must turn now, and it is probably the chief theme of Peter's first epistle.

18

SUFFERING AND SUBMISSION
1 Peter 1:2,18–21; 2:13–25; 3:1–7,17–22; 4:1–7,12–19: 5:1–11

Throughout Peter's first letter, the twin themes of suffering and submission intermingle: suffering, in relation to the persecution and unjust treatment that the Christians in these communities were facing; and submission, in connection with those relationships in which Christians found themselves — with state, employer, spouse and church leaders.

The theological quarry from which Peter took the ballast to steady these early disciples was the cross of Christ. If the motivating power for enduring unjust suffering comes through the patient example of Jesus' own unjust suffering, the power to enable submission to others comes also from the example of Jesus' humility in the passion and suffering on the cross, of which Peter himself was a witness.

In this chapter we shall look at these twin themes of unjust suffering and voluntary submission separately.

THE SUFFERINGS OF JESUS AND OUR SUFFERING

The overwhelming experience of the Christians in these dispersed communities through Asia Minor was one of vulnerability and danger. Strung out through this epistle is

Peter's awareness that to follow Jesus in the Roman world of the first century was to court difficulty and persecution. So Peter writes, "But even if you should suffer for what is right, you are blessed", or again, "For you have spent enough time in the past doing what pagans choose to do —living in debauchery, lust, drunkenness, orgies, carousing and detestable idolatry. They think it strange that you do not plunge with them into the same flood of dissipation, and they heap abuse on you."[1] So these Christians had at best to face the abuse and aggression of their neighbours whom they would not party with or, at worst, the full force of workplace or state persecution. This was the principal point of pressure in their lives. Naturally Peter, pastor as he was, gives them grounds for encouragement to maintain their Christian witness in such testing circumstances.

REDEMPTION

No sooner does this epistle open than we are made aware of the central place of the sufferings and cross of Christ. These dispersed Christians have been chosen by the Father, sanctified by the Spirit and sprinkled with the blood of Jesus.[2] Such language as "sprinkled with the blood of Jesus" can sound extremely strange to the modern mind, unacquainted as it is with the language of sacrifice, which is rooted in Old Testament traditions and fulfilled in Jesus. This particular phrase recalls both the consecration of Aaron and his descendants as priests in Israel upon whom blood was sprinkled, and the sacrifice which took place at the ratification of the covenant.[3] In both instances, consecration to a God-appointed task and the ratification of the covenant (made first with Abraham and then Moses at Sinai) involved a sacrifice. Likewise, the new covenant, in which forgiveness of sins and the gift of the Spirit are offered to those who will receive them through repentance and faith, is inaugurated and only made possible through the sacrifice of God's Son, Jesus. So this concept of "sprinkling" is one of personal involvement in which followers are redeemed and consecrated by this covenant sacrifice of Jesus. It is to the same concept of the purchasing and redeeming blood of Jesus that Peter returns in his subsequent call to holiness.

Again the idea of redemption is uppermost in Peter's mind when he writes, "For you know that it was not with perishable things such as silver or gold that you were redeemed from the empty way of life handed down to you from your forefathers, but with the precious blood of Christ, a lamb without blemish or defect. He was chosen before the creation of the world, but was revealed in these last times for your sake."[4] The theme of redemption has two meanings. The first meaning refers to the state or situation from which someone needs to be delivered, and the second meaning refers to the cost to another to do it. Restoration, a word with which we are more familiar than redemption, is not far from the idea of redemption.

In the recent popular UK television series "Restoration", a number of dilapidated but historic buildings are paraded in front of the viewer, from disused chapels to overgrown castles, for viewers to vote on which should win the possibility of restoration. In 2003, the Victorian Baths in Manchester won and they are being restored. Money is given or raised and the building is restored to its former glory. Likewise God has made it his business to redeem or restore the dilapidated state of human lives enslaved to what Peter calls, "...the empty way of life handed down to you from your forefathers."

This futility into which human life can easily fall is prevalent today where, in the West, we are so sated with materialism that there is a formidable loss of meaning and significance for many. Last year, my wife and I took my in-laws to a play called *Happy Days*, by Samuel Beckett. The popular British actress Felicity Kendal took the main part of Winnie. At first glance, and before booking, we thought that it would be an amusing evening, knowing some of the comic roles in which we have seen Felicity Kendal over the years. I should have known better! Samuel Beckett is not to be trifled with as a playwright. He chronicles the absurdity of living according to one's own lights. The entire play is spent with Winnie in a vice-like grip of a coiled plant into which she is gradually sinking. Her husband, Willie, is inconsequential, hardly ever properly seen, and of little use! Much of the early part of the play is spent with Winnie going through her handbag, the contents of which are trivial and unimportant. The play is a taste of the meaninglessness of living where there is no ultimate purpose. Living is just a string of inconsequential actions, without significance. This futility, from which we need to be redeemed, is all too common.

Peter teaches that we need to be redeemed from an empty way of life. And only restoration of meaning liberates us from the litany of the mundane.

Our contemporary world is full of many kinds of pain from which people need to be redeemed and freed. As well as the more obvious forms of physical suffering (not least AIDS) which afflict millions, in all parts of the world, there are increasing kinds of emotional pain. This category of suffering seems to be growing in our secular Western world, where human relationships so often suffer as a result of family breakdown, separation and isolation. Compared with some of the hideous pain caused by war and disease, such psychological anguish may seem less significant but, as Oliver James and others have pointed out, it is growing in the West by substantial proportions, with enormous social consequences.

One meaning of redemption is being lifted out of the pit. As the Psalmist says:

Praise the LORD, O my soul;
all my inmost being, praise his holy name.
Praise the LORD, O my soul,
and forget not all his benefits—
who forgives all your sins
and heals all your diseases,
who redeems your life from the pit
and crowns you with love and compassion,
who satisfies your desires with good things
so that your youth is renewed like the eagle's.[5]

The pit – or the empty way of living – can be read as a meta-phor for that general condition from which each needs to be redeemed. Peter uses a Greek word *mataios* to describe the emptiness, banality and meaninglessness of life prior to redemption. It is the same Greek word that is used thirteen times in the opening chapter of Ecclesiastes to denote the "vanity" referred to there.

If one theme of redemption is the mire from which we are taken, the other is the cost of that redemption. Peter makes it abundantly clear that it was inordinately costly. It is said that the ransom for Richard Coeur de Lion, the English crusading king taken hostage on his return from the Holy Land, nearly bankrupted England. The ransom of our souls by God, Peter teaches, was, "...the precious blood of Christ, a lamb without blemish or defect." It did not bankrupt God but it entailed the painful death of his Son. As Peter shows us, this was the timeless plan of God, in whose mind the sacrifice was known even before the creation of the world. That is a thought almost beyond thinking. If redemption is one of the themes that Peter draws out in considering the sufferings of Jesus, the other is that, in his own handling of unjust suffering, Jesus left us all a timeless example.

TO THIS YOU WERE CALLED

Peter has no comforting words anywhere in his first epistle for anyone in the Christian community who suffers for doing wrong; he repeatedly makes this clear.[6] But for any who suffer unjustly, and especially on account of their faith, there is a rich tradition of unjust suffering, which, as we have said, originates with Jesus himself. As Peter says, "But if you suffer for doing good and you endure it, this is commendable before God. To this you were called, because Christ suffered for you, leaving you an example, that you should follow in his steps."[7] Or again, in the following chapter, when writing about the characteristics of the Christian community, he says, "It is better, if it is God's will, to suffer for doing good than for doing evil. For Christ died for sins once for all, the righteous for the unrighteous, to bring you to God."[8]

As we have already seen, the dominant experience of many (probably mainly small and despised) churches in Asia Minor scattered through Pontus, Galatia, Cappadocia, Asia and Bithynia was the force of persecution from imperial Rome. Naturally, therefore, Peter takes them to the example of Jesus, whose redemptive sufferings were pre-eminently unjust. When Peter wrote, "...Christ suffered for you, leaving you an example...", the Greek word he employed for "example" is *hypogrammon*; it is of special significance, because in the whole of the New Testament this is its only appearance! The word is elsewhere used in Greek of the way children carefully copy writing set before them. Likewise, disciples need to imitate the example set by Jesus.[9] In particular, Peter holds before them the example of the patience of Jesus and his trust in the Father in the face of injustice. He was innocent (he committed no sin and no deceit was found in his mouth),[10] he was patient (when they hurled insults at him, he did not retaliate; when he suffered, he made no threats),[11] and he trusted in his Father (instead, he entrusted himself to him who judges justly.)[12] This combination of innocence, patience and trust was the pattern of the example that Jesus left others to follow who, like him, had been called to suffer unjustly. Here was the *hypogrammon* to follow, just like that child imitating letters on a Greek or Roman slate in a household classroom. The child would be commended for exact copying, and a Christian would be commended by his or her Lord, for following where Jesus had already been, so following in his steps. The cross is not only the way by which we are redeemed, but also inspiration concerning how to face injustice.

Does this mean that this is the only way in which a Christian may face unjust treatment? No, this is not the only model in the New Testament. There are times of legitimate complaint to authorities, as when Paul complained to them about his being incarcerated in the gaol at Philippi.[13] In our society we may use legal means to gain redress for injustice. But in an increasingly litigious society we do well to remember that our witness may be all the more powerful if it embodies the example of Jesus, who demonstrated innocence, patience and trust in the midst of his unfair and unjust treatment. And in situations where there is no easy redress because of the expense of legal action or the fear of unemployment, it may be right to be patient and trusting. However, if our actions would prevent the unjust treatment of others, then we may well have a duty to complain, "whistle-blow", and report to an authority or public body capable of getting redress. If that fails, it may even be necessary to mount a public campaign. Where the church is persecuted on account of her faith, and is attacked by the civic authorities, and where there is no likely redress, then, as has been instanced on so many occasions, Christians have no option but to follow in the steps of Jesus.

Finally, it is worth noting that Peter, although he is using the sufferings of Jesus as an example of how to face unjust suffering, is never content to leave it there without explaining the significance of the cross further. James Denny has pointed out that Peter customarily moves from the imitation of Jesus Christ to the centrality of his sacrifice in our place: the righteous for the unrighteous. Thus the exemplary death of Jesus does not stand in isolation from this central truth about his death atoning for sin.[14]

So Peter speaks of how, "He himself bore our sins in his body on the tree, so that we might die to sins and live for righteousness; by his wounds you have been healed"; and, "For Christ died for sins once for all, the righteous for the unrighteous, to bring you to God." The fact that after the second of these quotations Peter goes on to speak of the way in which Jesus "in the spirit" went on to preach to the spirits in prison from the time of Noah shows that, like Paul, he was occasionally hard to understand![15] When this "preaching tour" took place, who were the exact recipients of it, and for what purpose it was conducted, are all difficult questions to answer. But what it did show to Peter's readers, and this may well have comforted them in their persecution, is that nothing is outside the scope of the authority of Jesus, both past and present, and all are accountable to him.

As we survey Peter's teaching about the sufferings of Jesus and the cross, we see how Peter held together both the redemptive and exemplary character of Jesus' sufferings. As Tidball has rightly observed, Peter achieved a balanced presentation of the death of Jesus both as an example and as atonement, in a way that many other Christians since have not succeeded in doing.[16]

SUBMISSION

Alongside Peter's exhortation to keep the cross central to their believing and acting, there is another not unrelated exhortation to the believers in those scattered churches, namely to be submissive. In an age where such a concept is thought almost antediluvian, we must try to grasp what Peter means.

My first introduction to the word "submission" was as a boy in the context of wrestling, which used to be screened on late Saturday afternoon television. A successful hold in wrestling leading to the opposing wrestler's shoulders being pinned to the floor for a count of four would lead to a technical submission. Naturally, if you come to the meaning of a word, in this case submission, through such a context, then your ability to transpose the concept to a Christian's duty to either state, employer, husband or church leader will be somewhat strained. And in an age which places a high premium on independence and human rights, the thought of voluntarily yielding your obedience to someone or to some institution is very far from our modern mentality; and yet, in an unmistakeable way, Peter calls his readers, the Christian community, to submit in four areas of living: in relation to the state; the employer (or slave owner, if a slave); marriage; and the Christian community. We shall look at each in turn.

SUBMISSION TO THE STATE
1 Peter 2:13–17

Like Paul, Peter sees the state and its subservient authorities as being agents or ministers of God.[17] Paul says of the one in authority: "...he is God's servant to do you good."[18] The purpose of government ("the ruler") is depicted in similar terms: "...God's servant, an agent of wrath to bring punishment on the wrongdoer." So long as they do what they have been established for – namely the punishing of wrongdoing and the commendation of what is right – then the authorities are right to expect both the co-operation and the submission of the citizen to the laws of the state; but if they move to doing the opposite of their proper function, namely punishing those who do good and commending those who do evil, then they forfeit the right to submission and co-operation. But here in his teaching, Peter calls the Christians in the Roman Empire to submit to the emperor, who at that time was Nero, and who was beginning to persecute the church.

Presumably Peter must have thought the regime had not yet reached such a pitch of misgovernment that the Christians had no longer any duty to obey. Equally, the Christians were such a small and insignificant group in the empire that they had no means to change the way in which the emperor governed. In fact you could argue that through their willing submission to the empire, and the way in which they suffered persecution in the manner outlined by Peter here, they were able to change the empire in the long run more effectively than had they offered resistance to it. It is certainly one of the reasons given by Gibbon for the eventual victory of Christianity over paganism in his famous work *The Decline and Fall of the Roman Empire*.

However, in other situations Christians have felt it right either to take active steps as citizens to resist violently an evil state or to take part in civil disobedience when legitimate human rights have been curtailed.

The German Lutheran pastor Dietrich Bonhoeffer made this stance when, already himself imprisoned in Tegel prison, he took part in the plot against Hitler. Sadly, the plot failed; all the conspirators were executed in the final months of the war, even though the Reich was facing imminent defeat. If they had succeeded, the war might well have ended earlier, millions of lives would have been saved; and Bonhoeffer would have demanded that from the pulpits of all German Lutheran churches a confession would have been read of that church's guilt by acquiescence and silence in the face of both the Nazi terror and, above all, the fate of the Jews. As we know, terrible loss of life on all sides continued during the final year of the war. But this (albeit unsuccessful) act of resistance and defiance toward a dictator remains a classic example of God-fearing or Christian men and women taking legitimate action against an evil regime which had long since forfeited its right to govern. More recently, in the civil rights movement in the United States in the 1960s, in the campaign against apartheid in the 1960s and 1970s, and in the case of dissidents in the Soviet Union in the 1990s, there were movements of civil disobedience and non co-operation with either institutional racism or repressive governments. Nelson Mandela's defiance, and his long imprisonment on Robbin Island, was a classic case of such resistance.

At what point an authority or regime forfeits its right to co-operation from its citizens will be hard to discern. Sometimes, not to resist would imply complicity, but on the other hand to resist without good cause would be lawless; there is certainly a presumption that Christians ought to comply with the law of the land and co-operate with state agencies, unless this clearly conflicts with other biblical precepts.

It is clearly a New Testament principle of the greatest importance that the gospel imperative of witnessing to Jesus Christ and his saving power is a duty that ranks above submission to the state; that is evident both from the great commission and the willingness of the Christians to whom Peter wrote to accept martyrdom for the gospel's sake, if need be. So if a state seeks to muzzle Christians and prevent them speaking of the salvation available in Jesus, then Christians must, if need be, defy such a state in that matter, rather than submit to those of its decrees which forbid evangelism or the teaching of the Bible. There is evidence now of governments in the West, in the laudable pursuit of religious toleration, introducing legislation which may prevent the church from evangelising those of another faith (e.g. Islam) because the other faith regards such activity either as blasphemous or incitement to religious hatred. Such use of the law, although proposed with good intentions, is to be resisted.

SUBMISSION TO EMPLOYERS
1 Peter 2:18

Secondly, Peter calls slaves to submit to their masters. This should not be mistaken for approval of slavery as such. Once again, Christians were in no position to alter the institution of slavery. Slave rebellions ended in massive retribution, but the changing of society through the gradual infiltration of Christian values into it was going to be a more effective long term way of overturning this abuse, rather than a call to rebellion against slavery as a whole. So Peter gives a code of conduct which will lead to the maximum comfort for the Christian slave who found himself or herself in unjust situations, as well as offering the best possible witness to the gospel in the context of household slavery. Submission, respect and forbearance seem to be the watchwords for the slave/master relationship.

These same characteristics must describe the relationship of employer and employee today. The employee needs to be submissive, respectful and forbearing not because the boss is always worthy of that as an individual (he or she may well not be), but out of reverence for Christ.[19] Ways in which this can fruitfully work out in modern workplace practice have been well explored and described by a number of writers, including Mark Greene, David Kellett and Brian Allenby.[20] All would agree that the employee needs faithfully

245

to serve his employer, and seek to embody these biblical precepts in the working relationship.

Presumably Joseph had studied carefully the ways and needs of his master, Potiphar, in order to win his respect and trust. After Joseph arrived in Potiphar's house, we are told, "When his master [Potiphar] saw that the LORD was with him and that the LORD gave him success in everything he did, Joseph found favour in his eyes and became his attendant. Potiphar put him in charge of his household, and he entrusted to his care everything he owned."[21] Such promotion was due both to God's providence and Joseph's diligence. Indeed we should understand that promotion is as much a matter of God's providence as it is our own application.

As the Psalmist says,

> No-one from the east or the west
> or from the desert can exalt a man.
> But it is God who judges:
> He brings one down, he exalts another. [22]

Or again, as Jeremiah tells us, "Should you then seek great things for yourself? Seek them not...."[23]

Submission in the context of the workplace can take on many forms. It means studying to be useful to the boss. It means respecting the contract of employment and not taking illicit holidays. All too frequently now there is a mysterious amount of sick leave when the European or World Cup is on. Indeed, to cut down on "sickies", some employers have offered generous financial inducements to those employees who do not go beyond a certain number of sick leave days annually. Sadly there are even more ingenious ways of deceiving your employer. Apparently, for those taking hours or days off unjustifiably, mobile phones can imitate the background noise of supposed traffic congestion or roadworks, so that an employee can pretend to be caught in traffic when really still at home!

On the other hand, if there are cases of abuse at work, dubious work ethics or offensive behaviour then, as the town clerk said at Ephesus in quelling the riot, "the courts are open" —and there are tribunals to hear the complaint, or for the case to be heard.[24] In the meantime, the Christian vocation at work remains: be submissive, respectful and forbearing.

SUBMISSION IN MARRIAGE
1 Peter 3:1–7

If the practical meaning of submission in the modern workplace is hard to pin down, how much harder it is to define submission in a modern marriage! What does Peter mean by this?

We need to consider the congregations to which Peter addressed his teaching. It has been pointed out that there was a significantly high proportion of women in these Asian churches, and many had husbands who were not Christian. So, in that setting, the wives had a vital evangelistic role: they were to win their husbands for Christ through the way they behaved. Christian husbands were to live considerately with their wives. Indeed, Paul called all Christians to, "Submit to one another out of reverence for Christ", before launching his description of Christian marriage.[25]

In approaching Peter's important but culturally difficult teaching about marriage here, we need to think about how the wives of "not yet Christian" husbands should conduct themselves, what it means for Christian husbands to live considerately with their wives, and for wives to submit to their husbands. Whole books have been written on the subject, but we will attempt a reasonably pithy answer to these matters, based on Peter's teaching.

The key phrase of Peter's teaching about how to win an unbelieving husband is to set about it "without words".[26] Just as St Francis is commonly quoted as saying in the context of evangelism, "Win them by your actions and, if you must, use words", so here Peter definitely teaches that in the context of marriage it is far more effective to win your partner through attitude and action rather than words. It was St Augustine who recorded the effect of the prayers and actions of Monica, his mother, on the men of her family, namely Patricius, her husband, and Augustine himself. Augustine says of her, "She served her husband as her master, and did all she could to win him for you, speaking to him of you by her conduct, by which you made her beautiful. Finally, when her husband was at the end of his earthly span she gained him for you."[27] It seems likely that Patricius was a not untypical man, wanting most of one world before preparing himself for the next! But Monica marvellously fulfilled the teaching of Peter here, not only by prioritising action (above speech) but also by exemplifying the triumph of "the unfading beauty of a gentle and quiet spirit" over the outer glamour of "braided hair and the wearing of gold jewellery and fine clothes". In other words, it is the inner life which will, in the end, be more convincing to the husband than any outward display of female finery. In teaching this, Peter also places comforting confidence in husbandly discernment to see what is truly valuable in a wife, although history tells that it can take a long time for that particular penny to drop! In the case of Patricius it was the greatest part of his lifetime, so considerable patience is also, it seems, required on the part of the "gentle" wife. It can therefore be a long haul vocation in which the local church can provide ongoing support. I know a group in which several of the women are precisely in this position; their fellowship has a hugely important sustaining role as their vocation is worked out. The importance of faithful, persevering prayer, and standing on the biblical promises, is vital.[28]

Secondly, at this point in our approach to this teaching, it is worth noticing that husbands are called to live considerately with their wives. Peter writes, "Husbands, in the same way be considerate as you live with your wives, and treat them with respect as the weaker partner and as heirs with you of the gracious gift of life, so that nothing will hinder your prayers."[29] There are a number of points which are worth noting in interpreting the meaning of this instruction. Firstly, at least one biblical scholar has suggested, on the basis of manuscript evidence and Old Testament usage, that "live with" here refers to the sexual intercourse between husband and wife rather than other aspects of their life together. What Peter is here arguing is that husbands should treat their wives with respect in all areas of life, not putting self first, nor using their strength improperly. This latter point is underlined, because Peter says the female is the weaker partner. Now that might be a red rag to a feminist bull! So consider the views of a female writer on this. The broadcaster and author Anne Atkins has pointed out that, physically, most wives are not as strong as their husbands, who are therefore usually able to dominate. She goes on to stress, rightly, that a wife's wellbeing is to a degree dependent on her husband, and that the life of Christ can lead a husband to liberate his wife, rather than attempt to enslave.[30]

Peter's point is that consideration, respect, and acknowledgement that they are joint heirs, should inform all their mutual relations, including their sexual relationship, and such harmony will empower their prayer life together. But where that consideration is absent, their spiritual effectiveness will be greatly diminished. Where such consideration exists, the wife's response of "submission" is more likely —just as in Paul's teaching in Ephesians the husband is called to love his wife in the same way that Christ loved the church, and in that context, wives are called to "...submit to your husbands as to the Lord."[31] But what does this submission actually mean?

Imagine a financially independent, highly articulate, physically daring, well groomed, accomplished woman hearing that in marriage she is called to submit to her husband. Would that go down well? Would not many say that is outrageous in the assumptions made about her and her husband? Yet mutual submission is what we are called to, as we noted above. Likewise Peter says, "Wives, in the same way" [meaning as citizens and employees], "be submissive to your husbands."[32] There is a general calling here that all Christians are to be submissive to each other, in the same way that Jesus was submissive to his Father's will and "made himself nothing" for us.[33]

Submission will in fact be common to most of us in one or another area of our lives. The husband will probably have to be submissive to a boss at work; all of us must be appropriately submissive to the state; as Christians we must be submissive to our Lord. In the UK, even the Prime Minister should be submissive to Parliament. Although in each case there are patterns of behaviour or conduct that release us from the obligation to submission —if, for instance, the state consistently upholds evil and injustice; if the boss asks us to falsify information or lie; or if a husband asks his wife to do wrong, or treats her family with abuse. In those circumstances the general call to submission may be legitimately overridden. For example, if a husband asks his wife to say that she was driving when he broke the speed limit, so as not to incur more points on his licence which would make him lose his licence, and she refuses, then she would have been right not to have submitted to his will, however inconvenient that might be for the husband. In that example there is, of course, an obvious conflict between two duties of submission (to the law and to the husband), but the duty to be truthful rather than obliging will be pre-eminent.

So there is a calling to all of us to be submissive in one or more areas of our lives. None of us is called to be submissive where we are called or invited to do wrong; in such situations we may justifiably rebel; but nonetheless, the call of wives to submit to husbands is still there.

SUBMISSION TO THE CHURCH
1 Peter 5

The fourth and final category of submission about which Peter writes in his first letter is submission in the church. This is a passing instruction to the younger members of the church to be subject to the elders. These elders were not just older in age but elders (*presbuteroi*) in the sense of having an official pastoral office in the church. The elders had responsibilities which included leadership and pastoral supervision as well as disciplinary and financial matters. Since they had these duties, the young men were to be submissive to them. In fact the hallmark of their relations was to be humility. "All of you", says Peter, "clothe yourselves with humility towards one another."[34]

Two opposite forms of behaviour in church can prevent the harmonious relationship of leaders and led. All too often, ministers or clergy can use their own position to satisfy their need for either attention or power. In extreme cases this can even lead to the abuse of others. At the other end of the spectrum, those who are being led can frustrate or prevent any change which they dislike in the church.

One bishop visiting a rural parish in the north of England met a church leader, a churchwarden, who had been in office for thirty years.[35] "My," said the bishop, "you must have seen some changes!"

"Yes," said the churchwarden, "and I have opposed every one of them!"

In this case the churchwarden (though not a young man) had tried to hamper the work of the clergy he should have been helping. The manner in which we work together should be marked by humility, mutual listening and submission, so enabling God's mission to go forward.

But what should individual Christians and church leaders do when a particular church departs from orthodoxy, or embraces practices which are contrary to Scripture? Such situations are scarcely unknown in church history and can arise at any time. We must simply note here that submission in a truly biblical sense never means acquiescence or unquestioning obedience in the face of outright disobedience to God's law, no matter what ecclesiastical office any party may occupy. The Bible provides sound remedies in such circumstances, ranging from challenging a brother in an appropriate way to separation from those who persist in leading others astray.

So Peter calls his readers to these areas of submission. In doing so, under the inspiration of the Holy Spirit, he brings to bear both his own experience of dealing with civil and religious authorities (in Acts, as we have seen), and his perception of how Jesus conducted himself in his own sufferings; and he provided powerful (if perhaps at times unwelcome) instruction to those hard-pressed Christian communities to which he wrote. This was leadership of the highest order.

The word and concept of submission is hardly popular today. In the West we are conditioned to be independent, to stand up for our rights, and sometimes with little genuine reason we contract out of obligations rather than work through them. In the four areas we have looked at, namely state, employment, marriage and church, there is a call to submit our interests to others. But, as we have seen, Peter also teaches there may be times when Christians will suffer unjustly on account of their faith. This is still the case in many countries. Now, just as in the first century, the example of Jesus in his passion, his conduct and demeanour, is the most powerful encouragement for suffering Christians. Such was the quality of Peter's leadership that, although he had once been unprepared to suffer with his Lord, he was now ready to follow the pattern that Jesus had modelled, teaching and commending it to others. He knew first hand, from his ministry in Jerusalem, the truth of what he was teaching. He knew the truth of these words from his own experience: "And the God of all grace, who called you to his eternal glory in Christ, after you have suffered a little while, will himself restore you and make you strong, firm and steadfast. To him be the power for ever and ever. Amen."[36]

But persecution was not the only threat that the church faced. Another, to which we must turn now, was the challenge of false teaching.

19

FALSE TEACHERS

2 Peter 1:12–2:22

At the close of the apostolic age one of the chief concerns of the apostles was the infiltration of false teachers into the church. When Paul left the Ephesian elders at Miletus, he warned them, "I know that after I leave, savage wolves will come in among you and will not spare the flock. Even from your own number men will arise and distort the truth in order to draw away disciples after them. So be on your guard!"[1] Likewise, both in 2 Peter and Jude there are substantial warnings about the advent of false teachers or errorists into the church. In fact you could say that there were three main concerns besides the making known of Christ and the gospel in the apostolic writings of the New Testament: the unity of the church; the strengthening of the church in the face of persecution; and the exposure and correction of false teaching. This last part of their concerns fills a large section of apostolic correspondence in the New Testament.

The false teachers themselves can be placed into three main groups. There were the Gnostics, who in turn were linked to what is called antinomianism, the teaching that advocated freedom from observance of the moral law. There were Judaisers (at whom we have already looked, in the context of the Council of Jerusalem and Peter's role in that gathering), who sought to re-impose Jewish law upon the Gentile converts. And the third group, who were not unrelated to the first, and who came to the fore in the Arian controversy, were those who sought to diminish the true nature of Christ as both God and man. Before we say to ourselves that this is all a long way from where we are today, we need to be aware that this is far from true.

In every age, what Peter describes as "the way of truth" will be attacked, and this present age is no exception. There is presently a titanic struggle going on in my own denomination worldwide as to whether gay marriage is part of God's way for his church. It is a struggle which at the time of writing is in the process of being resolved.[2] And although it is clear to me that from Scripture, tradition and reason homosexual marriage is not warranted, there are many who argue passionately otherwise. If theirs is false teaching – that is, teaching based on either a misapprehension concerning Scripture, or misrepresentation of Scripture – how are they to be regarded and how should any false teaching be dealt with in the church? Peter's second letter is largely taken up with false teachers and how they should be regarded. He does not mince his words.

THE FALSE TEACHERS PETER EXPOSED

The group of false teachers that Peter confronts in his second letter could be termed the "antinomian Gnostics". If that leaves you cold and none the wiser, then some explanation is required. Of the two words in that expression, the more fundamental one is "Gnostic", which is derived from the Greek word *gnosis*, meaning knowledge. The particular putative "knowledge" that this group espoused concerned a supposed event prior to the creation of this world, which had, they believed resulted in mankind's ills and the existence of a divine element in the elect. The resulting present material world was seen by the Gnostics as being inferior and insignificant. Indeed there was an utterly false dualism underlying their perception, which is completely alien both to the Hebraic concept of man and the world and to the New Testament picture of God who cares for and loves people, and created the environment of which he made them stewards.

The Gnostic message was not far removed from Platonism, with its emphasis on the inferiority of all matter and the perfection of a non-material world which was thought to subsist in an idealised form. With its insistence that matter was inferior to the spirit, and that bodily actions could not endanger the spirit of a person, Gnosticism was only a short step from what is called "antinomianism"! Once again, the clue is in the Greek word: *nomos*, meaning law. The antinomians were those who believed that the law – in particular the moral law of God – might be broken with impunity.

Thus they completely misunderstood the nature of Christian transformation through faith in Jesus. Paul dealt with this misconception in his epistle to the Romans, where he famously asked, "What shall we say, then? Shall we go on sinning, so that grace may increase? By no means! We died to sin; how can we live in it any longer?"[3] The challenge that Paul was open to, in explaining the gospel of grace in Romans, was that if "...no-one will be declared righteous in his sight by observing the law", and the law is unable of itself to make any righteous, but only grace can, does that not mean that it does not matter if we sin, because grace only abounds all the more when we break the moral law? This, presumably, was a line of argument used especially by his Jewish critics when they thought (wrongly, as it happens) that he had abandoned the law. However, when a person believes in Jesus, he or she changes so that they no longer want (at least in their best moments) to sin, or to break the moral law. Paul makes this clear in the statement, "Therefore, if anyone is in Christ, he is a new creation; the old has gone, the new has come!"[4] So the antinomian "Christians" were quite clearly teaching and living a travesty of the gospel. They did not understand that receiving grace meant being changed from the inside out. These were the very people who Peter, it seems, had to deal with in the warnings in his second epistle.

As we would say now, it was a "full on" refutation of both their teaching and their conduct. Peter by now anticipates his imminent departure, of which Jesus had spoken in his conversation with him by the Sea of Galilee after the resurrection.[5] So Peter says, "I think it is right to refresh your memory as long as I live in the tent of this body, because I know that I will soon put it aside, as our Lord Jesus Christ has made clear to me. And I will make every effort to see that after my departure you will always be able to remember these things."[6] His reminder to them as to how they should live was, in part, a warning about the false teachers and their fate.

The characteristics of these false teachers or prophets were clear. Their teaching was a cloak for their desires. Their idea of pleasure is to "carouse in broad daylight" (i.e. they are shameless). They, "seduce the unstable, they are experts in greed." They appeal to "...the lustful desires of sinful nature", and they "...entice people who are just escaping from those who live in error." So Peter exposes the motivation of their conduct, which is the satisfaction of their own sexual or financial desires, conducted under the cover of false teaching. ("They will secretly introduce destructive heresies, even denying the sovereign Lord who bought them....")[7] But more than this, they were exploitative, so Peter says, "In their greed these teachers will exploit you with stories they have made up."[8]

You could say that their *modus operandi* was manipulation based on deceit. In fact they used their position particularly on those who were either unstable or new to the Christian faith, recent converts who were both unknowing and vulnerable. As Peter said, "...with eyes full of adultery.... they seduce the unstable." Powerful sexual motivation is cloaked both by their position and by their false teaching. Sadly, such moral depravity has been encountered from time to time in many churches and ministries through the ages, and our own age is no exception. Ministry can all too easily become a power trip, in which people become adjuncts to self-aggrandisement, or a place where a leader satisfies an unhealed desire for power or sexual conquest. It still remains one of the greatest temptations in spiritual leadership. It can exist under the cloak of orthodoxy as much as in outright false teaching. The irony of what the false teachers are doing to new converts is not lost on Peter: "They promise them freedom while they themselves are slaves of depravity —for a man is a slave to whatever has mastered him."[9]

This is the deception of this antinomian way: it promises freedom but ends up with enslavement, for true freedom involves being a slave to Christ. This is the paradox of Christian freedom. Peter was in no doubt, not only of the true character of these false teachers and prophets but also of their destiny.

FALSE TEACHERS WARNED

The fate of those who had traduced the way of righteousness and trashed the standards of God was well catalogued in Scripture. Peter gives a fairly comprehensive list of offenders and their deserts in 2 Peter 2:4–10. Beginning with the angels who lusted after earthly women and who were consigned to, "gloomy dungeons to be held for judgement",[10] he runs through a spiralling list of examples of those who have either been condemned or spared. His aim is to show that, "...the Lord knows how to rescue godly men from trials and to hold the unrighteous for the day of judgement...."[11] So both in the days of Noah and in the heyday of Sodom and Gomorrah, the earth in general and those cities in particular were judged, whilst at the same time the godly were spared.

One such godly man who was saved from his immoral surroundings was Lot. In the case of Lot, Peter gives him a write-up that seemingly goes beyond what his actions would merit in the original story.[12] J.N.D. Kelly has pointed out that Lot is portrayed as a man who does not seem to have seriously resisted the behaviour which was going on around him.[13] In early Christian and Jewish writings, nonetheless, Lot is depicted as virtuous.[14] The general sense which Peter wishes to convey, though, is clear: that false teachers like those he is lampooning can expect judgement, and those who resist as a minority against a tide of evil can expect deliverance or rescue. In every age, the church and its leaders must deal with the threat of false teaching. Identifying it, exposing it, and dealing with its perpetrators, have exercised the church and its leadership constantly.

HOLDING TO THE TRUTH AND MAINTAINING UNITY

As we have seen, the Christian community in every age does battle for the truth. This was envisaged and anticipated by the apostles. In their own day they manifestly battled for the truth of the gospel. Peter, Paul and John, three of the principal writers of the New Testament, by their teaching, were having to combat error. Paul, in his letters to the Galatians and Romans, showed there has only ever been one way of knowing the blessings of the covenant first made with Abraham, and that was through faith in God's promise. That promise fully came to light in Jesus, the redeemer of his people; and through faith in him and his sacrifice for human sin, men and women can be made new. Paul combated Judaism, and the false doctrine that it contained, which was that by observing the law anyone could be made righteous. Again, Paul took on the influence of Gnostic teaching, especially in his letter to the Colossians, in whose situation Paul encountered a mix of Christian teaching and elements of cultic beliefs, theosophy and unorthodox Judaism. Christians were at risk of being persuaded by heretical teachers to worship angels. The apostle John repeatedly in his writings emphasised the material and historical nature of Christian faith by saying, as he does at the opening of his Gospel, "The Word became flesh and made his dwelling among us...." In his first epistle, he stresses, "That which was from the beginning, which we have heard, which we have seen with our eyes, which we have looked at and our hands have touched —this we proclaim concerning the Word of life."[15] By emphasising the material and historical existence of Jesus, both John and Paul were combating the dematerialising and dualistic tendencies of the Gnostics.

Likewise, Peter in his second epistle substantiates the historical validity of the gospel by writing, "We ourselves heard this voice that came from heaven when we were with him on the sacred mountain."[16] So from what we might term the religious "right", or traditionalists, the apostles were confronted by the challenge of being dragged back into Judaism, and from the religious "left" or Gnosticism, they were confronted by a non-material, dualistic paganism. Courageously they held to an historical gospel of which they were witnesses, in which the divine and human Jesus redeemed his people so that Christians in their bodily life (i.e. the life of their whole person) might become a living sacrifice to the living God.

Today we face issues of comparable significance. Reality today is people's own experience. So we are all, in our Western society, children of existentialism, meaning, "What I experience is truth." This statement is both true and false. When the truth that I am experiencing is God-less, then it is not the final reality, but when it is God-full, it is! So the task of the church is to challenge those realities which are purely man-made, and to offer a new reality which is God-made and comes to us by the Holy Spirit. The question is therefore, "What is the reality to which I am called, and how do I find out what it is?" The answer is that we can only know the totality of that reality through the revelation of God in Scripture. So Peter writes: "...we have the word of the prophets" [meaning the entire Old Testament], "made more certain, and you will do well to pay attention to it, as to a light shining in a dark place, until the day dawns and the morning star rises in your hearts."[17] Scripture gives us true light and, when we attend to it, it is indeed like a new dawn; and it is Jesus himself who is in our hearts. An existential experience of Jesus through the Holy Spirit, in accordance with Scripture, is the reality we need and should aspire to. The purpose of our existence and the way we should relate to each other is explained in Scripture, and this is the truth which we must experience and proclaim. Anything less is not the way of truth.

This does not mean that if we can tick off a sound list of

doctrines, and adhere to a notional list of ethics, we are as we should be. Christianity is not a series of doctrinal and ethical abstractions. It is far more dynamic than that. Dry orthodoxy is a pale reflection of true Christian living. Being able to agree or sign off to a series of doctrinal propositions (as I am sometimes asked to do when speaking to certain Christian groups) may be a notional defence against heresy; but, as we know from the New Testament, it is possible both to search the Scriptures yet not come to Jesus for life, or to know the law (Torah) and have hearts far from God. No, the issue is whether we are living in a dynamic relationship with the Lord who is really, and therefore existentially, the Lord of our living. This surely is what Peter is getting at when he can say to the Christians to whom he is writing, "Though you have not seen him, you love him; and even though you do not see him now, you believe in him and are filled with an inexpressible and glorious joy, for you are receiving the goal of your faith, the salvation of your souls."[18] These people were in a heartfelt and dynamic relationship of love with their Lord, for whom they were prepared to suffer.

Leadership of the church today needs, as always, a rare combination of grace and truth. On the one hand it needs intellectual honesty to hold to what is revealed in the Scriptures about faith and life, but on the other hand it needs great compassion and sensitivity to the predicaments, moral and spiritual, in which people find themselves. In previous decades the debates were about the nature of the miraculous: could we believe in a bodily resurrection and the virgin conception? With the background of scientific rationalism so prevalent in the 1960s – 1980s, many thought it was time to abandon what they considered "myths" (curiously the same word that Peter had to contend with when he spoke of the divinity of Jesus and the way his appearance changed at the mount of transfiguration). But twenty years on, the domination of the scientific world view does not appear so strong; a new romanticism, which is a cocktail of new age ideas, supernatural awareness and fascination with the paranormal, has made the ideas of bodily resurrection less far fetched to the average secular mind, filled as it is with an amalgam of Lord of the Rings, Harry Potter and new age therapies! The task now is to challenge views which are nearer to Gnosticism, in which people are looking for a divine spark in all kinds of locations, from organic food to spiritual channelling, and tell them that we must look beyond created things to the one who created, with whom we may have a relationship based on grace.

Leadership of the church, at whatever level, requires not only the ability to refute what is false, in a humble and reasoning manner, but also the ability to challenge the church members themselves to a deeper unity. Just as our justification is based on faith, so our fellowship, too, is based on faith. As in secular society we have moved from the ideological world of the 1950s and 1960s, to a much more pragmatic world of the twenty-first century, so too in the church there is a greater willingness to commit to something that works rather than to something that is simply true. If you like, this is a move from ideology to intuition.

Reflecting this transition in the church, it is quite possible that our fellowship may be based increasingly on shared culture more than shared faith. So there is a danger that the style of the worship songs, the manner of the leader, the evidence of modern technology, become some of the determinative factors of belonging to a church, rather than deep attachment to the radical nature and content of the Christian faith. We must beware the homogenous church, which was the darling of the church growth gurus of the 1980s, in which like attracted like, and there was little room for the different. Such churches may be easier to grow, but what connections do they have with their communities? Of course we have to build a church into present cultural networks, but at the same time we must ensure that it does not become another Christian ghetto, unless we are deliberately founding a monastic movement!

Like Peter, leaders need to be courageous in defending what is non-negotiable in the gospel, concerning the lordship of Jesus and the way of salvation. We are not at liberty to use the imperative of love as a reason to derogate from the essentials of faith, but in secondary matters, where the truths of the faith are not at stake, being zealous for the faith does not remove the obligation to put love first.

As Richard Baxter, the Puritan pastor of Kidderminster, said, "In essentials, unity; in non-essentials, liberty; and in all things, charity" —a good motto for any spiritual leader, and one of which Peter would have approved. Any Christian leader will have the task of defining and holding to the truth. This will involve identifying right and wrong teaching, upholding the former and exposing the latter. It will mean a constant sieving of church practices and culture to discern what is or is not essential; and, having discerned what is basic, defending those beliefs and practices strongly, whilst not being prescriptive about those things which are not fundamental. This process has gone on in the church since its beginning, and will continue to the end. What that end is we must now consider. This end was for Peter, as for the other leading apostles, constantly in mind. They actively awaited a new cosmos as the outcome of their salvation.

20

THE NEW COSMOS

2 Peter 3:1–18

We come to the final piece of Peter's writing in his second letter, which is about a renewed cosmos. He is probably writing from Rome, where he was to be martyred. He is writing sometime after AD 64, when Rome suffered a severe fire during the reign of Nero. After the fire, the Christians were made scapegoats and were persecuted. It may well have been in this persecution that Peter was to lose his life. Of the three disciples intimate with Jesus, James the older son of Zebedee had already lost his life in an earlier persecution of the church by the Jewish authorities in Jerusalem. John, his brother, was still alive and after his exile in Patmos, where he received his Apocalypse, would live to ripe old age in Ephesus. Paul had been under house arrest in Rome, after his voyage under guard from Caesarea, via shipwreck in Malta. There is no knowing whether Peter would have visited Paul in Rome, but it is quite probable they would have met again there. Peter certainly knew of Paul's writings, for in this final chapter he remarks that Paul's letters, although in places hard to understand, were being twisted by those who wanted to mislead others.[1] John Mark, who wrote the Gospel of Mark (which was, as we recall, largely based on Peter's memories of Jesus' ministry, and culled from Peter's preaching ministry in Rome, and was first circulated in Rome for Gentile believers) was also with Peter in Rome.

The Roman church was by now well established. The church had been founded without any apostolic mission, by Christians travelling to Rome from other cities of the empire where the church had been previously founded. This is made clear by the long list of people whom Paul greets at the end of his epistle to the Romans. Paul greets twenty six individuals, some of whom, like Priscilla and Aquila, had already made their mark in the life of the early church. Aquila seems to have been an energetic disciple who, with his wife Priscilla, had a profound influence wherever he went. He had originally come from Pontus, and went to Rome from where, with other Christians, he was expelled at the command of the emperor Claudius, who blamed them for the riots in the city involving the Jews. During their temporary exile from Rome they went to Corinth, where they met Paul, who stayed with them and worked at tentmaking with them. Following the death of Claudius, when Christians were once again permitted to enter the city, Aquila and Priscilla returned to the church at Rome.

From then onwards, the church at Rome grew ever stronger, despite persecution. By AD 251, nearly two centuries later, it had forty six presbyters as well as its bishop, and many other ministers including fifty two exorcists![2] It supported no fewer than fifteen hundred widows and needy people, too. So we see a church here, admittedly well developed beyond its first century origins, which had spiritual power and was committed to the service of the poor —a fine example for any other church to follow. It was in the origins of this Christian community that Peter was to play an important part through his teaching and writing.

Quite when 2 Peter was written we cannot be sure, but in AD 64 Peter must have been in his early sixties if Jesus called him in his early twenties, around AD 27. Many of the disciples were almost certainly either late teenagers or in their early twenties when first called by Jesus —something those responsible for vocational ministries in the church today do well to remember! And surely this is an argument for extending the diaconate in the church so that more younger full-time ministers could be trained, with graded respons-ibilities, and then placed in larger churches where they could specialise.

Whether Peter was martyred during the Neronian per-secution of Christians which followed the great fire in Rome or later, we cannot be sure. If he survived a few more years, Peter's world would have been further drastically altered. In AD 66 in Judea, the great Jewish rebellion against the Romans took place, which ended with the destruction of Jerusalem by the armies of Titus. These were the events about which Jesus prophesied, and which Mark recorded in his great chapter on the last days: "When you see 'the abomination that causes desolation' standing where it should not belong – let the reader understand – then let those who are in Judea flee to the mountains."[3]

Unlike a previous occasion when the Jews had rebelled, under the leadership of Judas Maccabaeus in 169 BC against their ruler, the Seleucid king Antiochus IV, who had pro-vocatively profaned the temple, their rebellion this time in AD 66 led to a national disaster. Josephus records the events of the Jewish war against the Roman emperors Vespasian and Titus and tells how their rebellion, in which he had initially taken part, was brutally repressed. Jerusalem was besieged and destroyed, and the temple razed to the ground, leaving only a piece of it standing, prized by the Jews today, and known as the "Wailing Wall". Whether Peter knew any of those events we do not know, but he must have died within years of them taking place, and later writers of the New Testament certainly did.[4] In any event, Peter may have sensed that his closing years of life were witnessing great changes in the world order around him. The fire in Rome, the persecution of the church, the Jewish rebellion, were all background to this final chapter of his writings, in which he looks ahead, quite understandably, to a new cosmos. The renewal of the cosmos was the final act of salvation history. Already four acts had passed: the creation of the world; the fall of the first humans; the choosing of Israel; and the coming of Jesus, who dealt with human sin; but a fifth awaited fulfilment, and this was part of apostolic expectation. Each of the principal apostles, Peter, Paul and John, wrote of the renewal of the cosmos, and with this theme Peter ends his writings.

It was common amongst the early Christians to teach and expect the Lord's return. He himself had taught repeatedly on the subject and gave indications as to when it might be, not with calendar dates but by reference to the emergence of conditions in the world which would precede that event. Since the return of Jesus could be at any time,[5] it gave rise to both expectation and uncertainty: expectation that the *parousia* or second coming could happen at any time, but uncertainty as to precisely when. So with this teaching common in the early church, it predictably gave rise to some people "scoffing" that this hope was just an idle one. So Peter caricatures such sceptical questioning. "First of all, you must understand that in the last days scoffers will come, scoffing and following their own evil desires. They will say, 'Where is this "coming" he promised? Ever since our fathers [literally, their parents] died, everything goes on as it has since the beginning of creation.'"[6]

Peter's answer to such scoffing was both theological and physical. The theological argument he uses is that the heavens and world will be re-created in the same way that they were once created and would be judged in the future, namely through the fiat or power of the Word. Originally, God spoke and he created; later, he spoke and the selfsame world was judged during the time of the flood. Again he will speak, and heaven and earth will be re-created. The cosmos will be renewed following the second coming of Jesus. The elements used, in this process of creation, judgement and re-creation, are fire and water. Most cosmologists tell us that the universe we now know was created some 14 billion years or so ago through the coming together of dust following a vast explosion or "big bang". Whatever the timescale, the promise of salvation includes the provision of a renewed cosmos, ruled by a new humanity. This must be the overarching perspective to all Christian discipleship and leadership, without which it would be defective and impaired.

The second argument Peter employs, to explain the seeming delay in the fulfilment of the promise, is "physical" in the sense that it is a statement about time. Time is a measurement related to the planetary world of our solar system. The progress of the earth around the sun in 365 days determines the measurement of a year, the turning of the earth on its axis every twenty four hours determines night and day. But God's measurement of time is not simply planetary, it is quite unlike ours —just as his thoughts are not like our thoughts.

We can scarcely conceive what time is to God, who is infinite and eternal. The Psalmist bears witness to this great difference when he writes:

> For a thousand years in your sight
> are like a day that has just gone by,
> or like a watch in the night.[7]

A thousand years is like a day to him —in that sense there have only been two "days" since the coming of Jesus! The maker of the universe which includes our solar system is not himself measured by anything in creation. Therefore, any apparent "delay" in the return of Jesus does not signify its negation; rather, it provides an opportunity for all to respond. It should be seen as a display of unrivalled patience, so that all may come to know his grace, as he wishes none to perish.[8] What is sure, Peter teaches, is that the cosmos will be changed. When that will be, we do not know; but these considerations should dissuade even the wisest from hazarding a guess!

Irenaeus, who was familiar with 2 Peter (another argument for Peter's authorship of this epistle) wrote, "The world will come to an end in as many millennia as the days in which it was made. And therefore the scripture of Genesis says, 'And heaven and earth and all their adornment were finished. God finished on the sixth day all his works that he had made, and he rested on the seventh day from all his works that he had made.' This is an account of past events as they took place and a prophecy of the future. For 'If a day of the Lord is like a thousand years' and if creation was finished in six days, it is clear that the end of things will be the $6,000^{th}$ year!"[9] However, Irenaeus works from a theory, however neat, for which there is no biblical warrant.

The great fifth act of salvation history is the renewal of the cosmos, about which many authors in the both the Old and the New Testament write. Isaiah prophesies a new world order.[10] Paul, in Romans, describes how, "...the creation itself will be liberated from its bondage to decay and brought into the glorious freedom of the children of God."[11] John supremely, in Revelation, describes his vision of, "...a new heaven and a new earth, for the first heaven and the first earth had passed away, and there was no longer any sea."[12] And Peter describes how Christians are, "...looking forward to a new heaven and a new earth, the home of righteousness."[13] The culmination of God's saving acts is to be the renewal and re-creation of the world. It is truly amazing to consider even the possibility of a new heaven and earth, and yet this is the essence of Christian hope —and we will be ruled by a just and gentle king! However, what is alarming is the process Peter outlines, whereby this new creation will take place.

Peter forsees a process of new creation that involves a final conflagration of the heavens and earth. He writes of the day of the Lord involving, "...the destruction of the heavens by fire"; and he tells us that, "the elements will melt in the heat."[14] In Scripture, only Peter speaks of such a conflagration. Was he party to a piece of revelation that others did not have, or was his language in fact apocalyptic, describing metaphorically an event which would mark off the old order from the new? Time will tell, but any idea that the creation may itself be involved in a process of re-creation by fire is not an argument for trashing the earth or space now on the grounds that it will eventually one day be consumed. We have no way of knowing the relationship of the old earth to the new, except to say that the new earth (the "home of righteousness") will be better than the old. Our stewardship of the earth today is a sign of our commitment to stewardship of God's creation, both now and in the future. The prospect of final conflagration is not an excuse for present neglect. We should be concerned to preserve the inheritance we have been given in the first cosmos if we are to be entrusted with a new one. We are all familiar by now with the devastating effect of man's misuse of the earth's resources, flora and fauna. Species are being destroyed through mankind's greed, vanity and indifference; deforestation may threaten the very atmosphere we need to live in; and pollution of the oceans threatens the harvest of the seas for future generations.

But Peter's main point in bringing up the hope of a new earth and a new heaven is practical. His teaching poses a vital question: since everything will be destroyed in this way, what kind of people ought we to be?

LIVING IN THE SHADOW OF THE FINAL ACT

One of the titles Peter used of Jesus was 'Author of life'. It has been said that the appearance on a stage of a play's author marks its end. But it would perhaps be truer to say in this context that Christians believe that the Author's reappearance will mark the inauguration of a new order, including both judgment and the new heaven and new earth of which we read in the Scriptures.

Paul wrote that, "The night is nearly over; the day is almost here."[15] James, the Lord's brother and leader of the church in Jerusalem, wrote, "You too, be patient and stand firm, because the Lord's coming is near."[16] And John the beloved disciple wrote, "Dear friends, now we are children of God, and what we will be has not yet been made known. But we know that when he appears, we shall be like him, for we shall see him as he is."[17] There is no doubt that each of the apostles who taught the early church through their foundational writings believed that the Author of life would soon return. As Peter, Paul, James and John all made the return of Jesus central to their teaching, so Matthew and Luke also record in their Gospels Jesus' teaching about his own return. But for none of them was the purpose of this teaching merely speculation or conjecture; for each it was both the promised final act of salvation, heralded by the Author's re-appearance on the stage of life, but practically it was a call to live in the light of that glorious hope of what is to come. That was the vital, present significance of this teaching. Peter writes, "...what kind of people ought you to be?"[18] and John writes, "Everyone who has this hope in him purifies himself, just as he is pure."[19] And Paul writes, "So let us put aside the deeds of darkness and put on the armour of light. Let us behave decently, as in the daytime...."[20] And James writes, "Don't grumble against each other, brothers, or you will be judged. The Judge is standing at the door!"[21] Thus the promise of the return of Jesus, and new creation, is a call to behave with each other now as we will then. It means turning our back on, "...orgies and drunkenness", "...sexual immorality and debauchery", "...dissension and jealousy".[22] Invariably, it is a call to behaviour commensurate with this new existence to which the new humanity, renewed by Jesus, looks forward. This is a vital part of Peter's instruction. So if we ask what kind of people we should be, Peter's answer would be, "You ought to live holy and godly lives as you look forward to the day of God...."[23] To use the title of the first of this trilogy, we should be "becoming fully human".

To do this, we need to "make every effort" (a phrase that Peter uses twice in this epistle).[24] Effort is the product of grace, and adds to our character the qualities which have been disfigured by the Fall. Equally, anyone who aspires to leadership will be involved in such an effort. No leadership of a Christian kind is really possible without both the reception of grace and the exertion of effort; it is another of those balances of Christian living and leadership which must be discovered and embraced.

So Peter, at the end of his life and awaiting this new future existence, called on his readers to be aware of this final act of salvation. His teaching prepares us to begin to live now in this fallen world as we shall, finally, in the re-created one. We can only properly lead if we have this perspective, knowledge and conviction as to where we are going and what will assuredly greet us there. We are indeed looking forward, as Peter did, to a new heaven and a new earth, the home of righteousness.

CONCLUSION

The chronicler Sulpicius Severus wrote in his journal, "Thus a beginning was made of violent persecution of the Christians. Afterwards also laws were enacted and the religion was forbidden. Edicts were published: 'No one must profess Christianity.' Then Paul and Peter were condemned to death. The former was beheaded, Peter was crucified."

Sometime during the persecution which broke out against the church under Nero, after the fire in Rome which destroyed ten of the fourteen wards of the city, the two leading apostles were executed. Peter's own execution was in fulfilment of the words spoken by Jesus in his resurrection appearance by the Sea of Galilee during Peter's restoration, "'I tell you the truth, when you were younger you dressed yourself and went where you wanted; but when you are old you will stretch out your hands, and someone else will dress you and lead you where you do not want to go.' Jesus said this to indicate the kind of death by which Peter would glorify God."[1] It is highly probable, therefore, that the martyrdom of Peter took place in Rome —as mentioned by Severus and indicated both in Clement's letter to the Corinthians and Ignatius' letter to the Romans.[2] What is more, Christian tradition has it that Peter was crucified upside down, believing himself unworthy to be crucified in the same manner as his Lord.

By the time of Peter's execution, some thirty five years at least after the crucifixion and resurrection of Jesus, Peter must have been in his early sixties, though dating and therefore age calculation must remain an inexact science. During those years he surely had many moments to recall his extraordinary life, dividing as it does into three stages: the seemingly brief but tempestuous years with Jesus, beginning with his call in Galilee and ending with Jesus' ascension to the Father; secondly, his years in Jerusalem and Antioch, where Peter became the first bishop or leader of that church — years in which he saw the sudden growth of the church in Judea followed by the equally rapid growth of the church in the Gentile world of the Roman Empire; and finally, his years in Rome, from where he wrote his epistles to the growing but persecuted churches in the Roman provinces of present day Turkey. The events Peter not only witnessed but also played a part in shaped the course of human history. And yet, despite all of this, his would have been an ordinary life had he not been chosen by Jesus to be both the leading apostle and the rock upon which the Lord would build the church. In this sense, Peter's life was transformed by knowing, to use his own words, "...the Christ, the Son of the living God", as millions of other lives would be.[3] Without that "choosing" by Jesus, Peter would have spent a lifetime casting his net on the Sea of Galilee, catching fish!

Amongst his contemporaries Peter would have been known, warts and all, and there was never any conspiracy to hide the blunders of his discipleship; they were recorded for all to see and learn from. He was an ordinary man transformed by Jesus. But, over time, the tradition of Peter would grow, and with it the importance of the church in Rome. For a long time, in fact until the third century, the Roman church was simply *primus inter pares*, and there was no need for, or call for, a church at Rome with a sustained and theoretical claim of universal leadership. This evolved partly out of Rome's imperial position, but particularly through a controversy when a passionate disagreement arose between Cyprian of Carthage and Stephen of Rome about baptism. Stephen invoked the famous "Petrine text" (Matthew 16:18) as a way of pulling rank on Cyprian and defending his position. However, it was not until Damasus in 382 that sustained use of the Petrine text was made by the Roman church to shore up the teaching position of the Bishop of Rome, as well as to provide a scriptural basis for the claims of primacy. And, as they say, "the rest is history!"

The combination of the Petrine text, Peter's martyrdom in Rome (probably on the site of St Peter's), the development of the Petrine tradition through art, sculpture (not least that of Michelangelo) and buildings, and above all the papacy itself, has served to build an institution out of a life. But as we have already noted, that life would have been of no consequence without the call and grace of Christ. And Peter's life is given to us in Scripture so that, through prayer and reflection, we can learn what still makes a spiritual leader. As we have surveyed that life through its ups and downs, we have sought to draw out principles of spiritual leadership still vital for us today.

In conclusion, it is worth remembering Peter as the supreme pastor, for that is the role which Jesus gave him in their conversation by the Sea of Galilee, after the resurrection. Jesus said, "Take care of my sheep", and, "Feed my sheep."[4] It must have been Peter's most difficult and painful conversation with Jesus, and yet perhaps it was the most formative of all. Taking all the experience that Peter had gained by being with Jesus, whether easy or hard, he was now to direct it all towards the needs of the flock of God out of love for Jesus. At times in his life Peter was the great evangelist, notably on the day of Pentecost when thousands believed, and in the heady days of the early church in Jerusalem, when the sick were healed even when his shadow passed over them. He was the one used to bring both the Samaritans and the Gentiles into the kingdom of God but in the end Paul would take on the mission to the Gentiles in a spectacular way, explaining in his great epistles what is the essence of the gospel. By the end, Peter appears as the mature pastor-teacher of the church, and perhaps that is how we should best remember him.

Today the church needs those who will genuinely care for the flock of God as well as do the work of an evangelist; it needs those who with equal self sacrifice will give themselves to "tending the flock of God" wherever it is found —whether facing the rigours of persecution, as Peter did, or facing the materialism of Western society. Peter's message is a call to the church to be both distinctive and engaged with the world around it; distinctiveness is founded on holiness, and engagement means being willing to be involved with the public issues that confront all humankind.

The call to holiness, which is so strong in Peter's epistles, embraces both personal morality and public justice; and where the Christian comes off badly in the public arena, he or she (argues Peter, recalling our Lord's example) should be willing to suffer unjustly. Whatever forms the church may take – whether, in present day parlance, "new church" or "old church" – the form of church cannot supplant the need for mature and godly leadership. The danger is that we become so taken up with forms (a tendency that is a product of our culture) that either we lose the message the form is seeking to convey or we exchange true spiritual leadership for becoming managers of a process. Peter's call to us is to be true pastor-teachers of the flock of God, and to feed Jesus' sheep, as he did. There was never a more important time for Christians to become mature spiritual leaders.

The last word should go to Peter, who was called in Galilee, in his boat, who was prone to both inspiration and gaffe, who walked a few steps on the water before sinking, who both denied his master and was restored. We recall once again his teaching to those who are also called to lead: "Be shepherds of God's flock that is under your care, serving as overseers —not because you must, but because you are willing, as God wants you to be; not greedy for money, but eager to serve; not lording it over those entrusted to you, but being examples to the flock. And when the Chief Shepherd appears, you will receive the crown of glory that will never fade away."[5]

NOTES

Chapter 1
[1] See 1 Peter 1:1.
[2] Daniel 2:44.
[3] See Isaiah 40:3.
[4] Isaiah 40:1f.
[5] See Luke 3:7–14.
[6] See John 1:19–28.
[7] John 1:29.
[8] John 1:35.
[9] See John 1:41.
[10] Luke 5:4
[11] Luke 5:5
[12] See Exodus 3:3.
[13] See Genesis 15:5.
[14] Isaiah 6:1–9.

Chapter 2
[1] See Matthew 4:18–22.
[2] See Matthew 4:13; Mark 2:14; Matthew 8:5–13; Luke 7:1–10.
[3] See John 2:1–11.
[4] See John 4:46–54.
[5] See Luke 4:16–21.
[6] See Mark 1:21–28.
[7] See Matthew 23:1–4.
[8] See Luke 16:14.
[9] See Matthew 23:27f.

Chapter 3
[1] See Mark 2:1.
[2] See Mark 4:33f.
[3] See Mark 2:13ff.
[4] See Mark 2:10.
[5] See Mark 2:18.
[6] See Mark 7:1–5
[7] See Mark 2:25.
[8] See Mark 2:4; 3:7f; 3:20.
[9] See Mark 3:21.
[10] Mark 3:35.
[11] See Luke 6:12.
[12] See Luke 6:13.
[13] See Luke 10:1.
[14] See Luke 10:9.
[15] See Philip Yancey, *The Jesus I Never Knew*, p. 58
[16] See John 12:6; 13:21–30.
[17] See Acts 1:13f.
[18] See John 17:15; Luke 22:31f.
[19] See Matthew 9:35;10:1,7–11;14; Mark 6:6b–13; Luke 9:1–6.
[20] See Luke 10:21.

[21] See Matthew 14:12–14; Mark 6:30–34.
[22] See Matthew 14:14.
[23] Luke 9:11.
[24] John 6:6.
[25] See John 6:15.
[26] See John 6:27.
[27] John 6:51.
[28] Matthew 14.12.
[29] Matthew 14:12 and see14:23.
[30] See John 6:18.
[31] Romans 4:17.
[32] 2 Corinthians 5:7.
[33] John 6:25.
[34] See John 6:26.
[35] See John 6:38–40.
[36] See John 6:52.
[37] See John 6:66.
[38] John 6:68f.

Chapter 4
[1] Luke 9:18.
[2] Matthew 16:14.
[3] Matthew 16:16.
[4] See Luke 10:21–22 below.
[5] Luke 10:21–22.
[6] Mark 15:39.
[7] Ephesians 1:17–19a.
[8] Matthew16:18.
[9] See Romans 11:29.
[10] See Philippians1:6.
[11] Matthew 16:19.
[12] 1 Peter 2:4f.
[13] Matthew 16:23.

Chapter 5
[1] See Acts 17:16ff.
[2] 2 Peter 1:18.
[3] Exodus 24:17.
[4] 1 Kings 18:38.
[5] 1 Kings 19:11.
[6] 1 Kings 19:13.
[7] Luke 9:51.
[8] Luke 9:29.
[9] See Matthew 17:1.
[10] See Revelation 1:9ff.
[11] 2 Corinthians 4:6.
[12] Matthew 3:17; Mark 1:11; Luke 3:22.
[13] John 12:27–29.

[14] John 12:30.
[15] Luke 9:31.
[16] See Exodus 12:22.
[17] Exodus 12:26.
[18] Mark 9:5.
[19] 2 Peter 1:16–18.
[20] Acts 2:36b.
[21] See 2 Corinthians 12:3f.
[22] See 2 Corinthians 12:7.
[23] *The Distinguishing Marks of a Work of the Spirit of God*, p. 97.
[24] Daniel 8:27.

Chapter 6
[1] See Mark 9:29.
[2] Matthew 17:23.
[3] See Exodus 30:11–16.
[4] Matthew 22:17.
[5] Matthew 22:23ff.
[6] Matthew 22:36.
[7] See Romans 14:7; 1 Corinthians 8:13 and 9:12.
[8] 1 Peter 2:13ff.
[9] See Romans chapter 13.
[10] See Acts 16:3.
[11] See 1 Corinthians 9:19–23.
[12] In this case circumcision. See Galatians 2:15–16.
[13] Galatians 2:16.

Chapter 7
[1] e.g. Leviticus 26:18; Proverbs 24.16.
[2] 1 Peter 3:8f.
[3] See Did.1.3; Polycarp *Phil.ii.2*; J.N.D. Kelly, *The Epistles of Peter & Jude* Black's Commentary 1969, p. 135.
[4] See Matthew 19.1.

Chapter 8
[1] Matthew 20:20–27.
[2] See Luke 22:24.
[3] See Mark 9:34.
[4] See a fuller discussion of this encounter in *Meetings with Jesus*, Terra Nova.
[5] Luke 18:25.
[6] Acts 2:45; 4:32, 34f.
[7] Matthew 19:28.
[8] 1 Peter 5:2f.
[9] Hebrews 6:10.
[10] Hebrews 11:6b.

Chapter 9

[1] Matthew 21:5, and see Zechariah 9:9.

[2] John 13:9.

[3] John 13:2–5.

[4] John 13: 1b.

[5] Philippians 2:6–8.

[6] John 13:13–17.

[7] See Roald Dahl, *Boy.*

[8] See Ezekiel 34.

[9] 1 Peter 5:2f.

[10] The national structure of fees for weddings and funerals in the Church of England seems to be an exception to this, but since these are set by Parliament each year at least they are statutory and are the same across the country. But, from the above, an argument could be made for their abolition; although now no clergyman gains personally from their collection.

[11] v. 8.

[12] *Becoming Fully Human*, Terra Nova, 2003.

Chapter 10

[1] I Corinthians 10:12.

[2] Matthew 26:35.

[3] Luke 24:21a.

[4] Acts 1:6.

[5] John 12:27.

[6] Mark 14:38.

[7] Luke 22:31–32.

[8] See Luke 22:36.

[9] John 18:36.

[10] See Luke 22:51.

[11] See Mark 14:54, Matthew 26:58, Luke 22:54.

[12] See John 18:15.

[13] See John 18:15–16.

[14] See John 18:26.

[15] 1 Peter 5:8.

[16] Luke 22: 40, 46.

[17] See John 21:7.

[18] John16:7.

[19] Jim Wallis, *Faith Works*, SPCK 2002, p. 141.

Chapter 11

[1] Acts 1:3.

[2] See Matthew 3:11; Luke 3:16 and John 1:33; Mark1:7f., Acts 1:5.

[3] Luke 24:30f; 41–43.

[4] Matthew 28:17.

[5] See Acts 1:3.

[6] Acts 1:6.

[7] Acts 1:9.

[8] See Matthew 19:28.

NOTES

[9] Acts 1:21f.
[10] See Acts 1:21.
[11] See Acts 13:2.
[12] See Genesis 2:7.
[13] This was Donald Coggan, on visiting St Cuthbert's, York in the 1960s.
[14] See Ephesians 3:10.
[15] See Acts 2:6.
[16] See 1 Peter 3:15 .
[17] See 1 Corinthians 14:3.
[18] See Acts 2:21.
[19] Acts 2:36.
[20] See Acts 2:24 & 32.
[21] *The New Testament and the People of God*, SPCK 1992, p. 216.
[22] See Acts 2:30.
[23] Acts 2:38.

Chapter 12
[1] See Acts 4:20.
[2] See Acts 3:10.
[3] See Romans 15:18f.
[4] See Graham Tomlin, *The Provocative Church*.
[5] See Deuteronomy 18:15,18f.
[6] Acts 3:26.
[7] Acts 4:19.
[8] See Acts 5:27ff.
[9] Acts 5:28.
[10] See Acts 22:3.
[11] Acts 5:38f.
[12] See Acts 5:42.
[13] Acts 4:31.
[14] See Acts 4:29–30.
[15] See Acts 12:2.
[16] See Acts 12:5f.
[17] Acts 12:11b.
[18] See 1 Peter 1:1.

Chapter 13
[1] See the Church of England report *Mission Shaped Church*.
[2] See Genesis 15.
[3] Acts 2:44f.
[4] Acts 4:32–35.
[5] Acts 2:46f.
[6] See Acts 4:36–37.
[7] See Acts 5:4.
[8] See Joshua chapters 6 & 7.
[9] Matthew 16:19.
[10] Acts 6:2.
[11] Acts 6:3f.
[12] Acts 6:7.

Chapter 14
[1] See Matthew 16:19.
[2] See Acts 1:8.
[3] See Ezra 4:2ff.
[4] See John 4.
[5] See Luke 9:53.
[6] See Romans 5 & Galatians 3:5.
[7] Acts 8:14–17.
[8] See Genesis 12:2f. & 15:5.
[9] Luke 7:9.
[10] Mark 15:39.
[11] See Acts 10:15.
[12] Acts 10:28–30.
[13] Acts 10:38.
[14] Acts 11:12.
[15] Galatians 3:28f.
[16] See his book, *Changing World, Changing Church*.
[17] Genesis 15:6.
[18] See Romans 4:1–3.

Chapter 15
[1] Acts 8:1.
[2] Eusebius Mart. Pol 9:1–3.
[3] Tom Wright *The New Testament and the People of God*, SPCK 1992 p. 347f. Used by permission.
[4] Op. cit. p. 358.
[5] See Acts 16:4f.
[6] Acts 11:21.
[7] Acts 15:1b.
[8] Galatians 1:6.
[9] Galatians 3:11.
[10] Acts 15:8f.
[11] Acts 15:11.
[12] James 3:17f.
[13] John Stott *The Message of Acts*, IVP p. 242. Used by permission.
[14] Also supported by Lightfoot, Ridderbos and Cole.
[15] See Galatians 2:11–14.
[16] See also Acts 9:26–30; Acts 11:29–30.
[17] See Galatians 1:18.
[18] Galatians 2:2.
[19] Galatians 2:7f.
[20] See Galatians 2:12.
[21] See Acts 15:39.
[22] See Romans chapters 9–11.
[23] "Babylon", see 1 Peter 5:13.

Chapter 16

[1] Suetonius' account of the life of Claudius.
[2] See 1 Peter 5:13.
[3] See Acts 15:38.
[4] See 1 Peter1:1,17.
[5] See *Becoming Fully Human*, Terra Nova, 2003.
[6] See 1 Peter 1:7.
[7] 1 Peter 1:3–5.
[8] Romans 8:24f.
[9] 2 Peter 1:4.
[10] See 1 Peter 1:3f.
[11] 1 Peter 1:6f.
[12] 1 Peter 1:8.
[13] See 1 Peter 1:23ff.
[14] Romans 8:3f., my addition in brackets.
[15] 1 Peter 1:19.
[16] 1 Peter 1:15.
[17] 1 Peter 1:13.
[18] See 1 Peter 1:14, 22.
[19] Ed. J.B. Bury, *Decline and Fall of the Roman Empire*, Book 2, Methuen 1909.
[20] See 1 Peter 1:22.
[21] 2 Peter 1:11.
[22] 2 Peter 1:3.
[23] 1 Peter 1:23.
[24] See 2 Peter 1:3f.
[25] See 2 Peter 1:8.
[26] 1 Peter 1:22.
[27] See 1 Peter 1:17–21.
[28] See 2 Peter 1:10.

Chapter 17

[1] 1 Peter 2:4.
[2] See Acts 4 and 5.
[3] 1 Peter 2:5.
[4] 1 Peter 2:9.
[5] 1 Peter 2:11.
[6] See Deuteronomy 26:5.
[7] See Exodus 25 & 26 and 2 Chronicles 6–7.
[8] See 1 Samuel 8.
[9] Jeremiah 2:2f,13.
[10] See *How to be Good*, Nick Hornby, Penguin, 2001, p. 186.
[11] 1 Peter 3:8–9.
[12] See Graham Tomlin *The Provocative Church*, SPCK p. 101. Used by permission.
[13] James 1:22.
[14] 1 Peter 3:15.
[15] See *Fraser and Prayer* , OMF 1963, p. 31.
[16] 1 Peter 1:22. The Byzantine text adds a "pure" heart with a formidable array of supporting mss.

[17] John 15:12.
[18] Galatians 5:6b.
[19] 1 Peter 4:9
[20] 1 Peter 4:10
[21] See Nehemiah 10:32, 35.
[22] See Bill Hybels, *Courageous Leadership*, chapter 7.
[23] *The First Epistle of Peter* SCM 1950, p. 108.
[24] Op. cit. *The Provocative Church*, SPCK
[25] 1 Peter 5:4.
[26] See Rob Parsons, *What they didn't teach me in Sunday School*,
Hodder 1997.
[27] 1 Peter 5:6.
[28] 1 Peter 5:8.
[29] 1 Peter 5:10.
[30] See Psalm 30:5.

Chapter 18
[1] 1 Peter 3:14, 4:3f., see also 2:20b.
[2] See 1 Peter 1:2.
[3] See Exodus 29:21& 24:8.
[4] 1 Peter 1:18–20.
[5] Psalm 103:1–5.
[6] See 1 Peter 2:20 & 1 Peter 4:15.
[7] 1 Peter 2:20b–21.
[8] 1 Peter 3:17.
[9] See Derek Tidball, *The Message of the Cross*, IVP 2001.
[10] See Isaiah 53:9 & 1 Peter 2:22.
[11] See 1 Peter: 2:23.
[12] 1 Peter 2:23b.
[13] Acts 16:37–40.
[14] See James Denny, *The Death of Christ*, Tyndale Press 1951, p. 63.
[15] See 2 Peter 3:16.
[16] Op. cit. *The Message of the Cross*, p. 289.
[17] See Romans 13:1.
[18] See Romans 13:4.
[19] See Colossians 3:23–24, Titus 2:9–10.
[20] See Mark Greene, *Thank God It's Monday*, SU 1994.
See also David Kellett, *Champions for God at Work*, Terra Nova and
Brian Allenby, *Witness and Work*, Terra Nova and *Witness and Work Resources*,
Terra Nova.
[21] Genesis 39:3f.
[22] Psalm 75:6f.
[23] See Jeremiah 45:5.
[24] See Acts 19:38.
[25] Ephesians 5:21.
[26] See 1 Peter 3:1.
[27] Augustine *Confessions* IX. 19–22.
[28] See Lynn Forrester, *When Jesus Wins Your Husband's Heart*, Terra Nova.

She writes about a number of couples in which the wives prayed for many years before seeing them come to faith in Christ.

[29] 1 Peter 3:7.

[30] See Anne Atkins, *Split Image*, Hodder, 1998.

[31] Ephesians 5:22.

[32] 1 Peter 3:1.

[33] See Philippians 2:7.

[34] See 1 Peter 5:5f.

[35] A churchwarden is an office holder in the Anglican Church.

[36] 1 Peter 5:10f.

Chapter 19

[1] Acts 20:29f.

[2] After the Windsor Report the Primates (leaders) of the Anglican Communion have met, to both reinforce orthodox teaching in this area and ask ECUSA and the Anglican Church of Canada to think again.

[3] Romans 6:1f.

[4] 2 Corinthians 5:17.

[5] See John 21:18f.

[6] 2 Peter 1:13–15.

[7] 2 Peter 2:1b.

[8] 2 Peter 2:3.

[9] See also John 8:34, James 1:15.

[10] See 2 Peter 2:4.

[11] See 2 Peter 2:9.

[12] See Genesis 19:15ff.

[13] Op. cit. p. 333.

[14] See Wisdom 10.6 & 1 Clement 11.1.

[15] 1 John 1:1.

[16] 2 Peter 1:18.

[17] 2 Peter 1:19.

[18] 1 Peter 1:8f.

Chapter 20

[1] See 2 Peter 3:16.

[2] See Henry Chadwick, *The Early Church* p. 57.

[3] Mark 13:14.

[4] Matthew, Luke and John probably knew of these events.

[5] See 2 Peter 3:10.

[6] 2 Peter 3:4f.

[7] Psalm 90:4.

[8] See 2 Peter 3:9b.

[9] In his *Against Heresies* 28:3. See Genesis 2:1–2 and 2 Peter 3:8.

[10] See Isaiah 66:22.

[11] Romans 8:21.

[12] Revelation 21:1.

[13] 2 Peter 3:13.

[14] See 2 Peter 3:12.

[15] Romans 13:12.
[16] James 5:8.
[17] 1 John 3:2.
[18] 2 Peter3:11.
[19] 1 John 3:3.
[20] See Romans 13:12f.
[21] James 5:9.
[22] See Romans 13:13.
[23] See 2 Peter 3:11.
[24] See 2 Peter 1:5.

Conclusion
[1] John 21:18f.
[2] See Henry Chadwick, *The Early Church* p. 17.
[3] Matthew 16:16.
[4] John 21:15–17.
[5] 1 Peter 5:2–4.